God's Character:

Unraveling 52 Attributes of the Almighty

God's Character

Unraveling 52 Attributes of the Almighty

Vinu V Das

T̈P
Tabor Press

ISBN 978-0-9940194-9-3

Table of Contents

Introduction

Welcome to a journey of discovery into the very nature of God as revealed through Scripture. This book invites you to explore the multifaceted attributes of the Divine—from His unfathomable wisdom to His gentle, protective care—and to see how these qualities shape both our understanding of God and our lives. As we delve into these themes, we encounter a God who is both transcendent and intimate, powerful yet compassionate, and sovereign while remaining accessible to every soul.

Throughout the pages that follow, each chapter highlights a distinct characteristic of God. We begin with the mystery of His incomprehensibility, where we learn that while our finite minds can only grasp a glimpse of His infinite nature, He graciously reveals Himself through creation, Scripture, and ultimately in Jesus Christ. We then move to the attributes of provision and protection, discovering that God meets every need and stands as an unwavering fortress in times of trial. These truths provide believers with assurance that nothing in our lives is random; every joy, every hardship, and every moment is woven into a grand, purposeful design.

A significant part of our exploration focuses on God's relational qualities. The intimate, fatherly nature of God invites us into a deep, personal relationship marked by love, trust, and acceptance. Jesus' own description of Himself as "gentle and lowly in heart" exemplifies a leadership that is caring, compassionate, and dedicated to the restoration of the broken. In His life, death, and resurrection, we see a redemptive power that transforms suffering into hope and despair into renewal. This theme of healing—both physical and spiritual—is a recurring promise throughout Scripture, affirming that God not only rescues us from our pain but also renews us for a flourishing future.

Moreover, the book examines the supreme authority of God—a truth that anchors all other attributes. His sovereignty, omniscience, and perfect moral character assure us that His plans are unassailable. Even when human efforts falter, divine authority remains steadfast, guiding history and individual lives toward the ultimate fulfillment of His redemptive purposes. This comprehensive governance of the cosmos offers a stable foundation in a world often marked by uncertainty and chaos.

Each chapter builds on these interwoven themes to present a holistic picture of a God who is absolute in character and purpose. This divine tapestry not only provides theological insight but also practical guidance. Believers are encouraged to reflect these attributes in their own lives—cultivating hope, integrity, and compassion in personal relationships and communities, and engaging the world with courage and conviction.

As you journey through these pages, may you find encouragement, deepen your understanding, and be inspired to live out a faith that mirrors the glory and goodness of the One who is beyond measure. This book is not just an academic exploration; it is a call to experience a transformative relationship with God—a relationship that promises eternal significance, personal renewal, and a harmonious future under His loving reign.

Chapter 1: The Holiness of God

God's holiness is at the very heart of His identity. In Christian theology, holiness signifies not only moral purity but also the absolute separateness and transcendent majesty of the Divine. It is the quality that sets God apart from all creation, highlighting His uniqueness and otherness. Every other attribute of God—His love, justice, righteousness, power, and etc—must be understood in light of His inherent holiness. This chapter explores the concept of holiness, its biblical foundations, its nature, and the profound effects it has on believers.

1.1 Understanding the Nature of Holiness

Defining Holiness: Set Apart and Unique

The term "holy" derives from the Hebrew *qadosh* and the Greek *hagios*, both emphasizing being "set apart" or "dedicated." In the biblical worldview, God's holiness means He is utterly different from the finite, unclean, or profane. This separation is not to imply remoteness; rather, it underlines that God's very essence is distinct. He is not merely one moral being among many, but the unique and incomparable Creator whose presence sanctifies all that it touches.

More Than Moral Purity

While moral purity is a significant aspect of holiness, it is only one facet of God's nature. His perfection in righteousness and justice is well known, yet His holiness also speaks to an overwhelming uniqueness that transcends everyday morality. Throughout Scripture, whenever God's presence appears—transforming a place or person—it marks that space as sacred. In essence, holiness conveys both the moral perfection and the ineffable mystery of God's being, inviting worship that acknowledges His absolute difference from the created order.

Transcendence and Mystery

God's holiness also points to His transcendence—His existence beyond the finite limits of human comprehension. This dimension reminds us that no human thought or image can fully capture the Divine nature. Biblical warnings against idolatry emphasize that any attempt to confine God within our limited ideas diminishes His mystery. Although God reveals Himself in Scripture and through Jesus Christ, His transcendent holiness calls for an approach imbued with humility and awe.

1.2 Biblical Foundations of Holiness

Old Testament Revelations

The Old Testament offers vivid depictions of God's holiness. In Exodus, Moses encounters God in the burning bush—a seemingly ordinary bush set aflame by a holy fire. This encounter forces Moses to remove his sandals, symbolizing the need to approach the Divine with reverence (Exodus 3:1–6). Similarly, the elaborate rituals of the Tabernacle and Temple were designed to remind Israel of the sacred gap between the holy God and ordinary humanity. The Holy of Holies, accessible only to the high priest once a year, underscored the gravity of approaching a holy God without purification and atonement.

Isaiah's Vision

One of the most striking visions of God's holiness appears in Isaiah 6:1–5. In this vision, the prophet sees the Lord enthroned in glory, attended by seraphim who proclaim, "Holy, holy, holy!" This thrice-repeated declaration not only affirms God's moral perfection but also accentuates His transcendent nature. Overwhelmed by his own unworthiness in the presence of such radiant holiness, Isaiah is transformed through a symbolic act of purification that prepares him for prophetic ministry. This encounter underscores that true awareness of God's holiness brings both fear and transformative grace.

New Testament Affirmations

The New Testament reiterates the uncompromising holiness of God. Jesus, who embodies compassion and approachability, nonetheless reflects the same divine separation from sin. His authority over evil and His embodiment of God's glory reveals that holiness is not confined to the Old Testament but remains a core aspect of the New Covenant. In 1 Peter 1:15, believers are exhorted to reflect God's character by being holy in their conduct—a direct echo of the Old Testament call in Leviticus. Additionally, the celestial worship depicted in Revelation, with its recurring cry of "Holy, holy, holy," confirms that the recognition of God's holiness transcends time and remains central to the Christian faith.

1.3. Experiencing and Responding to Divine Holiness

The Impact of Encountering Holiness

Encounters with God's holiness often provoke profound fear and awe. Throughout Scripture, figures such as Moses, Isaiah, and even Peter are depicted as falling to their knees or trembling in the presence of the Divine. This reaction is not a sign of weakness but a recognition of the vast gulf between the infinite purity of God and the flawed nature of humanity. Such holy fear, or reverence, is essential. It drives believers to repentance, fosters a deep sense of humility, and leads to a greater desire to align one's life with God's perfect will.

Transformation and Renewal

A genuine encounter with holiness is never a static experience. Instead, it catalyzes personal transformation. For Isaiah, the encounter with God's radiant presence not only highlighted his own sinfulness but also set him on a path of redemption and prophetic service. Likewise, modern believers often experience a renewal of purpose when they truly grasp the magnitude of God's holiness. In moments of worship, prayer, or even quiet reflection, the awareness of God's pure and majestic nature inspires a turning away from sin and a recommitment to a life of integrity and obedience.

Worship and Submission

When believers recognize God's holiness, their response naturally flows into worship and submission. True worship involves more than ritual or formality; it is the full alignment of heart and mind with the Creator. This kind of worship is not confined to church services but permeates every aspect of life. As believers yield to the authority of a holy God, their everyday actions—how they work, relate to others, and make decisions—become acts of devotion. In this way, the experience of God's holiness transforms daily routines into continuous offerings of praise and gratitude.

1.4. Living Out a Life of Holiness

Confession and Repentance

The recognition of God's holiness invariably brings a heightened awareness of personal sinfulness. Much like Isaiah's confession of unclean lips, believers are called to confront their imperfections honestly. Confession is the first step toward transformation, as it involves acknowledging where one has fallen short. This awareness naturally leads to repentance—a turning away from sin and a decisive move toward aligning one's life with God's will. Far from being a one-time event, this process is an ongoing journey that refines and renews the believer through the work of the Holy Spirit.

The Call to Personal Holiness

Scripture commands believers not only to admire God's holiness but also to pursue it in their own lives. As stated in 1 Peter 1:15, we are to be holy in all our conduct, reflecting the character of the One who has called us. This pursuit is not about achieving perfection through human effort alone; rather, it is an invitation to partner with the divine grace that empowers us to overcome temptation and live righteously. Practical expressions of personal holiness might include resisting the lure of sin, actively seeking justice, and showing selfless love to others. Each of these acts, however small, is an opportunity to mirror the radiant character of God.

Embracing an Eternal Perspective

Understanding and embracing God's holiness also reorients our focus toward eternity. When we grasp that our lives are lived in the light of an eternal, unchanging God, our priorities shift. Temporal concerns—personal comfort, wealth, or fame—diminish in importance compared to the call to honor and serve a holy God. An eternal perspective encourages believers to invest in spiritual growth, nurture loving relationships, and serve others selflessly. By anchoring our hope in God's immutable holiness, we find strength and confidence even amid the brokenness of the world.

In Conclusion, in every dimension of Scripture, from the burning bush in Exodus to the celestial scenes in Revelation, God's holiness stands as a defining and transformative reality. It reveals not only His moral perfection and transcendent majesty but also invites every believer into a relationship marked by reverence, transformation, and renewal. The call to recognize and respond to this holiness is not a relic of an ancient covenant; it is the dynamic heartbeat of the Christian life.

To encounter God's holiness is to be awakened to the truth of our own limitations and the vastness of His grace. It calls us to confess our shortcomings, to turn away from sin, and to live in continual submission to His divine authority. This journey transforms everyday actions into acts of worship and aligns our lives with an eternal purpose. In embracing the tension between our unworthiness and God's perfect purity, we are invited to a deeper, more intimate walk with the Creator—a walk that is both humbling and exhilarating.

May we continually seek to understand, revere, and reflect the holiness of God in every aspect of our lives. In doing so, we not only honor the One who is completely unique and supremely good but also discover the profound joy and purpose that come from living in His eternal light.

Chapter 2: Righteousness

God's righteousness is central to understanding His character. While Chapter 1 focused on God's holiness—the attribute that underscores His distinct, pure nature—righteousness reveals how that divine purity is applied in action. Righteousness embodies God's moral perfection, justice, and reliability. Everything He does is aligned with what is right, just, and true. In this chapter, we examine the biblical foundations, theological insights, and practical consequences of God's righteousness.

2.1 Defining Divine Righteousness

Biblical Meanings

In Scripture, the idea of "righteousness" is primarily conveyed by two key words: the Hebrew *tsedeq* (and its variant *tsedaqah*) and the Greek *dikaios* (and *dikaiosunē*). These terms evoke images of straightness, moral rectitude, and right relationships. They do more than simply "doing the right thing"—they suggest complete fidelity to God's own standards. When we say God is righteous, we affirm that His every action and judgment reflects perfect fairness and an unwavering commitment to truth.

Righteousness versus Holiness

Although closely related, righteousness and holiness highlight different aspects of God's nature. Holiness, as discussed in Chapter 1, focuses on God's absolute purity and separateness from sin. Righteousness, however, speaks to the dynamic application of that purity in how God governs, judges, and sustains relationships. God's holiness is the essence of His being, while His righteousness shows us that every act He performs is consistent with what is just. In this sense, God's righteousness is the practical outworking of His pure nature.

2.2 Biblical Foundations of Righteousness

The Covenant with Abraham

A foundational story in the Old Testament reveals God's righteous character through His dealings with Abraham. In Genesis 12:1–3, God promises Abraham that he will become the father of a great nation. Later, Genesis 15:6 records that "Abraham believed the Lord, and He counted it to him as righteousness." This verse emphasizes two important points:

- **Covenant Faithfulness:** God makes promises and always fulfills them. His actions are consistently aligned with what is right.

- **Trust and Alignment:** Abraham's trust in God not only secured his place in God's plan but also demonstrated that righteousness is imparted to those who rely on God's trustworthy character.

Another moment in Abraham's journey occurs when he pleads for Sodom (Genesis 18:22–33), appealing to God's inherent sense of justice. In asking, "Shall not the Judge of all the earth do what is just?" Abraham acknowledges that all of God's decisions stem from His perfect righteousness.

Righteousness in the Law

The Torah—the first five books of the Old Testament—contains detailed laws covering worship, justice, and societal conduct. These laws are not arbitrary rules but reflections of God's moral order. For example, commands that ensure fair treatment of the poor and vulnerable (see Leviticus 19:9–10 and Deuteronomy 24:17–18) reveal that God's righteousness extends to issues of social justice. The psalmists, too, celebrate the wisdom and reliability of God's commands (as in Psalm 119), emphasizing that obedience to these laws is a way of aligning one's life with God's righteous will.

2.3 New Testament Affirmations

Jesus: The Embodiment of Righteousness

In the New Testament, Jesus Christ is presented as the perfect manifestation of God's righteousness. Jesus not only fulfilled the Law (Matthew 5:17) but redefined its intent by addressing the heart and mind behind human actions. In His teachings—especially in the Sermon on the Mount (Matthew 5–7)—He went beyond mere external adherence. For instance, He taught that anger and contempt are as much a violation of righteousness as overt acts of violence, and that lustful thoughts undermine the sanctity of marriage (Matthew 5:21–28). Through His sinless life and compassionate ministry, Jesus demonstrated that righteousness is not about ticking off commandments but about cultivating a heart that mirrors God's moral perfection.

Paul's Theology of Righteousness

The Apostle Paul further develops the concept of righteousness in his letters, particularly in Romans and Galatians. Paul starkly declares, "None is righteous, no, not one" (Romans 3:10), highlighting humanity's universal need for divine intervention. According to Paul, it is only through faith in Jesus Christ that we receive God's righteousness. In Romans 3:21–22, Paul explains that righteousness is made available as a gift through Christ's atoning sacrifice. This teaching brings together two essential truths:

- **Universal Need:** Every person, regardless of background, falls short of God's standard.

- **Divine Provision:** God extends His righteousness to those who believe, ensuring that His judgments remain just even as He redeems the sinner.

2.4 The Nature of God's Righteousness
Moral Perfection in Action

God's righteousness means that His every action is in complete harmony with absolute goodness and truth. Unlike human justice, which can be partial or flawed, divine justice is perfect. Whether delivering judgment or bestowing blessings, God's decisions are unerring because they are grounded in His omniscience and moral excellence. This assurance means that even when human systems fail or injustice seems to prevail, ultimate justice is assured by God's righteous nature.

Justice and Accountability

Linked inseparably with righteousness is the concept of justice. In Scripture, God's justice involves addressing wrongdoing in a manner that upholds His moral law. This dual nature can be both comforting and challenging. It comforts us to know that God notices and rectifies injustice, yet it also serves as a stern reminder that every act of evil is recorded and will ultimately be judged. The prophets, for example, repeatedly denounce the exploitation of the poor and oppressed, insisting that a just society must reflect God's righteous standards (see Isaiah 1:17 and Micah 6:8).

2.5 Encountering God's Righteousness
Blessings and Judgment

One often overlooked aspect of God's righteousness is how it manifests in both blessing and judgment. For those who live in accordance with His principles—showing integrity, mercy, and faithfulness—God extends blessings that may come in many forms: spiritual enrichment, inner peace, and a deep sense of His presence (Psalm 1:1–3). Conversely, persistent rebellion against His righteous standards leads to divine judgment. Whether through immediate consequences or long-term outcomes, God's judgment confirms His commitment to maintaining moral order.

Transformation Through Grace

A crucial element of experiencing God's righteousness is the transformation it brings through grace. The New Testament teaches that through Christ, believers are not only declared righteous but also gradually transformed into His likeness (2 Corinthians 5:21). This process of sanctification is ongoing and is empowered by the Holy Spirit. The Spirit convicts of sin, encourages repentance, and strengthens believers to live in ways that reflect God's justice and truth. In this way, righteousness is both a gift and a journey—a continuous cooperation with God's transforming power.

2.6 Living Out Righteousness in Daily Life

Imitating God's Righteous Character

Paul's instruction in Ephesians 4:24 calls believers to "put on the new self, created after the likeness of God in true righteousness and holiness." This means that the reception of divine righteousness should be reflected in every aspect of our lives:

- **Devotion:** Regular prayer and engagement with Scripture deepen our understanding of God's ways.

- **Character:** Honesty, kindness, patience, and courage are tangible expressions of living in God's truth.

- **Growth:** A lifestyle of continual repentance and improvement ensures that we remain aligned with God's standards.

This pursuit of righteousness is not about earning God's favor; it is a grateful response to the gift of salvation that we have received through Christ.

Social Justice and Advocacy

God's righteous character extends beyond individual conduct to include a concern for social justice. The Bible consistently portrays God as a defender of the vulnerable—whether it is the provision for widows and orphans in the Old Testament or Jesus' mission to liberate the oppressed in the New Testament (Luke 4:18–19). For Christians, living out righteousness means advocating for fairness and justice in society. This can involve working against human trafficking, opposing racial discrimination, ensuring fair wages, or improving access to education. Such actions are not merely political stances but are rooted in the desire to mirror the compassionate and just nature of God.

Personal Integrity and Community Impact

Finally, personal integrity is a powerful testimony of God's righteousness. When believers consistently choose truth and fairness, they become beacons of divine justice in their communities. Whether in business, family, or social settings, integrity speaks volumes about the influence of God's character. Moreover, communities that prioritize transparency and mutual accountability create an environment where righteousness flourishes. These communities not only foster individual growth but also serve as a collective witness to a world in need of God's transformative justice.

In Conclusion, God's righteousness is both the standard and the manifestation of divine moral perfection. It is revealed in the covenant promises given to Abraham, in the laws of the Torah, and in the life and teachings of Jesus Christ. Through the writings of Paul, we understand that while all humans fall short, God graciously provides righteousness through faith. This righteousness is not a static quality—it is active in the way God delivers justice, blesses the faithful, and transforms lives through His grace.

As believers, recognizing God's righteousness calls us to trust in His perfect judgments, to live lives marked by integrity, and to advocate for justice in our communities. It challenges us to transform our hearts and actions, aligning them with a standard that is both transcendent and attainable through the power of the Holy Spirit.

In contemplating and embodying God's righteousness, we are invited into a dynamic relationship where judgment and grace meet—a relationship that not only reassures us of ultimate justice but also empowers us to be agents of that justice in a broken world. May we continually seek to reflect this divine standard, knowing that our righteous God is both judge and redeemer, lawgiver and life-giver, guiding us toward a future where His perfect justice reigns.

Chapter 3: Loving

God's love is the most profound expression of His character—a force that not only defines who He is but also transforms every heart it touches. In the Christian faith, God is not simply loving among other attributes; He is love itself (1 John 4:8). This truth sets the stage for exploring a love that is as foundational as it is transformative, reaching from creation through redemption and into the everyday lives of believers.

3.1 The Biblical Foundation of Divine Love

Love in the Old Testament

The Old Testament, often remembered for its laws and judgments, is equally rich with expressions of God's tender affection. From the moment of creation, when God fashioned humanity in His own image and entrusted them with stewardship over the earth (Genesis 1:26–28), we see a love designed for relationship and flourishing.

Throughout Israel's history, God's love is expressed through the Hebrew term *hesed*, a word that captures "lovingkindness," "steadfast love," and "covenant faithfulness." This covenant love is central to God's relationship with His people. In His promises to Abraham (Genesis 12:1–3; 15:1–6), God assures that His favor is not based on human merit but on His enduring commitment. Even when Israel faltered, God's love remained unbroken—a patient, merciful force ever ready to forgive. Prophets like Hosea use vivid imagery, portraying God as a devoted bridegroom or a compassionate father, reinforcing the idea that divine love is about restoring and nurturing a fractured relationship.

Love in the New Testament

The New Testament brings an even more personal dimension to God's love with the advent of Jesus Christ. Jesus not only taught about love but embodied it in every aspect of His ministry. His compassion—healing the sick, embracing the marginalized, and ultimately offering Himself on the cross (Romans 5:8)—reveals a love that is sacrificial and redemptive.

The apostolic writings deepen this understanding. John declares unequivocally, "God is love," affirming that love is not just an action of God but His very essence. Paul, in letters such as Ephesians 3:17–19, describes this love as immeasurable in its dimensions—beyond what human hearts can fully comprehend. Moreover, salvation itself is a product of this divine love; it is by grace—God's unearned favor—that believers are saved (Ephesians 2:8).

3.2 Distinctive Qualities of God's Love

Unconditional Love

Human love often comes with conditions or expectations of reciprocity. By contrast, God's love is entirely unconditional. The parable of the prodigal son (Luke 15:11–32) vividly illustrates this truth: no matter how far one strays, the loving father runs to embrace and restore his wayward child. This radical love does not waver in the face of human failure or doubt—it is offered freely, regardless of merit.

Sacrificial Love

A defining characteristic of divine love is its sacrificial nature. God does not merely offer loving words; He enters into human suffering. Jesus' life is a testament to this, from His gentle acts of service—washing the disciples' feet (John 13:1–17)—to His ultimate sacrifice on the cross. His willingness to endure pain and humiliation reveals a love that overcomes selfishness and uplifts humanity, setting a higher standard for how we relate to one another.

Steadfast and Enduring Love

Scripture repeatedly celebrates the permanence of God's love. The refrain "His steadfast love endures forever" found throughout Psalms (e.g., Psalm 136) reminds us that God's love does not fluctuate with circumstances. It is a constant, reliable source of hope and security. No matter the trials or setbacks in life, believers can trust that God's love remains unshaken and everlasting.

Transformative Love

Beyond providing comfort, God's love transforms lives. When individuals encounter His love, it brings healing, freedom, and renewal. As the Apostle John writes, "We love because He first loved us" (1 John 4:19). This transformative power not only changes personal lives but also empowers believers to extend love to others, breaking cycles of pain and creating communities marked by forgiveness and compassion.

3.3 Theological Insights into Divine Love

Love and the Trinity

A key to understanding God's love lies in the Christian doctrine of the Trinity—Father, Son, and

Holy Spirit. In the eternal relationship among the three persons, love is not an afterthought but the very substance of God's being. This perfect communion exemplifies the self-giving nature of divine love, setting an example for human relationships and revealing that love is at the core of cosmic reality. Through Christ, believers are invited to share in this eternal love, becoming part of the divine family.

Love and Salvation

Salvation, at its heart, is an expression of God's love. John 3:16 proclaims that God loved the world so much that He gave His only Son, not as a reluctant concession but as a bold declaration of His desire to redeem humanity. This love confronts the reality of sin and offers a path to reconciliation and new life. It is the driving force behind the gospel message—God's initiative to restore a broken world through a sacrificial act of love.

The Holy Spirit: The Empowerer of Love

The Holy Spirit plays a crucial role in making divine love a lived reality. Romans 5:5 tells us that God's love has been poured into our hearts through the Holy Spirit. This abundant outpouring equips believers to overcome natural limitations, enabling them to love with patience, forgiveness, and kindness. The Spirit transforms abstract love into concrete actions, allowing communities of faith to embody the love of God in everyday interactions.

3.4 The Transformative Power of God's Love

Healing and Restoration

One of the most powerful effects of divine love is its ability to heal and restore. Whether healing personal wounds from sin, betrayal, or trauma, God's love acts as a balm for the broken-hearted. Biblical narratives abound with examples—from the forgiving encounter with the adulterous woman (John 8:1–11) to the radical transformation of Zacchaeus (Luke 19:1–10) and even the conversion of the Apostle Paul (Acts 9). In every case, an encounter with God's love ignites a process of healing and renewal that redefines identity and purpose.

Liberation from Bondage

Divine love is also liberating. It breaks the chains of addiction, fear, and shame that so often trap individuals in cycles of despair. As 1 John 4:18 reminds us, love casts out fear. When people grasp that they are unconditionally loved by God, the power of past failures and present anxieties diminishes, replaced by a renewed sense of worth and possibility. This liberation is not achieved through human effort alone but by embracing the transformative grace of God.

Catalyzing Service and Ministry

Experiencing God's love compels believers to serve others. When one is filled with the awareness of being deeply loved, the natural response is to extend that love outward. This impulse has driven countless acts of charity, from the compassionate ministry of Mother

Teresa to modern humanitarian efforts in disaster zones and underserved communities. In practical terms, service becomes a means of expressing gratitude for God's love, turning personal transformation into communal impact.

3.5 Living in the Light of God's Love

Receiving and Abiding in Love

To fully benefit from God's love, believers must learn to receive it. This involves embracing the truth that, regardless of past failures, God's love is a constant gift. Scriptures such as Romans 8:38–39 assure us that nothing can separate us from this love. But receiving love is only the beginning. Abiding in it—through prayer, reading Scripture, worship, and fellowship—ensures that it continually shapes our hearts and actions. Jesus' command to "Abide in my love" (John 15:9) is a call to an intimate, ongoing relationship with the Creator.

Loving Others in Response

The transformative power of God's love is meant to be shared. Believers are commanded to "love one another as I have loved you" (John 13:34–35). This means extending grace, forgiveness, and kindness even when it is challenging. In practical terms, loving others can mean mending fractured relationships, showing compassion to those who have wronged us, or simply choosing selflessness over convenience in daily interactions. The biblical portrait of love—patient, kind, and truth-rejoicing (1 Corinthians 13)—serves as a blueprint for building communities that reflect God's heart.

Overcoming Barriers to Love

Despite its power, living out God's love can be challenging. Past hurts, cultural influences, and personal insecurities may hinder our ability to fully embrace and express divine love. Overcoming these obstacles requires intentional effort—through prayer, counseling, and supportive community—to break down barriers and invite God's healing grace. With perseverance and humility, believers can replace fear and resentment with hope and openness, allowing love to flourish in every aspect of life.

In conclusion, in a world often marked by pain and uncertainty, God's love stands as an unwavering beacon of hope. This hope is not naive wishfulness but a confident trust in the One who governs history with perfect love and justice. The promise that "I am with you always" (Matthew 28:20) assures believers that even in the darkest moments, God's presence is constant. This assurance transforms trials into opportunities for growth, reinforcing the belief that divine love sustains us and guides us toward an eternal future where every tear is wiped away (Revelation 21:4).

Chapter 4: Good

"God is good." This familiar declaration echoes in prayers, sermons, and hymns, yet its profound meaning often remains unexamined. To affirm that God is "good" is to acknowledge a multifaceted reality: a divine moral excellence combined with a boundless benevolence that actively cares for creation. In a world where human goodness can be limited or conditional, God's goodness stands as the supreme standard—a perfect and consistent expression of care, provision, and love. This chapter explores the nature, foundations, and implications of God's goodness, examining how it informs our understanding of creation, redemption, and the hope that sustains believers through life's trials.

4.1 Understanding Divine Goodness

Moral Excellence and Benevolence

When we declare "God is good," we are speaking of two interwoven qualities. First, His moral excellence: God is the ultimate standard of purity and righteousness, entirely free from corruption or wickedness. As the source of all moral law, He defines what is right and just. Second, His benevolence: God's goodness is not passive or abstract; it is an active, loving disposition toward His creation. He consistently works for the well-being of all He has made, offering care, sustenance, and hope.

In everyday language, calling someone "good" might suggest that they are kind or helpful. Yet the biblical concept of goodness reaches far deeper. It describes a Creator who not only embodies moral perfection but also purposefully extends grace and blessing. His actions are never arbitrary; they are always aimed at fostering a flourishing, ordered creation where every living thing can thrive.

Distinguishing Goodness from Holiness and Righteousness

While closely related to holiness and righteousness, divine goodness emphasizes a unique relational dimension. Holiness speaks to God's otherness and purity, setting Him apart from sin. Righteousness reveals that His actions are perfectly just. In contrast, goodness highlights His heartfelt kindness and generosity toward creation. It is the gentle aspect of His nature that reassures us of His care even in a fallen world.

4.2 Biblical Foundations of God's Goodness

The Goodness of Creation

The opening chapters of Genesis vividly illustrate God's goodness. As He speaks creation into existence, God repeatedly pronounces His work "good" (Genesis 1). Each element—light, sky, land, plants, animals—is declared good, culminating in the creation of humankind, which is deemed "very good" (Genesis 1:31). This narrative is not merely a description of an ordered universe; it is a testament to the benevolent intent of the Creator. In forming a world characterized by beauty, harmony, and life, God reflects His own good nature in every facet of creation.

The idyllic state of Eden further underscores this truth. In the garden, humanity experienced an unbroken fellowship with God—a relationship marked by care, provision, and abundance. Although sin later disrupted this harmony, the original design of creation continues to remind us that God's intent is for blessing, not for chaos or suffering.

Testimonies in Israel's History

Throughout the Old Testament, the narrative of Israel's journey is imbued with the evidence of God's goodness. In times of distress—such as the enslavement in Egypt—God's response was swift and decisive. He raised up Moses to deliver His people, guiding them from oppression into a promised land described as "flowing with milk and honey." The recurring refrain found in Israel's songs and psalms—"Give thanks to the Lord, for He is good; His steadfast love endures forever" (e.g., 1 Chronicles 16:34; Psalm 107)—confirms that even amidst challenges, God's benevolence remains constant.

Even when Israel faced judgment for its unfaithfulness, God's actions were not vindictive but redemptive. His discipline served to restore and guide His people back to the path of blessing, demonstrating that divine goodness is intrinsically linked to mercy and hope.

The Teaching and Ministry of Jesus

The New Testament offers an even more intimate portrait of God's goodness through the life and teachings of Jesus Christ. Jesus not only spoke about God's goodness but lived it out through His interactions with people. He taught His followers to call God "Our Father," evoking the image of a loving parent who desires the best for His children (Matthew 6:9–13). In His ministry, Jesus healed the sick, fed the hungry, and embraced the marginalized—each act a tangible expression of the Father's benevolent heart.

Perhaps the most profound demonstration of divine goodness is found in the cross. Jesus' sacrificial death reveals a God who is willing to bear suffering and injustice for the sake of humanity. His ultimate act of love assures us that God's goodness is not limited by human failure or sin; it extends even into the realm of redemption and new life.

4.3 God's Goodness in a Broken World

The Tension of Suffering

Believers frequently wrestle with the question: How can a good God allow suffering, natural disasters, and human cruelty? This tension between divine goodness and the presence of evil is as old as humanity itself. The Bible teaches that much of the pain and chaos in the world stems from human free will and the corrupting influence of sin. In many cases, suffering arises as a consequence of human choices—actions that stray from God's perfect design.

Yet, even in the midst of suffering, God's goodness is evident. Scripture reveals that God is actively at work to bring about growth, renewal, and even unexpected blessings through trials (see Genesis 50:20; Romans 8:28). His presence does not eliminate pain, but it offers a redemptive purpose—a promise that every hardship can be transformed into an opportunity for deeper reliance on Him.

Acts of Consolation and Compassion

A crucial aspect of God's goodness is His compassion toward the afflicted. The Psalms assure us that the Lord is close to the brokenhearted (Psalm 34:18), and the prophets remind us that He cares for orphans and widows (Deuteronomy 10:18). In the New Testament, Jesus' own tears at Lazarus' tomb (John 11:35) reveal a Savior who is deeply moved by human suffering. The Holy Spirit, too, serves as a Comforter, instilling strength and peace in the midst of trials.

For believers, these acts of divine consolation are not abstract promises but experienced realities. Whether through personal prayer, the support of a caring community, or the timely reminder of Scripture, God's compassionate presence helps transform suffering into a context for healing and hope.

4.4 Theological Dimensions of Divine Goodness

Goodness as Intrinsic to God's Nature

One theological question arises: Is God good by necessity or by choice? Traditional Christian theology holds that God's goodness is intrinsic to His nature—it is not something He must perform under compulsion but a fundamental aspect of who He is. His moral perfection and benevolence flow naturally from His eternal character. Unlike human beings, whose notions of good can change with circumstances or personal biases, God's goodness is unchanging and reliable. This immutable nature assures us that His intentions toward creation are always for our ultimate welfare.

Common Grace and Providential Care

The concept of "common grace" further illustrates God's all-encompassing goodness. Common grace refers to the unmerited kindness God bestows upon all people, regardless of their spiritual status. Sunlight, rain, creative talents, and the beauty of nature are gifts that reveal the benevolence of a Creator who delights in the flourishing of His creation. This grace is visible in everyday life, inviting every human heart to recognize and respond with gratitude.

Providence, or God's ongoing governance of the world, is another facet of His goodness. Biblical accounts, such as Joseph's rise from slavery to leadership in Egypt (Genesis 37–50), demonstrate how God orchestrates events—even those marked by human wrongdoing—to achieve a benevolent outcome. While believers may face trials and uncertainties, the assurance of God's providence provides a foundation of trust that, ultimately, every aspect of history is subject to His good purpose

4.5 Responding to the God Who Is Good

Imitating Divine Goodness

Recognizing God's goodness calls believers not only to receive His blessings but also to become channels of that goodness. As beings created in God's image, we are invited to mirror His kindness in our interactions. This may involve acts of charity, advocacy for the vulnerable, or simply everyday gestures of compassion and honesty. The call to "do good works" (Ephesians 2:10) is a practical outworking of a life transformed by divine grace, showing the world that God's goodness can be reflected in human relationships.

Trust, Surrender, and Perseverance

Trust in God's goodness is essential, especially during challenging seasons. Believers are encouraged to surrender personal ambitions and fears to a God whose intentions are eternally benevolent. This surrender does not equate to passive resignation but to a confident reliance on His promises. When doubts arise, the testimony of God's past faithfulness—recorded in Scripture and experienced in community—serves as a powerful reminder that His good purposes prevail.

This trust nurtures a steadfast hope, empowering believers to persevere in faith. Even in moments of uncertainty, the conviction that "the Lord is good" can transform despair into determination and encourage a spirit of contentment and joy.

Overcoming Doubts and Embracing Joy

It is natural to encounter moments of doubt when confronted with life's hardships. In such times, reflecting on the consistent evidence of God's goodness—whether in personal experiences or the broader narrative of redemption—can restore faith. Testimonies of answered prayers, communal support during trials, and the enduring nature of God's promises all reinforce the truth that His goodness endures.

This understanding ultimately leads to a deep-seated joy and contentment. Believers find that when their lives are anchored in the knowledge of God's unchanging goodness, they can face each season with gratitude and hope, confident that even the smallest blessings are expressions of His gracious care.

In conclusion, embracing the truth that "God is good" transforms how we view ourselves, our relationships, and the world around us. Divine goodness is not a fleeting sentiment but a profound reality that shapes every aspect of creation—from the beauty of a sunrise to the redemptive work of Christ on the cross. It is a love that establishes moral excellence, offers relentless benevolence, and assures us that no trial is beyond God's redeeming reach.

For believers, the call is twofold: to trust in this goodness with all their hearts and to actively reflect it in their daily lives. In doing so, we become living testimonies to the benevolent heart of our Creator—a heart that heals, restores, and offers hope that transcends all circumstances. May our lives continually mirror this divine goodness, inspiring us to care for one another and to hold fast to the promise that His mercy and faithfulness endure forever.

Chapter 5: Merciful

Mercy is a defining hallmark of the God revealed in Christianity—a compassionate response that reaches into the depths of human suffering, sin, and frailty. Rather than remaining aloof or indifferent, God's mercy is an active, restorative force. It suspends immediate judgment, offers second chances, and seeks to heal broken lives. In this chapter, we explore the nature of divine mercy, its biblical foundations, and its transformative impact on believers.

5.1 Understanding Divine Mercy

The Heart of Mercy

Mercy, though closely related to love, focuses more specifically on those who are suffering, guilty, or weak. Whereas love reflects God's broad benevolence toward all of creation, mercy is His compassionate response toward human need. It is as if God's own heart, tender like that of a caring parent, is moved to act on behalf of those in distress. In the Old Testament, the Hebrew words *racham* and *rachamim*—terms that evoke the nurturing closeness of a womb— capture this intimate, protective quality. In the New Testament, the Greek *eleos* similarly conveys a heartfelt pity that leads to relief and rescue.

Mercy versus Grace

While mercy and grace are often mentioned together, they highlight different facets of God's kindness. Grace refers to the unmerited favor God gives—blessings and gifts that no one can earn. Mercy, on the other hand, addresses the immediate need to relieve suffering or avert deserved judgment. In essence, while grace bestows undeserved blessings, mercy spares us from the full consequences of our wrongdoing. Together, they offer a complete picture of a God who is both lavishly generous and deeply compassionate.

5.2 Biblical Foundations of God's Mercy

Old Testament Illustrations

1. **The Story of Jonah** In the book of Jonah, God's mercy is vividly displayed when He calls a repentant city to transformation. Jonah is sent to warn the people of Nineveh—a city notorious for its wickedness. Despite Jonah's initial reluctance and prejudice, God's compassionate nature prevails. When the Ninevites repent, God withholds the judgment He had planned. Jonah's complaint—lamenting that God is "a gracious God and merciful, slow to anger and abounding in steadfast love" (Jonah 4:2)—reveals how mercy can challenge our notions of who deserves compassion.

2. **Israel's Deliverance** Throughout Israel's history, God's mercy is evident in His repeated deliverance of His people. When the Israelites suffered under oppression or the consequences of their disobedience, they cried out, and God responded by raising leaders like Moses or the Judges to rescue them. This recurring pattern—sin, oppression, repentance, deliverance—demonstrates that even when His people falter, God's mercy remains available, always inviting them back to a relationship of blessing and hope.

3. **The Psalms** The Psalms are rich with expressions of God's merciful character. Verses such as Psalm 86:15 and Psalm 103:8 remind us that God is "gracious and merciful, slow to anger and abounding in steadfast love." In these prayers, lament turns into praise as the psalmists find comfort in the assurance of God's compassionate care.

New Testament Revelations

1. **Jesus' Compassionate Ministry** In the Gospels, Jesus exemplifies divine mercy through His actions and teachings. He healed the sick, fed the hungry, and reached out to sinners, demonstrating a mercy that does not discriminate. For example, when a blind beggar named Bartimaeus called out for help (Mark 10:46–52), Jesus stopped and restored his sight—a clear sign that divine mercy meets urgent human need.

2. **Parables of Mercy** Jesus frequently used parables to illustrate the nature of God's mercy. In the parable of the Good Samaritan (Luke 10:25–37), mercy is shown as a compassionate response that transcends social and ethnic boundaries. Likewise, the parable of the Prodigal Son (Luke 15:11–32) depicts a father who eagerly forgives and restores his wayward child, embodying the merciful heart of God.

3. **The Cross as the Ultimate Expression** The crucifixion of Jesus is perhaps the most powerful demonstration of divine mercy. Although humanity was steeped in sin, God did not wait for perfection. As Romans 5:8 reminds us, "while we were still sinners, Christ died for us." At Calvary, God absorbed the full penalty of sin so that sinners might be offered forgiveness and reconciliation—a mercy that redefines what it means

to be saved.

5.3 Dimensions of Divine Mercy

Forgiveness and Pardon

A central aspect of mercy is the forgiveness of sins. Instead of requiring us to bear the full consequences of our wrongdoings, God's mercy lifts the burden of guilt. Through sincere confession and repentance (1 John 1:9), believers are granted pardon, restoring their relationship with God and freeing them from the weight of condemnation.

Restoration and Healing

Mercy extends beyond forgiveness—it brings restoration and healing. Emotional wounds, physical ailments, and spiritual brokenness are met with God's tender care. Jesus' healing of outcasts and the cleansing of lepers demonstrate that divine mercy not only forgives but also renews, reintegrating individuals back into community and purpose.

Divine Forbearance

God's mercy is also evident in His forbearance—His willingness to delay judgment. Throughout Scripture, God "bears with" human failings, offering multiple opportunities for repentance (2 Peter 3:9). This patient forbearance highlights a divine desire for transformation rather than retribution, inviting us to change our ways and embrace His loving discipline.

5.4 Receiving and Embracing God's Mercy

The Call to Confession and Repentance

To experience divine mercy, one must first acknowledge personal sin and need. Genuine confession and heartfelt repentance open the door to God's forgiveness. As believers come before Him with humility, they are cleansed and set on a path of renewal.

Trusting in God's Character

Many struggle to accept God's mercy, believing their sins too great to be forgiven. Yet Scripture assures us that God is "rich in mercy" (Ephesians 2:4). Trust in His unchanging character helps us overcome shame and despair, enabling us to receive His compassion wholeheartedly.

Embracing Transformation

Receiving mercy is not a passive act; it calls for active cooperation with the Holy Spirit. As we allow God's mercy to heal our wounds and transform our lives, we learn to live in a way that reflects His restorative power. This transformation brings inner freedom, renewed purpose, and a deeper commitment to following God's will.

5.5 Reflecting God's Mercy in Daily Life

Personal Compassion

Believers are called to mirror God's mercy in their interactions with others. This means extending forgiveness, offering help to those in distress, and refraining from harsh judgment. Jesus' words in the Sermon on the Mount—"Blessed are the merciful, for they shall receive mercy" (Matthew 5:7)—remind us that living mercifully is both a response to God's grace and a witness to His character.

Social Justice and Advocacy

Mercy has a broader societal dimension. Throughout Scripture, God shows special concern for the oppressed, the orphaned, and the marginalized. Christians are therefore urged to engage in social justice—addressing poverty, discrimination, and exploitation—as an expression of God's compassionate heart. By advocating for systemic change, believers help create communities that reflect divine mercy and uphold the dignity of every individual.

Cultivating a Community of Mercy

Churches and faith communities should serve as havens of mercy—places where individuals find support, restoration, and a nonjudgmental welcome. This means fostering environments that encourage confession, provide practical help, and emphasize accountability tempered by compassion. When communities embody mercy, they become powerful testimonies of God's transformative love.

5.6 The Transformative Power of Divine Mercy

Deliverance from Shame

One of the most liberating aspects of God's mercy is its ability to free us from the chains of shame. Unlike guilt, which focuses on specific actions, shame attacks our very identity. Divine mercy reaffirms our inherent worth and reminds us that we are beloved, regardless of our failures. This profound release from shame enables personal growth and healthy relationships.

Breaking Cycles of Harm

Mercy has the power to interrupt destructive cycles. In families and communities marred by bitterness or abuse, the decision to respond with compassion rather than retaliation can lead to reconciliation and healing. When mercy is extended, it disrupts the cycle of harm and creates an opportunity for lasting change.

Deepening Worship and Gratitude

Experiencing God's mercy naturally deepens our worship. The Psalms are filled with exclamations of wonder at a God who "does not deal with us according to our sins" (Psalm 103:10). As we reflect on how mercy has touched our lives, our gratitude grows, inspiring us to praise and worship with renewed fervor. This deepened sense of worship is both a personal and communal response—a testimony to a God who transforms our hearts with His boundless compassion.

In conclusion, God's mercy is not a passive sentiment but an active, redemptive force. It reaches into the darkest corners of human experience—offering forgiveness to the guilty, healing to the wounded, and hope to the desperate. For believers, this mercy transforms our understanding of ourselves and our relationships. It frees us from the heavy burden of shame, invites us to trust in God's unchanging character, and calls us to extend the same compassion to others. In a world marked by pain and injustice, God's mercy stands as a beacon of hope— a promise that no one is beyond redemption.

May we continually receive, embrace, and reflect this divine mercy, allowing it to shape our lives, our communities, and our worship. In doing so, we join in the sacred work of restoration, becoming living testimonies of a merciful God whose compassion never fails, whose forgiveness renews, and whose love transforms every heart it touches.

Chapter 6: Compassionate

God's compassion reveals His profound empathy and tender-hearted care toward all His creatures. More than mere sympathy, divine compassion is an active, relational force that moves God to respond to human suffering with decisive care. It is the emotional dimension of His benevolence—a willingness to enter into our deepest pain and brokenness and transform it through healing, restoration, and hope. In this chapter, we explore the foundations, expressions, and transformative power of God's compassion and how it shapes our relationship with Him and with one another.

6.1 Understanding Divine Compassion

The Heart of Compassion

Compassion is the intimate, visceral response that arises when one truly encounters another's suffering. In Scripture, this quality is vividly portrayed by the Hebrew word *racham*, which is linked to the image of a womb—a symbol of nurturing and deep care. In the New Testament, the Greek term *splagchnizomai* conveys a gut-level reaction to distress. Unlike detached pity, divine compassion is an active, empathetic engagement that sees human pain and is stirred to act.

Compassion Compared to Mercy and Love

While related to mercy and love, compassion has its own distinct focus. Mercy involves withholding judgment or alleviating punishment, and grace provides unmerited favor. Compassion, however, zeroes in on the immediate emotional response to suffering. It bridges the gap between God's transcendent nature and human frailty by showing that He is not indifferent to our pain. His compassionate heart reaches down to rescue the oppressed, comfort the grieving, and restore the broken.

Old Testament Illustrations

1. **The Exodus Narrative** In the book of Exodus, the plight of the Israelites in Egyptian bondage calls forth God's compassionate intervention. Their cries for deliverance are not ignored; instead, God "hears" their groaning, remembers His covenant, and raises Moses as their deliverer. Through dramatic acts—confronting Pharaoh, sending plagues, and parting the Red Sea—God demonstrates that His compassion moves Him to rescue those who suffer under oppression.

2. **The Prophets' Lament and Hope** The prophets frequently portray God as deeply moved by the pain of His people. Hosea, for instance, uses the image of a betrayed husband who still yearns to restore his unfaithful wife, underscoring that even when Israel strays, God's heart "recoils within" Him, seeking to heal and restore (Hosea 11:8–9). Jeremiah, too, depicts God weeping over the destruction brought by sin, showing that divine compassion is intertwined with both justice and hope.

3. **The Psalms** The Psalms echo this compassionate character. Verses such as Psalm 34:18 affirm that "The Lord is close to the brokenhearted," and countless laments turn to praise as the psalmists experience God's tender care. These prayers reveal a God who is intimately acquainted with human suffering and who offers comfort amid despair.

New Testament Revelations

1. **Jesus's Compassion in Action** In the Gospels, Jesus is repeatedly described as being "moved with compassion." Whether feeding the hungry, healing the sick, or restoring sight to the blind, His ministry is marked by an immediate response to need. One striking example is the raising of a widow's son (Luke 7:13), where Jesus, seeing her grief, is deeply moved and restores life. In every act, Jesus models a compassion that is personal, proactive, and transformative.

2. **Parables Illustrating Compassion** Jesus' parables further reveal the heart of divine compassion. In the parable of the Good Samaritan (Luke 10:25–37), the Samaritan's caring response to a wounded stranger transcends social and cultural barriers. Likewise, the parable of the Prodigal Son (Luke 15:11–32) portrays a father who runs to embrace his wayward child even before any plea for forgiveness—a vivid picture of a compassionate God eager to restore the lost.

3. **The Cross as the Ultimate Act of Compassion** The crucifixion of Jesus stands as the pinnacle of divine compassion. While humanity was steeped in sin, God chose to bear its penalty by offering His Son as a sacrifice. Romans 5:8 reminds us that "while we were still sinners, Christ died for us." The Cross is not only an act of atonement but also the supreme demonstration that God is deeply moved by human suffering, willing

to enter into our worst condition to bring redemption and new life.

6.3 Expressions and Dimensions of Divine Compassion

Emotional Resonance and Active Intervention

One of the most striking aspects of God's compassion is that He genuinely "feels" our pain. Far from being a distant judge, God is moved to act. His compassion is not passive; it propels Him to intervene—whether by delivering the Israelites from bondage or by healing the sick and comforting the brokenhearted. This active intervention gives hope that our cries are heard and that no suffering is overlooked.

Inclusiveness and Universal Reach

Although Scripture often focuses on Israel, God's compassionate care extends to all peoples. The Psalms and prophetic writings affirm that all nations are within God's concern. In the New Testament, Jesus' outreach crosses ethnic, cultural, and social boundaries—ministering to Samaritans, Romans, and outcasts alike. Divine compassion breaks down barriers, demonstrating that no one is beyond the reach of God's loving embrace.

6.4 Compassion in the Midst of Suffering

Addressing the Problem of Suffering

A common question is: If God is so compassionate, why does suffering persist? The Christian response acknowledges that much of human suffering results from the misuse of free will and the broken state of creation following sin. God permits human freedom and the consequent disorder of a fallen world; yet, His compassion is ever-present, offering comfort, hope, and redemptive purpose even amid pain. This is further underscored by the eschatological promise in Revelation 21:4, where a future without tears affirms that God's compassion will ultimately prevail.

The Cross: Compassion Conquering Suffering

The Cross uniquely encapsulates the tension between suffering and divine compassion. In taking on human sin and experiencing the agony of betrayal and death, Jesus did not stand apart from our pain but immersed Himself in it. His resurrection then offers the promise that suffering is not the final word—it can be transformed into hope and renewal. This profound mystery assures believers that God's compassion is active even in the darkest moments.

6.5 Receiving and Experiencing God's Compassion

Opening Up to Divine Presence

To experience God's compassion, one must be willing to be vulnerable. Scripture models this through the raw, honest prayers of the psalmists, who poured out their fears, sorrows, and doubts before God. Authenticity in our struggles invites God's comforting presence, assuring us that His heart is tender toward every human wound.

Spiritual Practices for Nurturing Compassion

Regular prayer, meditation on Scripture, and participation in communal worship help us attune our hearts to God's compassionate voice. As we engage in these practices, we become more receptive to the Holy Spirit's work in binding up our brokenness and offering comfort. These disciplines not only deepen our relationship with God but also transform our capacity to empathize with others.

Healing and Restoration

Experiencing divine compassion leads to healing—not just physical or emotional, but spiritual renewal. Many find that the healing of deep wounds, whether from trauma, shame, or loss, opens the door to a renewed sense of self-worth and purpose. Through the counsel of caring communities and the direct work of the Spirit, the places of deepest hurt can become sites of profound restoration and growth.

6.6 Reflecting Divine Compassion in the World

Personal Kindness and Empathy

Believers who have experienced God's compassion are called to extend it to others. This begins with simple, everyday acts: listening to a friend in distress, forgiving past wrongs, or offering help to those in need. The Apostle Paul urges us in Ephesians 4:32 to "be kind to one another, tenderhearted, forgiving one another, as God in Christ forgave you." Personal acts of compassion reflect the transformative power of a heart touched by God's love.

Compassion in Community and Church

Church communities should be places where compassion thrives. By creating environments that welcome the vulnerable and support those in crisis, churches serve as living testimonies of God's care. Whether through support groups for grief or outreach programs for marginalized individuals, the church can embody a culture of mercy that both comforts and challenges.

Social Engagement and Justice

Beyond personal interactions, divine compassion compels Christians to address broader social issues. This includes advocating for policies that protect the oppressed, challenging systems of injustice, and mobilizing resources to alleviate suffering in communities worldwide. Historical movements for social justice have often been fueled by a deep conviction that God's compassion extends to every person, demanding that we work for a society that reflects His values of dignity and care.

Spiritual Growth and Unity

When believers embrace a lifestyle of compassion, they experience profound spiritual growth. Compassion encourages us to move beyond self-interest, interceding for others and deepening our understanding of God's character. This, in turn, fosters unity within the community of faith. As we share in each other's burdens and joys, our bonds strengthen, and the church becomes a more effective witness to a world in need.

Healing Broken Relationships

Compassion has the power to mend fractured relationships. When individuals choose to approach conflicts with empathy and understanding rather than judgment or resentment, they create opportunities for reconciliation and forgiveness. In doing so, they reflect God's own heart—a heart that does not abandon but restores.

In conclusion, divine compassion offers hope. It assures us that no matter how deep our suffering or how broken our world may seem, God's tender care is at work. This hope is not naive; it is rooted in the historical and redemptive reality of a God who has repeatedly demonstrated His willingness to intervene. As we reflect on the Cross and the promise of a renewed creation, we are reminded that compassion is not merely an ideal—it is a dynamic, life-changing force that points us toward a better tomorrow.

Chapter 7: Gracious

God's graciousness is a cornerstone of the Christian faith—a lavish, unmerited favor that defines His relationship with humanity. It is not earned by human merit but freely given, inviting both sinners and saints into a transformative relationship with the Divine. Graciousness undergirds salvation, shapes our identity in Christ, and calls us to reflect this generosity in our daily lives.

7.1 Defining Divine Graciousness

The Essence of Grace

In Scripture, the concept of grace—often expressed by the Hebrew word *chen* and the Greek *charis*—speaks of unmerited favor, kindness, and goodwill. God's graciousness is His predisposition to bestow blessings, forgiveness, and renewal regardless of human merit. Unlike rewards that are earned, grace flows freely from God's generous character. It is not an afterthought but the very heartbeat of His interaction with creation.

Grace Versus Reward

A reward is given in return for effort or obedience; grace, however, is a gift without any prerequisite. This paradox—that we cannot earn God's favor yet receive it abundantly—is central to Christian theology. Salvation, spiritual gifts, and daily blessings all spring from this divine generosity, inviting believers into deeper fellowship with a God who delights in redeeming even the unworthy.

7.2 Biblical Foundations of Graciousness

Old Testament Foundations

1. **Patriarchal Narratives** Early in Scripture, God demonstrates His gracious character through His interactions with Abraham, Isaac, and Jacob. For example, God calls

Abraham out of obscurity to be the father of many nations (Genesis 12:1–3) despite his flaws. Similarly, Jacob—despite his deceit—receives a covenantal promise and is renamed Israel, signifying that God's grace surpasses human imperfection.

2. **Covenant and the Law** The giving of the Law at Sinai, though seemingly strict, is rooted in a history of deliverance. God reminds the Israelites that their freedom from Egyptian bondage was an act of grace, setting the stage for a relationship built on forgiveness and guidance. Even as the people repeatedly fall short, God's patient forbearance underscores His desire to restore rather than condemn.

3. **Psalms and Wisdom Literature** The poetic texts of the Old Testament frequently extol God's gracious nature. Verses like Psalm 86:15 declare, "You, O Lord, are a God merciful and gracious," reinforcing that His benevolence is an intrinsic aspect of His identity. Through these writings, worshipers are reminded that grace is a constant, sustaining force in their lives.

New Testament Revelations

1. **The Incarnation and Ministry of Jesus** The clearest demonstration of divine graciousness is found in the person of Jesus Christ. In taking on human flesh (John 1:14), God enters our broken world, identifying with our struggles and extending His unmerited favor. Jesus' teachings, miracles, and sacrificial love reveal a grace that transforms lives and restores hope.

2. **Parables Illustrating Grace** Jesus' parables, such as the Laborers in the Vineyard (Matthew 20:1–16) and the Great Banquet (Luke 14:15–24), challenge conventional notions of merit. They depict a kingdom where generosity triumphs over strict fairness—where even the last are given the same gift as the first. These stories underscore that grace is not a reward for hard work but a free, unearned gift.

3. **Healings and Miracles** Beyond parables, Jesus' healings highlight the gracious dimension of His mission. Outcasts and sinners receive not only physical restoration but a renewed sense of dignity and acceptance. This radical kindness reinforces the truth that God's favor reaches beyond human standards, embracing all who come to Him.

7.3. Theological Implications of Divine Graciousness

Centrality in Salvation

Grace is inseparable from the Christian concept of salvation. As Paul explains in Ephesians 2:8–9, we are saved "by grace through faith"—a gift from God, not the result of human effort. This unearned favor transforms our relationship with God, shifting it from one of striving for approval to one of grateful acceptance. Our salvation is secured not by our deeds but by His generosity.

New Identity and Empowerment

Receiving God's grace reshapes our identity. Instead of being defined by our failures or self-righteous efforts, we are adopted into God's family as beloved children. This new identity empowers us to live transformed lives—marked by humility, gratitude, and a commitment to share His grace with others. Our empowerment is not self-generated; it flows from the Spirit, enabling us to resist sin and actively pursue righteousness.

A Call to Humility

Recognizing that every blessing is unmerited demolishes any grounds for pride. Since we can boast in nothing but the gift of grace, believers are called to live with profound humility. This humility is the foundation of the Christian community, where individuals are encouraged to extend the same patience, generosity, and forgiveness they have received from God.

7.4 Receiving and Living Out Divine Graciousness

Embracing Grace Through Faith and Repentance

To receive God's grace, one must come before Him in humble faith and genuine repentance. Faith is the posture of open hands—an acknowledgment of our need and a trust in God's generosity. While repentance involves turning away from sin, it is not a condition for grace but rather the means by which we continuously hold fast to it. As 2 Corinthians 7:10 explains, godly sorrow leads to repentance and healing.

Daily Reliance on Grace

Grace is not a one-time event but a daily reality. Believers are called to rely on God's unmerited favor in every aspect of life—overcoming temptation, enduring trials, and seeking wisdom for each decision. This ongoing dependence nurtures intimacy with God and reinforces the truth that our strength and hope come from His limitless generosity.

7.5 Reflecting Divine Graciousness in Relationships

Gracious Speech and Attitude

Scripture exhorts believers to let their communication be "gracious, seasoned with salt" (Colossians 4:6). Our words and attitudes should mirror the kindness and generosity we have received. When we speak with understanding, empathy, and forgiveness, we extend the tangible reality of God's grace to those around us.

Forgiveness and Conflict Resolution

In relationships, grace enables us to overcome grudges and resentment. By choosing forgiveness over revenge, we dismantle barriers to reconciliation. This approach does not condone sin but reflects a heart transformed by grace—a heart that understands that every person is in need of mercy and second chances.

Generosity and Hospitality

The gracious nature of God inspires us to be generous and hospitable. Sharing our resources, welcoming strangers, and caring for the disadvantaged become natural expressions of a life touched by divine favor. The early church's practice of communal living (Acts 2:44–45) is a powerful testament to how grace can forge bonds of unity and compassion, providing a witness to a world driven by meritocracy.

7.6 Misconceptions and Challenges

Avoiding "Cheap Grace"

A potential pitfall is the notion of "cheap grace," where the gift of God's favor is taken lightly as a license to live without moral accountability. True grace transforms; it does not excuse sinful behavior but leads to a sincere pursuit of holiness. Recognizing the high cost of Christ's sacrifice keeps us mindful that grace is both a profound gift and a call to responsible living.

Reconciling Grace with Fairness

Human logic often demands that rewards be earned. Yet divine grace upends this notion by demonstrating that salvation and blessing come unconditionally. While this may seem unfair by worldly standards, it reveals a higher order—a reality where love and mercy triumph over strict merit. Embracing this mystery requires humility and trust in God's sovereign goodness.

Overcoming Cultural Barriers

In cultures that prize self-reliance and hard work, accepting grace can be challenging. Many struggle with feelings of unworthiness or the belief that they should earn God's favor. However, the message of grace is radical: it is precisely for those who cannot achieve perfection on their own. Recognizing our need and receiving grace invites us into a liberating relationship with God, where our value is defined not by our efforts but by His unchanging love.

In conclusion, God's graciousness is a transformative force—a lavish, unmerited favor that redefines our relationship with Him and with one another. From the patriarchs to the giving of the Law, from the Psalms to the life and sacrifice of Jesus, Scripture testifies that grace is at the heart of God's character. It is the gift that saves us, empowers us, and calls us to live with humility and generosity.

Chapter 8: Faithful

God's faithfulness is the rock-solid foundation upon which believers place their hope. Unlike human reliability, which can falter with changing circumstances, divine faithfulness remains unwavering across time, culture, and even in our own shortcomings. To call God "faithful" is to affirm that He consistently keeps His promises, remains true to His word, and provides an unshakable anchor for trust and hope. This chapter explores the biblical basis for God's faithfulness, its expression in both the Old and New Testaments, and how it shapes the Christian life.

8.1 The Nature of Divine Faithfulness

Unchanging Reliability

At its core, faithfulness means loyalty, consistency, and dependability. God's faithfulness is not a conditional quality that ebbs and flows—it is inherent in His nature. Unlike human loyalties that can be influenced by self-interest or fleeting emotions, God's commitment is immutable. He is the steadfast rock amid life's storms, providing a secure foundation for the covenant relationship He establishes with His people. Even when we fail, His promises endure, inviting us to return in repentance and find restoration.

Distinct from Love and Mercy

While love and mercy highlight God's desire to care for and forgive His creation, faithfulness emphasizes His unwavering commitment to the promises He makes. Love may inspire Him to act, and mercy may soften judgment, but faithfulness guarantees that He will never abandon His word. This quality assures us that every promise—whether of salvation, provision, or restoration—is a certainty, not a mere possibility.

Old Testament Foundations

Covenant as the Anchor: The concept of covenant is central in the Old Testament, where God's promises to figures like Noah, Abraham, and David reveal His enduring loyalty. Consider the covenant with Abraham: despite human shortcomings, God promised descendants, land, and blessing (Genesis 15), and He remains true to that promise across generations. These covenants demonstrate that God's faithfulness is not contingent on human perfection but is rooted in His own character.

Stories of Deliverance and Restoration: Throughout Israel's history, God's faithfulness is evident even in the midst of human failure. In the story of Joseph, for example, a series of betrayals and hardships ultimately lead to his rise in Egypt—a turning point that preserves an entire nation from famine. Similarly, during the periods of the monarchy, exile, and prophetic warning, God repeatedly shows that He never forsakes those who turn to Him. The prophetic writings affirm that even when Israel strays, a faithful remnant is preserved and restored.

Poetic Testimonies: The Psalms and other poetic writings celebrate God's unchanging reliability. Phrases like "Your steadfast love, O Lord, extends to the heavens" (Psalm 36:5) serve as reminders that His faithfulness is as vast as the universe. In times of despair, the psalmists shift from lament to praise, confident that God's promises remain secure no matter how dire the circumstances.

New Testament Affirmations

Christ as the Fulfillment of Promises: The New Testament reveals God's faithfulness most fully in the person of Jesus Christ. Jesus' life, ministry, death, and resurrection are the ultimate fulfillment of the promises foretold in the Old Testament. In His words, Jesus affirmed that He came not to abolish the Law and the Prophets but to fulfill them (Matthew 5:17). His sacrificial obedience, culminating on the Cross, stands as proof that God completes what He begins. The resurrection, in particular, assures believers that God's redemptive work is both decisive and everlasting.

Apostolic Exhortations: The apostles further underscore God's faithfulness in their writings. Paul reminds the Corinthians that "God is faithful, by whom you were called into the fellowship of his Son" (1 Corinthians 1:9) and assures them that God will not allow them to be tempted beyond what they can bear, but will also provide a way out (1 Corinthians 10:13). In Hebrews, the call to "hold fast the confession of our hope without wavering" (Hebrews 10:23) is rooted in the assurance that "he who promised is faithful." These teachings encourage believers to trust in God's reliability, even in the face of personal or communal challenges.

Revelation's Promise: The Book of Revelation offers a cosmic perspective on God's faithfulness. Amid apocalyptic visions of conflict and tribulation, the triumphant image of God on His throne and the Lamb who reigns eternal underscore that nothing can thwart His plan. The promise of a new heaven and a new earth, where suffering is no more, reaffirms that God's faithfulness will ultimately bring complete restoration.

8.3 The Theological Implications of God's Faithfulness

Certainty of Promises

Because God is faithful, His promises are not mere hopes but certainties. This conviction transforms how believers live, pray, and face the future. Hope is not an empty wish but a confident expectation that God will fulfill His word—whether that is the promise of salvation, daily provision, or eternal life. When we pray, we do so with the assurance that our petitions align with a loving, reliable God.

Comfort in Suffering

In times of suffering, the knowledge of God's faithfulness offers deep comfort. Believers can trust that even when circumstances seem bleak, God remains present and active. Romans 8:28 assures us that "in all things God works for the good of those who love Him." This promise helps us understand that suffering, while painful, is not the final word; God is using it to shape our character and draw us closer to Him.

Empowerment for Growth

God's faithfulness also underpins our spiritual growth. As Philippians 1:6 reminds us, "He who began a good work in you will carry it on to completion." This means that our journey of sanctification—becoming more like Christ—is supported by a God who is unwavering in His commitment to transform us. We can persevere in spiritual disciplines, confident that our struggles are met with divine strength and guidance.

8.4 Living in the Light of Divine Faithfulness

Cultivating Trust and Dependence

Recognizing God's unchanging reliability transforms our everyday lives. Trusting in His faithfulness allows us to step out in obedience and make decisions without fear, knowing that He directs our paths. This dependence on God converts anxious striving into deliberate, prayerful action. Instead of fretting over uncertain outcomes, believers rest in the assurance that God's promises are secure.

Gratitude and Worship

A heart attuned to God's faithfulness naturally overflows with gratitude. Worship, both corporate and personal, becomes a celebration of His constant presence and unwavering love. When we recall past instances of divine rescue and provision, our prayers turn into praises that honor the One who is always true. This gratitude not only deepens our relationship with God but also encourages us to reflect His reliability in our interactions with others.

Reflecting Faithfulness in Relationships

Encountering God's steadfast loyalty compels us to mirror that quality in our relationships. Whether in our families, friendships, or communities, being faithful means keeping promises, standing by others in times of need, and fostering trust. When we honor our commitments and show consistent care, we become living testimonies of the divine faithfulness that sustains us.

8.5 Overcoming Doubts and Embracing Assurance

Addressing Uncertainty

There are moments when God's faithfulness may seem obscured by unanswered prayers or prolonged trials. The Bible itself includes raw expressions of doubt—from Jeremiah to Job—but these moments invite deeper engagement with God's past acts of reliability. Reflecting on the long history of divine rescue, from the covenants of old to the resurrection of Christ, helps us reframe our present hardships within the larger narrative of God's unwavering fidelity.

The Role of Lament

Lament is not a sign of weak faith but a vital expression of honest grappling with pain. Through lament, we can bring our doubts and grief before God, trusting that He hears us. The Psalms often transition from sorrow to renewed hope as the psalmist remembers that God's steadfast love endures. Such expressions pave the way for a deeper, more resilient faith that is rooted in the certainty of God's promises.

Intergenerational Assurance

One of the most comforting aspects of divine faithfulness is its continuity through generations. The stories passed down through families and recorded in Scripture serve as reminders that God's reliability is not limited to one season but spans the entirety of history. This legacy of faith encourages each generation to trust in the same promises that sustained their ancestors, creating a community bound by the certainty of God's word.

In conclusion, to proclaim that God is faithful is to declare that He never wavers from His promises or His character, no matter how chaotic the world may seem. From the covenants of the Old Testament to the fulfillment of those promises in the life, death, and resurrection of Jesus Christ, Scripture resounds with the assurance that God's loyalty is unbreakable.

This truth transforms our daily lives: it grounds our prayers in hope, comforts us in suffering, and empowers us for spiritual growth. It also calls us to reflect His faithfulness in our own relationships as we strive to be trustworthy and steadfast in our commitments. Even when doubts arise, the collective testimony of God's unchanging nature offers us a secure foundation upon which to build our future.

Chapter 9: Patient (Long-Suffering)

God's patience, often expressed as "long-suffering," is a vital aspect of His character. It reveals a Divine willingness to endure human failings, rebellion, and repeated mistakes without rushing to judgment. Unlike mere tolerance, God's patience is active, purposeful, and redemptive—providing time for repentance, growth, and restored relationship. This chapter explores the biblical foundations of God's patience, its theological implications, and practical ways believers can emulate this long-suffering love in daily life.

9.1 Understanding Divine Patience

A. The Nature of Long-Suffering

Divine patience is more than simply putting up with offenses—it is a deliberate restraint of judgment aimed at giving humanity the opportunity to repent and transform. God's long-suffering is not born of indifference; rather, it reflects His deep commitment to restoring relationships. He has the power to judge immediately but chooses instead to delay judgment, showing a heart that longs for reconciliation over retribution.

B. Distinguishing Patience from Mercy and Compassion

While mercy relieves immediate suffering and compassion shows empathetic care, patience focuses on the temporal dimension of God's dealings with sin and rebellion. God's patience spans extended periods, offering repeated chances for people to turn toward Him. It is this enduring forbearance that underscores His commitment even when human efforts falter.

9.2 Biblical Foundations

A. Old Testament Examples

1. **Self-Revelation in Exodus** In Exodus 34:6, God describes Himself as "merciful and gracious, slow to anger, and abounding in steadfast love." This self-disclosure, given

after Israel's sin with the golden calf, highlights that God's patience is an intentional aspect of His covenant commitment. His reluctance to deliver immediate punishment underscores a desire to bring His people back into the relationship.

2. **Narrative Illustrations**

   o **Pre-Flood Generation:** Despite the rampant wickedness of humanity, God gave Noah ample warning and time to build an ark. This delay shows God's patient opportunity for repentance, even though the Flood eventually demonstrates that unrepentant sin has consequences.

   o **Wilderness Wanderings:** During Israel's 40-year sojourn in the desert, despite repeated complaints and acts of idolatry, God continued to provide manna, water, and guidance. This period of discipline and care taught Israel that even in failure, His patience offers room for learning and growth.

3. **Psalms and Prophetic Voices** The Psalms frequently attest to God's enduring patience. When the psalmists transition from lament to praise, they remind themselves that God does not abandon His people despite their repeated failures. Prophets like Jeremiah and Hosea depict a God who, though just, is slow to anger and always ready to restore those who repent.

B. New Testament Affirmations

1. **Jesus' Ministry** Jesus exemplifies divine patience in His approach to sinners and outcasts. In the parables of the Prodigal Son and the Barren Fig Tree, He illustrates that God patiently waits for repentance rather than immediately condemning wrongdoing. When Jesus healed the sick or forgave sins, He showed that divine patience underpins both His miraculous acts and His teachings.

2. **Apostolic Teaching** Paul explains in Romans 2:4 that God's kindness is meant to lead people to repentance. Similarly, 2 Peter 3:9 emphasizes that the Lord is patient, "not wishing that any should perish, but that all should reach repentance." These passages affirm that God's apparent delay in judgment is purposeful—providing opportunities for transformation rather than permitting unchecked sin.

3. **Eschatological Perspective** In Revelation, the final triumph of God over evil is depicted as the fulfillment of His long-suffering patience. Amid cosmic conflict, the certainty of God's eventual judgment and renewal of all things reminds believers that His timing, though sometimes inscrutable, is perfectly aligned with His redemptive plan.

9.3 Theological Implications

A. Space for Repentance and Growth: God's patience creates a temporal window during which individuals and communities can reflect, repent, and realign themselves with His will. If every misstep were met with instant judgment, there would be no room for spiritual maturation. Divine patience thus embodies God's redemptive purpose, offering chances for genuine transformation rather than immediate retribution.

B. The Mystery of Divine Timing: The "delay" of God's judgment can be perplexing, especially when injustice and suffering persist. However, His timing reflects a providence that surpasses human understanding. God balances the need to rectify wrongdoing with a broader plan for redemption. This tension invites believers to trust in His sovereign timing, even when the reasons behind delays remain hidden.

C. Interplay with Justice: God's long-suffering does not negate His commitment to justice. Rather, it postpones judgment to allow for repentance and restoration. The eventual fulfillment of divine justice, as seen at the Cross and in the promise of a new creation, shows that God's patience is part of a larger narrative where mercy and justice converge.

9.4 Living in the Light of Divine Patience

A. Cultivating Humility and Gratitude: Recognizing God's extended patience encourages humility. Every believer has, at some point, benefited from His forbearance—whether through second chances or gradual growth. This awareness dismantles self-righteousness and instills deep gratitude, prompting a worshipful response that honors God's enduring kindness.

B. Perseverance in the Spiritual Journey: Understanding that growth is a gradual process helps believers persevere through setbacks and slow progress. Just as a gardener patiently tends to a vine, God nurtures us steadily. When progress seems slow, the knowledge of His long-suffering inspires believers to continue in faith, trusting that every step of their journey is undergirded by divine care.

C. Extending Patience to Others: God's example of patience challenges us to practice long-suffering in our own relationships. This means bearing with one another's weaknesses, forgiving repeatedly, and investing time in helping others grow. In families, churches, and communities, a commitment to patience fosters reconciliation and strengthens bonds, reflecting the very character of God.

D. Responding to Injustice and Suffering: For those facing injustice or waiting for divine vindication, embracing God's patience involves a posture of trust and perseverance. While it is natural to cry out for immediate intervention, the biblical perspective encourages a deep trust in God's eventual, redemptive action. This trust transforms waiting into an active, hope-filled endurance, even amid profound suffering.

9.5 Challenges in Embracing Divine Patience

A. Avoiding Misinterpretation as Indifference

A common misunderstanding is to equate God's patience with indifference. However, Scripture makes it clear that God is not apathetic; He is actively restraining judgment for a higher purpose. Recognizing this helps believers avoid complacency and remain vigilant, not misusing God's forbearance as an excuse for continued sin or inaction.

B. Coping with the Pain of Delay

Long periods of injustice or suffering can test our faith. The cry of "How long, O Lord?" (Psalm 13:1) reflects genuine anguish. In these moments, believers are called to cling to the testimony of God's past faithfulness, trusting that His patience is both purposeful and redemptive—even if the full realization of His promises is deferred.

C. Embracing Lament as Part of Faith

Lament is a healthy expression of the tension between suffering and hope. Far from signifying weak faith, it allows believers to honestly express their pain honestly while simultaneously affirming God's enduring faithfulness. Such honest dialogue with God deepens our reliance on Him and prepares us for eventual renewal.

9.6 Eschatological Hope and Ultimate Redemption

A. The Final Revelation of Justice

Christian eschatology teaches that God's patience will ultimately yield to His final act of justice and renewal. The Second Coming of Christ will bring a complete and perfect fulfillment of all His promises—a day when every tear is wiped away, and all wrongs are righted. This future hope offers a powerful incentive for faithful endurance today.

B. Balancing Patience with Eager Expectation

Believers are called to hold in tension the hope for immediate change with the reality of God's gradual work. This balance—eager expectation tempered by patient endurance—motivates ethical living, steadfast service, and a hopeful outlook despite current challenges.

In conclusion, God's patience, or long-suffering, is a profound testament to His redemptive love. It reveals a Divine character that is not quick to anger but always ready to give opportunities for repentance, growth, and reconciliation. From the Old Testament accounts of Israel's wandering and the forewarning of the Flood to Jesus' parables and the apostolic teachings, Scripture consistently portrays a God who withholds immediate judgment for the sake of restoration.

For believers, this attribute provides comfort in suffering, encourages perseverance in the spiritual journey, and challenges us to extend similar patience in our relationships. It reminds us that while divine justice is inevitable, the current season is marked by a grace that invites transformation.

In a world that demands instant results, God's long-suffering offers a countercultural message: true growth, healing, and redemption require time. As we learn to trust in His perfect timing and embrace His patient heart, we are empowered to reflect that same enduring love to a hurting and hurried world.

May we continually rest in the assurance of a God who, in His infinite patience, is always working to bring about our ultimate good and the restoration of all things.

Chapter 10: Omnipotent

God's omnipotence—being all-powerful—is one of the most awe-inspiring attributes of the Divine. It means that God can accomplish anything that is consistent with His nature and purposes. This power is not arbitrary but operates in harmony with His holiness, love, and wisdom. In every act—from creation to redemption—God's omnipotence underscores that no force or circumstance can thwart His will. This chapter explores the biblical foundation, theological challenges, and practical implications of divine omnipotence, offering believers a secure basis for trust and hope.

10.1 Understanding Divine Omnipotence

The Core Meaning: Omnipotence means possessing the ability to do all that is logically possible and consistent with God's nature. It does not imply doing the logically impossible (e.g., creating a square circle or committing evil), as such actions contradict the very nature of a holy, good God. Rather, God's power assures us that nothing can thwart His redemptive purposes.

Common Misunderstandings: Critics sometimes pose paradoxes—like the "rock so heavy" question—to challenge omnipotence. However, these are based on conceptual errors. True omnipotence means God operates without contradiction, always in accordance with truth and reason, as befits His perfect nature.

Interconnected Divine Attributes: God's omnipotence does not exist in isolation. It is interwoven with His other attributes. His power is always exercised in light of His holiness, ensuring that His actions are just, and in the context of His love, which directs His power toward blessing and redemption. Thus, His might is never arbitrary but always aims at the ultimate good of creation.

10.2 Biblical Foundations
Old Testament Testimonies

1. **Creation and Sovereignty:** In Genesis 1–2, God speaks the world into existence, demonstrating His power to create order from nothing. Each "Let there be…" is fulfilled instantaneously, emphasizing that no external force can thwart His command. Throughout the Old Testament, God is depicted as the Maker of heaven and earth, whose dominion extends over all nature—as seen in events like the parting of the Red Sea and the halting of the Jordan River.

2. **Dominion over Nations:** The Old Testament also portrays God's omnipotence in His control over kings and empires. He raises and deposes rulers, directing the course of nations. The account of Nebuchadnezzar in Daniel 4, for example, reminds us that even the most powerful earthly leaders bow before a higher authority whose will governs all of creation.

B. New Testament Affirmations

1. **Jesus' Miracles and Authority:** In the New Testament, Jesus' ministry provides clear evidence of divine omnipotence. He calms storms, multiplies loaves and fish, heals the sick, and even raises the dead. These miracles reveal not only His power over nature but also His authority over sin and death. His ability to forgive sins further attests that only God can restore the broken relationship between humanity and the Divine.

2. **The Resurrection and Ascension:** The resurrection is the ultimate demonstration of omnipotence. By conquering death, Jesus shows that God's power transcends even the ultimate human limitation. His ascension to the Father's right hand confirms that all authority in heaven and on earth is vested in Him, marking the beginning of a new era of salvation and hope.

3. **Apostolic Witness:** The writings of the apostles reinforce the theme of divine omnipotence. Paul, for instance, declares that God can do "far more abundantly than all that we ask or think" (Ephesians 3:20), inviting believers to trust in a power beyond human comprehension. The Book of Revelation envisions a future where God's reign restores all things, underscoring that His ultimate plan will prevail.

10.3 Theological Considerations

The Problem of Evil: One common challenge to omnipotence is the existence of evil and suffering. Critics ask: if God is all-powerful and good, why does He allow pain? Christian theology explains that while God has the power to eliminate evil, He permits human freedom and the natural consequences of a fallen world. The cross, where God absorbs suffering to redeem humanity, demonstrates that His omnipotence works in conjunction with mercy, justice, and redemptive love. Thus, the reality of evil does not diminish God's power; it rather frames it within a larger narrative of restoration.

Divine Freedom and Necessity: Some argue that if God is all-powerful and wholly good, His actions are predetermined by His nature, limiting true freedom. However, God's omnipotence is the source of both His ability and His will to act, ensuring that His choices are perfectly aligned with goodness. His freedom is not constrained by external conditions because He is the standard of moral perfection.

Human Agency and Omnipotence: A further discussion concerns the balance between divine power and human free will. While God is capable of orchestrating all events, He often works through human decisions, preserving authentic moral agency. This dynamic interaction affirms that God's omnipotence is not diminished by human choices but rather encompasses them, directing history toward His redemptive purposes.

10.4 Practical Implications

Trust and Security: Belief in God's omnipotence offers profound comfort. In times of crisis— be it natural disasters, personal trials, or societal upheaval—faith in an all-powerful God provides a secure foundation. Even when immediate answers seem elusive, believers can trust that no circumstance is beyond His control. This assurance transforms fear into hope and anxiety into confident dependence on divine providence.

Prayer and Worship: Understanding that God is all-powerful shapes our approach to prayer. Rather than mere wishful thinking, prayer becomes an active engagement with a God who can and does intervene. Corporate worship, filled with hymns and declarations of His might, reinforces the connection between the Creator of the universe and the everyday life of His people.

Empowerment for Service: A belief in divine omnipotence also empowers believers to act. Knowing that God's plan will prevail encourages Christians to engage in ministries that address injustice, alleviate suffering, and share the gospel. Paul's assertion in Philippians 4:13, "I can do all things through him who strengthens me," reflects the confidence that God's power works through our limitations, enabling us to fulfill His purposes.

Ethical Responsibility: Finally, acknowledging God's omnipotence reminds us of our ethical obligations. When we recognize that all power ultimately belongs to God, we are less likely to become self-reliant or to misuse our own authority. Instead, we are called to exercise stewardship and humility, ensuring that our actions honor the Creator and contribute to the well-being of the world.

In conclusion, God's omnipotence is not an abstract concept but a dynamic reality that permeates every aspect of creation—from the formation of the cosmos to the redemption of human souls. It assures believers that nothing can thwart God's will, that every promise He makes is certain, and that His power is exercised in perfect harmony with His holiness, love, and wisdom.

This truth transforms how we live: it grounds our prayers in confident expectation, inspires ethical service, and nurtures a resilient hope in the midst of adversity. Moreover, it challenges us to live in humility and dependence, recognizing that our strength and security come from a God whose power is limitless and whose purposes are unchanging.

In a world marked by uncertainty and shifting loyalties, the doctrine of God's omnipotence offers a steadfast beacon—a promise that the same power that created the stars and governs the heavens is at work in our lives, guiding us toward ultimate redemption. May we embrace this truth, allowing it to shape our worship, empower our service, and sustain our hope until that final day when all things are made new.

Chapter 11: Omniscient

God's omniscience—His capacity to know all things—is a defining attribute of the Divine. It means that nothing in the cosmos, from the vast workings of nature to the innermost thoughts of the human heart, lies hidden from Him. This all-encompassing knowledge shapes our understanding of divine guidance, prayer, human freedom, and even scientific inquiry. In this chapter, we explore the biblical foundations, theological implications, and practical impacts of God's omniscience.

11.1 The Nature of Divine Omniscience

Perfect and Unlimited Knowledge To say that God is omniscient means He possesses complete and perfect knowledge of all that is, was, and will be. Unlike human knowledge—which is partial, evolving, and often inferred—God's understanding is immediate and exhaustive. He knows every detail of creation and every possibility, including all outcomes that could occur under various circumstances. Importantly, God's omniscience operates outside of time. While we experience events sequentially as past, present, or future, He perceives all moments simultaneously from an eternal perspective.

Clarifying Misunderstandings A common misconception is that if God knows every outcome, He predetermines every event, thereby nullifying free will. However, knowing all possibilities does not equate to forcing them. God's foreknowledge coexists with genuine human agency; He fully comprehends our choices without causing them. Another error is to assume that divine omniscience makes God emotionally detached. In fact, Scripture reveals that His perfect knowledge deepens His compassion and involvement in human affairs, much like a loving parent who understands every need.

11.2 Biblical Foundations

Old Testament Testimonies The Old Testament presents numerous examples of God's all-encompassing knowledge.

- **Early Narratives:** In Genesis, after Adam and Eve's disobedience, God asks, "Where are you?" not because He is ignorant of their actions, but to invite accountability and restoration. Similarly, His inquiries to Cain reveal an intimate awareness of human hearts.

- **The Flood:** Genesis 6:5 tells us that God saw the corruption in every inclination of the human heart. Yet, even as He prepares judgment through the Flood, He provides Noah with a way to preserve life—a sign that His knowledge informs both warning and mercy.

- **Psalms and Prophets:** Psalm 139 beautifully portrays a God who knows every thought and word before it is uttered, providing comfort to those who feel deeply known and understood. Prophets like Isaiah demonstrate that God's foreknowledge extends to the destiny of nations, as seen in His predictions concerning future rulers like Cyrus, long before their arrival.

New Testament Revelations The New Testament further develops the doctrine of omniscience through the life and teachings of Jesus and the writings of the apostles.

- **Jesus' Ministry:** Jesus exhibits divine insight when He interacts with individuals. For instance, He discerns Nathanael's character and the Samaritan woman's hidden life, showing that His understanding goes beyond surface appearances. His predictions about His own betrayal, crucifixion, and resurrection underscore that His foreknowledge is part of His divine nature.

- **Apostolic Testimony:** Paul and other apostles stress that God's knowledge is integral to His redemptive plan. In Romans 8, Paul explains that God works all things together for good—a process that relies on His complete awareness of every detail. The early church, as recorded in Acts and Revelation, held firm to the conviction that God's omniscience guarantees the fulfillment of His promises.

11.3 Theological and Philosophical Implications

Foreknowledge and Human Freedom A central theological debate is how God's complete knowledge of future events interacts with human free will. Several perspectives exist:

- **Calvinism** sees divine foreknowledge as part of God's sovereign decree, yet still upholds human responsibility.

- **Arminianism** distinguishes between knowing an outcome and causing it, asserting that human freedom remains intact even under divine foreknowledge.

- **Molinism** suggests that God knows what free creatures would do in any circumstance. Despite differing views, all affirm that God's omniscience does not nullify moral accountability.

The Problem of Evil If God is all-knowing, He is aware of every instance of evil and suffering. This raises the question: why does He allow such pain? Christian thought teaches that while God is fully aware of all evils, He permits them in a world where free will and genuine love are possible. The cross is pivotal here; through Christ's suffering, God not only confronts the reality of evil but transforms it into an avenue for redemption and hope.

The Relationship Between Knowledge and Action God's omniscience is intimately connected with His omnipotence and omnibenevolence. His comprehensive knowledge does not render Him passive; instead, it informs His active engagement in creation. Every act of divine intervention, from miraculous healings to the orchestration of historical events, is carried out with complete awareness and purpose.

11.4 Practical Implications for the Christian Life

Trust in Divine Guidance Belief in an omniscient God gives believers confidence that no matter how complex life may seem, nothing escapes His notice. When making decisions or facing trials, Christians are encouraged to seek His guidance through prayer, trusting that He understands all aspects of their situation. This fosters humility and reliance on divine wisdom over limited human insight.

Comfort in Suffering Knowing that God sees every hidden tear and understands every sorrow provides immense comfort. The assurance that He comprehends the depths of our pain reassures us that we are never truly alone in our struggles. This intimate knowledge of our lives enables God to offer precise comfort and encouragement, making our burdens lighter.

Encouragement to Live with Integrity The awareness that God knows every thought, word, and action can inspire believers to live authentically and with integrity. Rather than succumbing to hypocrisy or secret sin, the conviction that nothing is hidden from God encourages honest repentance and transparency. This realization nurtures a spirit of accountability and continual growth.

Integration with Scientific Inquiry In an age of expanding scientific discovery, God's omniscience reminds us that while human knowledge grows, it remains finite. The intricate design of the universe—revealed through advancements in science—points to a Creator whose understanding surpasses all human comprehension. This perspective does not diminish scientific endeavor but invites a harmonious view where faith and reason coalesce in awe of the divine intellect.

In conclusion, the doctrine of divine omniscience is woven throughout Scripture, affirming that God is the all-knowing Creator who sees every detail of the universe and every nuance of the human heart. From Genesis to Revelation, the Bible presents a God whose perfect knowledge informs His redemptive actions, sustains His promises, and offers profound comfort to believers.

Theologically, omniscience challenges us to reconcile divine foreknowledge with human freedom and to confront the reality of evil with hope in God's redemptive plan. Practically, it transforms our approach to prayer, decision-making, and personal integrity. In a world where human understanding is limited and ever-changing, the certainty of God's all-encompassing knowledge provides a steadfast anchor—a reminder that nothing is too small or too great to escape His notice.

For Christians, embracing divine omniscience is both an invitation and a call to trust. It encourages us to live with humility, knowing that our lives are fully known and cared for by a loving God. In turn, this trust fosters resilience and inspires us to seek wisdom, integrity, and a deeper relationship with the One who holds all knowledge. Ultimately, the omniscience of God is not a cold, detached attribute but a dynamic, comforting presence—a beacon of hope in an ever-complex world.

Chapter 12: Omnipresent

God's omnipresence—the reality that He is present everywhere at all times—is one of the most comforting and profound truths of the Christian faith. It affirms that no place or moment escapes His watchful care, and that His presence sustains all of creation. This chapter explores the biblical foundations, theological nuances, and practical implications of divine omnipresence, helping believers understand what it means to live in the constant, reassuring presence of God.

12.1 Defining Omnipresence

All-Exhaustive Presence To say God is omnipresent means He exists fully and simultaneously in every part of His creation. Unlike physical objects that occupy one specific location, God's presence is not limited by space or time. He knows every detail of the universe—from the vast workings of galaxies to the smallest nuances of our inner lives—and does so from an eternal perspective. This timeless view means God sees all events—past, present, and future—"all at once" without being confined by human concepts of time.

Beyond Pantheism Christian omnipresence is distinct from pantheism. While pantheism identifies God with the universe, Christian theology maintains that God is both immanent and transcendent. He is present in and sustains all things, yet remains distinct from them. This understanding, sometimes described as panentheism, affirms that while all creation is infused with His presence, the fullness of God transcends the material world.

Unfragmented Attention God's omnipresence also implies that His attention is not divided or limited. Unlike human beings who can focus on only one thing at a time, God's infinite capacity allows Him to be fully attentive in every situation simultaneously. Whether He is comforting a grieving heart, orchestrating the laws of nature, or guiding nations, His presence is complete and unbounded.

12.2 Biblical Foundations

Old Testament Witness

1. **Patriarchal Encounters:** The early narratives of Genesis offer vivid glimpses of God's pervasive presence. When Hagar flees into the wilderness, she encounters "the angel of the LORD," and names God "El Roi"—"the God who sees me"—indicating that even in isolation, one is never beyond His sight. Similarly, Jacob's dream of a ladder connecting earth and heaven (Genesis 28) reminds him—and us—that God is present even in unexpected places, turning ordinary locations into sacred meeting points.

2. **Psalms and Prophets:** Psalm 139 is a powerful meditation on omnipresence. The psalmist marvels, "Where shall I go from your Spirit? Or where shall I flee from your presence?" (Psalm 139:7–8), affirming that whether one ascends to heaven or sinks into the depths, God is there. Prophets like Isaiah and Jeremiah expand on this idea by declaring that God's knowledge and presence extend to all nations and future events, guiding history according to His divine plan.

New Testament Affirmation

1. **Jesus' Teachings and Ministry:** Jesus redefined the concept of worship by emphasizing that God is not confined to a specific temple or mountain. In His conversation with the Samaritan woman at the well, He foretells a time when true worshipers will worship "in spirit and truth" (John 4:24), highlighting that God's presence is accessible everywhere. His miracles—calming storms, healing the sick, raising the dead—demonstrate that divine power is at work throughout creation, unhindered by physical limitations.

2. **The Role of the Holy Spirit:** Following Jesus' ascension, the promise of the Holy Spirit reinforces God's omnipresence. At Pentecost, the Spirit descends on believers from every nation, uniting them in the understanding that God's presence transcends cultural and geographical boundaries. Jesus' promise, "I am with you always, to the end of the age" (Matthew 28:20), assures Christians that God remains ever-present through His Spirit, guiding and sustaining His church.

3. **Apostolic Witness:** Paul, addressing diverse audiences in his letters, reminds them that "in him we live and move and have our being" (Acts 17:28). This reinforces the idea that God's sustaining presence is not limited to isolated communities but permeates all aspects of life. The apostolic teaching ties God's omnipresence to the certainty of His promises, giving believers a secure foundation for hope and action.

12.3 Theological Reflections

Immanence and Transcendence The doctrine of omnipresence harmonizes two seemingly paradoxical truths: God is both immanent—closely involved in every detail of creation—and transcendent—exceeding all that is created. While He fills the world with His presence, He is not confined by it. This balance ensures that God remains exalted yet intimately accessible, providing comfort without diminishing His majesty.

Localized Manifestations vs. Universal Presence Biblical narratives sometimes describe extraordinary manifestations of God's presence, such as the glory descending on the tabernacle or temple. These episodes highlight moments when God's presence is experienced with heightened intensity. However, they are special revelations that do not limit His universal, ongoing presence throughout all time and space.

Omnipresence and the Problem of Hell A challenging question is whether God is present in Hell. Christian theology asserts that while God's sustaining power reaches every part of creation, in places of judgment the experience of His presence is profoundly different— marked by the absence of His redeeming warmth, resulting in alienation rather than comfort. Thus, God's omnipresence remains, but the relational experience of it varies with one's state of communion with Him.

12.4 Practical Implications

Sustaining Hope and Security The belief in an ever-present God provides profound comfort. In moments of loneliness, crisis, or despair, the assurance that God is with us—that no one is ever truly alone—offers a secure foundation for hope. Passages like Psalm 23 remind us that even in "the valley of the shadow of death," God's presence is a constant source of guidance and protection.

Accountability and Integrity Understanding that God is present everywhere motivates ethical living. When believers recognize that every thought and action is known to God, they are encouraged to cultivate honesty and integrity. This awareness not only promotes personal moral growth but also fosters transparent relationships, as nothing is hidden from the all-seeing Creator.

Global Mission and Service The omnipresence of God undergirds the call to mission. Since God's care extends to every part of the world, no region is beyond His concern. This conviction compels Christians to engage in service and evangelism in every sphere—be it urban centers, remote villages, or digital communities—trusting that the same God who is with them is also reaching out to others.

Mindfulness in Prayer and Worship Knowing that God's presence pervades all of creation transforms prayer into an intimate dialogue. Believers are invited to rest in the knowledge that God is already near, making prayer less about summoning His presence and more about attuning to the one who is already there. This awareness also enriches worship, as congregations around the globe can unite in the shared experience of a God who transcends physical boundaries.

12.5 Community and Eschatological Hope

Global Fellowship The doctrine of omnipresence naturally extends to the idea of global church unity. Despite geographical and cultural divides, all believers share in the same divine presence. Modern communication technologies further echo this truth, enabling believers worldwide to connect, worship, and support one another under the same omnipresent God.

Eschatological Consummation Christian eschatology envisions a future where God's presence is experienced in its fullest and most unobstructed form. In the new heaven and new earth described in Revelation 21, the boundary between the Creator and His creation is dissolved. The promise of "seeing God face to face" (1 Corinthians 13:12) reflects the ultimate revelation of His presence, where every barrier is removed, and the fullness of His glory is embraced by redeemed humanity.

In conclusion, God's omnipresence is a profound and multifaceted truth that assures believers of His constant, intimate involvement in every part of creation. From the early narratives of Genesis to the eschatological visions of Revelation, Scripture consistently affirms that no place is too remote and no moment too insignificant for God's presence. His all-encompassing knowledge and care provide a secure foundation for trust, ethical living, and global fellowship.

Theologically, omnipresence harmonizes God's immanence and transcendence, ensuring that while He is exalted above creation, He is also intimately near to every heart. Practically, this doctrine encourages believers to live with integrity, engage in prayer with confidence, and extend God's love through acts of service and compassion. It offers comfort amid suffering and inspires hope for a future where the full glory of God's presence is realized.

In a world marked by isolation and fragmentation, the assurance of an omnipresent God reminds us that we are never alone. Whether in times of trial or in moments of joy, God is always near—guiding, sustaining, and inviting us into deeper communion with Him. May this truth inspire us to live boldly, love generously, and worship with the awareness that the Creator of all is ever-present in our lives, now and forever.

Chapter 13: Eternal

God's eternity is one of the most awe-inspiring and foundational truths of the Christian faith. To say God is eternal means that He has no beginning and no end; He exists beyond the confines of time while still engaging intimately with creation. This doctrine challenges our finite understanding, yet it offers profound hope and stability in a transient world. Here, we explore the biblical foundations, historical-theological perspectives, and practical implications of God's eternal nature.

13.1 Understanding Divine Eternity

Transcending Time When Christians affirm that God is eternal, they mean that He exists outside the limitations of linear time. Unlike human beings who experience life in distinct past, present, and future moments, God perceives all events simultaneously. He is not merely unending in duration; His very being is independent of time. Some theologians describe this state as "atemporal"—a condition where change, decay, or succession do not affect His nature. Yet, while God remains constant, He still interacts with the temporal world, guiding history and redeeming creation.

The "Eternal Now" A key aspect of divine eternity is the concept of the "eternal now." For God, every moment—past, present, and future—is equally present. This means He fully comprehends every event and possibility without the limitations of human memory or foresight. This expansive perspective ensures that no event is "too late" or "too early" for His intervention. The eternal now provides believers with assurance that God's timing is perfect, even when human circumstances seem chaotic or delayed.

13.2 Biblical Foundations

Old Testament Witness

1. **Everlasting Existence:** Psalm 90:2 proclaims, "Before the mountains were brought

forth, or ever you had formed the earth and the world, from everlasting to everlasting you are God." This vivid expression emphasizes that God's existence is not measured by time; He is the unchanging foundation upon which all things rest. The phrase "everlasting to everlasting" captures the belief that God's being transcends creation, underscoring His absolute self-existence.

2. **Divine Self-Revelation:** In Exodus 3:14, God reveals Himself to Moses as "I AM WHO I AM," a declaration that emphasizes His self-sufficient, eternal nature. Unlike the deities of surrounding cultures, who had origin myths, the God of Israel simply is— existing before and beyond the universe He created.

3. **Narrative Examples:** In Genesis, God's encounters with individuals like Hagar and Jacob illustrate His omnipresence and eternal watchfulness. Hagar names God "El Roi," meaning "the God who sees me," while Jacob's dream of a ladder connecting heaven and earth reveals that God's presence is not confined to one location. These narratives remind us that, regardless of where we are or what we experience, God's eternal presence is a constant.

New Testament Developments

1. **Christ's Preexistence and Role:** The New Testament expands on the theme of eternity by identifying Jesus as the eternal Logos. John 1:1–2 states, "In the beginning was the Word, and the Word was with God, and the Word was God." Jesus' claim in John 8:58, "Before Abraham was, I am," further affirms that He exists beyond time. His life, death, and resurrection reveal that the eternal nature of God is not distant but intimately involved in human history.

2. **Eternal Life as Relationship:** Eternal life in the New Testament is more than endless existence; it signifies an unbroken, intimate relationship with the eternal God. In John 17:3, Jesus defines eternal life as knowing the only true God and Jesus Christ, suggesting that participating in God's eternal nature transforms our experience of time and existence.

3. **Apostolic Reflections:** Paul and other apostles frequently reflect on the eternal character of God as a source of hope. For instance, in Colossians 1:16–17, Paul writes that Christ is "before all things, and in him all things hold together," reinforcing that God's eternal power sustains the universe. Similarly, Romans 8 assures believers that nothing can separate them from the love of God—a promise anchored in His unchanging, eternal nature.

13.3 Theological and Philosophical Reflections

Eternity and Time The relationship between God's eternity and temporal existence has been a central theme in Christian thought. Some theologians argue that time is a created reality, and since God exists beyond creation, He is not bound by it. Others suggest that God, while eternal, chooses to engage in sequential, historical acts. Both views uphold that God's eternal nature does not conflict with His dynamic presence in time; rather, it enhances our understanding of His perfect timing and sovereignty.

The Problem of Evil and Suffering The eternal nature of God also provides a framework for understanding the presence of evil and suffering. Although temporal suffering can be overwhelming, God's eternity assures believers that no evil is permanent. His redemptive plan, as revealed in the cross and resurrection, offers a future where pain is transformed into glory. Thus, while human experience is marked by impermanence, God's eternal perspective ensures that ultimate justice and restoration will prevail.

Eternal Perspective and Human Life Understanding God's eternity reshapes how believers view life. It invites us to see our daily struggles, joys, and relationships in light of an everlasting reality. This eternal mindset transforms our values, urging us to invest in what truly matters—love, justice, and the spread of the gospel—knowing that our actions echo into eternity.

13.4 Practical Implications for Faith

Hope Amid Impermanence Human life is transient, but God's eternal nature offers a stable anchor for hope. Believers are encouraged to view temporal hardships as part of a larger, everlasting narrative. As 2 Corinthians 4:18 reminds us, "what is seen is transient, but what is unseen is eternal." This perspective helps us endure loss, change, and uncertainty by focusing on the eternal promises of God.

Worship and Reverence Recognizing God's eternal nature deepens our worship. Liturgical traditions and hymns that proclaim God as the "everlasting Father" or the "eternal King" remind us that our worship is directed to a God who transcends time. Such worship not only uplifts the spirit but also connects believers with a rich heritage of faith that spans generations.

Ethical Living and Legacy A belief in God's eternity influences daily choices. When we see our actions as part of an eternal framework, ethical decisions gain lasting significance. Acts of love, justice, and mercy are not just momentary gestures but investments in God's eternal kingdom. This eternal perspective encourages believers to build legacies that honor God, such as supporting long-term missions, educational initiatives, and community projects that will impact future generations.

Global and Interpersonal Unity The doctrine of omnipresence naturally extends to the idea of an eternal God who unites all believers. Despite cultural, geographical, or temporal differences, Christians around the world share in the worship of the same eternal God. This shared belief fosters a sense of global unity and encourages collaborative efforts in ministry, social justice, and interfaith dialogue.

In conclusion, the doctrine of God's eternity stands as a cornerstone of Christian belief, offering a profound counterpoint to the transitory nature of human existence. Rooted in the biblical witness—from the timeless declarations of the Old Testament to the revelation of Christ in the New Testament—God's eternal nature assures us that He is unchanging, omnipresent, and fully in control of history.

Theologically, understanding God's eternity invites us to reconcile the mysteries of time, the problem of evil, and the dynamics of human freedom with divine sovereignty. Practically, it shapes how we live, worship, and engage with the world: providing hope amid impermanence, encouraging ethical and legacy-building choices, and uniting believers in a global community.

In our daily lives, the reality of an eternal God transforms our perspective, allowing us to trust Him with our past, present, and future. It reassures us that every moment is held within His everlasting care and that our ultimate destiny is secured in His eternal promise. As we align our lives with this timeless truth, we find both comfort and inspiration, living each day in the light of a God whose eternal nature not only defies time but also redeems it, weaving our finite moments into an everlasting tapestry of divine love and grace.

Chapter 14: Infinite

God's infinity is one of the most awe-inspiring aspects of Christian theology. To call God "infinite" means that His nature, power, and wisdom have no limits; He transcends every boundary that defines our finite existence. In every attribute—be it power, knowledge, or presence—God exceeds all measures. This chapter explores the biblical foundations of God's infinite nature, examines historical and theological reflections, and considers how His boundlessness shapes our worship, ethics, and hope.

14.1 Defining Divine Infinitude

Boundlessness in Every Aspect When we describe God as infinite, we assert that He is not confined by space, time, or any other limitation. Unlike created beings who have finite lifespans, limited capacities, and measurable attributes, God exists beyond all external and internal limits. His power, wisdom, and love are not subject to expansion or contraction; they are eternally abundant. In essence, God's infinity means that no aspect of His being or work can be fully measured, for He transcends the very categories we use to understand the world.

The "Infinite Now" A useful way to grasp this concept is the idea of the "eternal now." While humans experience time sequentially—past, present, and future—God perceives all moments simultaneously. Every event, every possibility, and every outcome is equally present to Him. This eternal perspective reassures us that God's timing is perfect, for nothing is "too early" or "too late" for His redemptive work.

Distinction from Pantheism Christian theology holds that while God is infinite, He is not identical to creation. Unlike pantheism, which equates God with the universe, the biblical view maintains that God is both immanent and transcendent. He fills and sustains all creation with His presence while remaining distinct from it. This means that although every part of the universe testifies to His infinite power, creation itself is not a measure of His essence.

14.2 Biblical Foundations for Infinity

Old Testament Insights The Old Testament, though rarely using the term "infinite," is replete with imagery that captures God's immeasurable nature.

- **Cosmic Imagery:** In Isaiah 40:12–17, the prophet marvels at how God can measure the oceans in the hollow of His hand and weigh the mountains on a scale. Such language underscores that earthly dimensions are negligible compared to the Divine. Similarly, Psalm 147:5 proclaims, "Great is our Lord, and abundant in power; his understanding is beyond measure."

- **Everlasting Existence:** Psalm 90:2 declares, "Before the mountains were brought forth, or ever you had formed the earth and the world, from everlasting to everlasting you are God." This poetic expression emphasizes that God's existence stretches infinitely backward and forward, independent of the created order.

- **Transcendence in Covenant:** In 1 Kings 8:27, Solomon observes that "the heavens, even the highest heavens, cannot contain you," suggesting that not even the vastness of the cosmos can confine God's being.

New Testament Revelations The New Testament deepens our understanding of God's infinity through the person of Jesus Christ and the writings of the apostles.

- **Christ's Preexistence:** The Gospel of John opens by asserting, "In the beginning was the Word, and the Word was with God, and the Word was God" (John 1:1–2). Jesus' declaration, "Before Abraham was, I am" (John 8:58), affirms that He exists beyond the confines of time.

- **The Fullness of God's Love:** Ephesians 3:18–19 speaks of the "breadth, length, height, and depth" of Christ's love—a metaphor that points to an immeasurably vast, infinite quality.

- **Apostolic Testimony:** Paul proclaims in Romans 11:33, "Oh, the depth of the riches and the wisdom and the knowledge of God! How unsearchable are His judgments and His ways!" Such expressions remind believers that no human inquiry can fully grasp the infinite nature of God.

14.3 Theological and Historical Perspectives

Early Church and Medieval Reflections Early Church Fathers like Athanasius and Augustine emphasized God's unchanging and boundless nature as central to His identity. Augustine's reflections, for example, celebrated God as "everywhere entire"—a poetic recognition of His limitless presence. Medieval theologians, notably Thomas Aquinas, further developed these ideas by arguing that God's essence is pure act, fully actualized and without any potentiality. Thus, God is not merely "very large" but qualitatively infinite, transcending every created measure.

Reformation and Modern Thought The Reformers underscored God's sovereignty and majesty, reaffirming that His infinite nature sets Him apart from all creation. In modern times, theologians continue to engage with the mystery of God's infinity, often in dialogue with scientific discoveries about the vastness of the universe. Rather than undermining faith, these insights often enhance our reverence, as every astronomical discovery points to a Creator whose wisdom and power are limitless.

Philosophical Reflections The challenge of understanding an infinite God has led to various philosophical models. While human language falls short, analogies like the "eternal now" or comparisons to an unbounded ocean help convey the concept. Importantly, Christian theology asserts that God's infinity is not an abstract mathematical notion but is intimately tied to His character—His omnipotence, omniscience, and omnipresence all flow from an infinite essence that upholds and redeems all things.

14.4 Practical Implications for Christian Life

Hope Amid Impermanence Human life is transient, marked by change, decay, and uncertainty. In contrast, God's infinite nature provides a secure foundation for hope. Believers can trust that while our circumstances are temporary, God's unchanging presence endures forever. This perspective empowers us to face challenges with confidence, knowing that every moment is held within the embrace of an eternal God.

Worship and Reverence Recognizing God's infinity deepens our worship. Liturgical expressions, hymns, and prayers that extol the "everlasting Father" or the "eternal King" remind us that we are engaging with a God whose glory and power surpass all human understanding. This reverence fosters a sense of awe and humility, encouraging us to worship not just with our voices but with our lives.

Ethical and Legacy-Building Living An eternal perspective reorients our priorities. When we view our actions against the backdrop of infinity, ethical choices take on lasting significance. Acts of kindness, justice, and mercy are not just momentary gestures; they become part of a larger, eternal tapestry. Believers are encouraged to invest in legacies—through community service, educational initiatives, or mission work—that honor God's eternal reign and bring lasting good to future generations.

Global Unity and Vision The doctrine of God's infinity unites believers across time and space. Since God is infinite, no culture or nation is beyond His concern. This truth encourages a global perspective in ministry and fosters unity within the diverse body of Christ. Whether in local congregations or international missions, believers share in the common hope that God's eternal purposes will ultimately prevail.

In Conclusion, God's infinity is a majestic reality that redefines how we view time, creation, and our own existence. From the Old Testament's poetic declarations of "everlasting" God to the New Testament's portrayal of Christ as the eternal Word, Scripture affirms that our Creator transcends every limitation. His boundless nature means that no event, no detail of our lives, escapes His notice.

Theologically, the concept of infinity challenges us to grasp a reality that surpasses human limitations—inviting us to trust in a God whose power, knowledge, and love are limitless. Historically, the reflections of Church Fathers and modern theologians alike have enriched our understanding of an eternal God who is both transcendent and intimately involved in His creation.

Practically, an eternal perspective transforms our lives. It offers hope in the face of impermanence, deepens our worship, and guides our ethical decisions. It also unites us with believers around the world in a shared confidence that the same God who created the cosmos continues to sustain and redeem us.

In a world where everything seems fleeting, the promise of an infinite God reminds us that our ultimate destiny is secure. His eternal nature is a constant source of comfort, inspiring us to live with integrity, worship with passion, and invest in legacies that reflect His unending grace. As we embrace the reality of a God without limits, we are called to reflect that same boundless love and wisdom in every aspect of our lives—trusting that the eternal Creator is ever-present, guiding us toward a future filled with hope and everlasting joy.

Chapter 15: Sovereign

God's sovereignty is a cornerstone of Christian theology. It means that God holds ultimate authority and dominion over all creation—every nation, every event, and every detail of human life falls under His wise, righteous control. This doctrine, far from depicting a remote, arbitrary ruler, reassures believers that God's rule is good, purposeful, and redemptive, even when it incorporates human choices and the realities of a fallen world.

15.1 Understanding Divine Sovereignty

Supreme Authority When we speak of God's sovereignty, we affirm that He is the ultimate King—"King of kings"—with authority that flows directly from His nature as Creator. God did not receive His power from an external source; rather, His power is intrinsic because He is the origin of all that exists. His rule is not based solely on raw force but on a harmonious blend of power, wisdom, and love. In this view, His decisions are not capricious but are consistently directed toward the ultimate good and the fulfillment of His redemptive plan.

Sovereignty and Human Freedom A central question is how divine sovereignty interacts with human freedom. While God is in complete control, human beings still make genuine moral choices. Theologians explain this interplay in various ways: some see God's meticulous plan encompassing human freedom, while others emphasize that although our decisions are free, they ultimately operate within the bounds of God's overarching will. In either case, God's sovereign plan uses human actions—both good and bad—to accomplish His purposes, without nullifying our responsibility.

15.2 Biblical Foundations

Old Testament Testimonies

1. **Kingship and Covenant:** The Old Testament frequently portrays God as the supreme King. The Psalms, for example, celebrate Him as the eternal ruler over all the earth

(Psalm 47:7–8; 93:1). This imagery extends beyond national borders; God is not merely Israel's deity but the Lord over all creation. The covenant relationship between God and His people, established through Moses and David, reinforces that while human obedience is expected, God's promises remain secure irrespective of human failings. For instance, even when Israel faltered, God's judgment was tempered by mercy and the call to return to Him.

2. **Sovereignty Over Nations:** Prophetic literature further demonstrates God's reign over political and cultural powers. In books like Isaiah, God uses empires such as Assyria and Babylon as instruments of judgment and discipline, only to humble them when their pride becomes excessive (Isaiah 10:5–19; 14:3–23). Daniel's account of King Nebuchadnezzar (Daniel 4:35) illustrates that even the mightiest rulers ultimately acknowledge that no human force can restrain God's will.

3. **Personal Deliverance:** Stories of individual deliverance, like Joseph's rise from slavery to rulership, reveal how God's sovereign plan transforms human suffering into avenues for blessing. In Joseph's story, betrayal and hardship are repurposed to preserve a nation, underscoring that God can work through even the darkest human circumstances.

New Testament Revelations

1. **Jesus' Kingdom:** The New Testament brings the theme of sovereignty to its climax in the person of Jesus Christ. Jesus proclaims, "The kingdom of God is at hand" (Mark 1:15), announcing that God's rule is breaking into human history in transformative ways. His miracles, teachings, and parables illustrate a kingdom not established by force but by love, mercy, and self-sacrifice. Even as Jesus challenges worldly expectations—eschewing political rebellion for spiritual renewal—He affirms that God's reign is both present and decisive.

2. **Christ's Exaltation:** After His resurrection, Jesus is exalted to the right hand of God (Acts 2:33–36; Ephesians 1:20–22). This exaltation signals that Christ now exercises divine authority over all things, confirming that every power—whether seen or unseen—will eventually be subject to His rule. The New Testament also envisions a final consummation, when Christ will deliver the kingdom to God the Father, ensuring that God's ultimate plan is fulfilled.

3. **Apostolic Teaching:** The apostles, particularly Paul, consistently emphasize that God's sovereign will is at work in history. Romans 11:33 declares, "Oh, the depth of the riches and the wisdom and knowledge of God! How unsearchable are His judgments and His ways!" Such language encourages believers to trust that even the most perplexing events are orchestrated by a God whose purpose is ultimately good.

15.3 Theological and Historical Perspectives

Early Church and Medieval Reflections Early Christians and medieval theologians, such as Augustine and Thomas Aquinas, elaborated on God's sovereignty as an expression of His unchangeable nature. They argued that all earthly authority is derivative, while God alone possesses inherent, unlimited rule. Aquinas, for example, described God's essence as "pure act," meaning that His power is fully actualized and free from any potentiality that limits finite beings.

Reformation and Modern Debates During the Reformation, theologians like John Calvin and Martin Luther stressed that salvation is entirely the result of God's sovereign grace. They maintained that even human disobedience is ultimately subservient to God's redemptive plan. Modern theologians continue to grapple with the tension between divine sovereignty and human freedom, but all agree that God's rule is the secure framework within which all of life unfolds.

Philosophical Challenges Questions often arise about whether sovereignty implies fatalism or diminishes human responsibility. Biblical narratives, however, repeatedly affirm that while God's sovereign plan is assured, human choices carry real weight. The story of Jonah, for example, shows that repentance genuinely alters God's intended judgment. Thus, divine sovereignty does not render our actions irrelevant but rather incorporates them into a grand, redemptive design.

15.4 Practical Implications

Comfort in Uncertainty Belief in God's sovereignty offers deep comfort during times of crisis. Whether facing personal hardships or societal turmoil, Christians trust that no circumstance is beyond God's control. The assurance that "all things work together for good" (Romans 8:28) provides a steady foundation for hope, even when immediate outcomes are unclear.

Prayer and Obedience Understanding that God is in complete control encourages a more robust prayer life. Believers are urged to seek God's guidance in all matters, confident that He knows every detail of their lives. This trust fosters a spirit of obedience and humility, as Christians submit their plans to a Sovereign King whose wisdom surpasses all human understanding.

Ethical Living and Stewardship Recognizing divine sovereignty motivates ethical behavior. Knowing that every action is observed by an all-powerful, righteous God encourages integrity and accountability. This awareness transforms private life as well as public conduct, guiding believers to act justly, love mercy, and walk humbly with God (Micah 6:8).

Global and Communal Vision The doctrine of sovereignty also shapes how Christians engage with society. It prevents the idolization of political powers by reminding us that true authority belongs to God alone. This perspective inspires efforts in social justice, community building, and global missions—work undertaken in the conviction that God's rule extends to every corner of the earth and that no human institution can claim ultimate control.

In conclusion, God's sovereignty is the foundation upon which all other divine attributes rest. It assures believers that the Almighty, who created and upholds the universe, governs history with wisdom, love, and justice. From the Old Testament's portrayal of a King who holds even empires in His hand to the New Testament revelation of Christ's exaltation, Scripture consistently affirms that nothing escapes God's authority.

This doctrine does not render human freedom irrelevant; rather, it invites a mysterious interplay where our choices contribute to the unfolding of God's redemptive plan. It provides comfort in the midst of life's uncertainties and calls us to live ethically and courageously in a world that is under divine supervision.

In a culture often marked by uncertainty and shifting loyalties, the belief in a sovereign God offers a steadfast anchor. As believers, we are encouraged to approach life with confidence, knowing that every event, no matter how small or large, falls under the watchful eye of a benevolent King. Through prayer, ethical living, and active engagement in society, we participate in the fulfillment of God's eternal purposes.

Ultimately, God's sovereignty is not a distant, abstract concept but a dynamic reality that impacts every facet of life. It inspires reverence, fuels hope, and calls us to a deeper trust in the One who rules above all. As we embrace this truth, we are reminded that the same power that governs the cosmos is also at work in our daily lives—guiding us, sustaining us, and leading us toward the ultimate realization of His redemptive, eternal kingdom.

Chapter 16: Self-Existent

One of the most profound truths of Christian theology is that God is self-existent—He exists by Himself, independent of anything external. This doctrine, often called "aseity" (from the Latin *a se*, "from oneself"), means that unlike all creation, which depends on external causes and sustaining forces, God's being comes solely from His own nature. This chapter examines the biblical and theological foundations of God's self-existence, its historical development, and its profound implications for faith, worship, and daily life.

16.1 Understanding Divine Aseity

Defining Self-Existence To say that God is self-existent is to affirm that He is uncreated and independent. While every created thing requires something external to come into being or to be sustained—whether it be parents, natural processes, or physical laws—God's existence is intrinsic. He is the necessary, self-sufficient Source of all life, possessing within Himself the complete reason for His being. This means that God does not rely on any external factors or resources, and His nature is not subject to change or depletion.

Contrasting with Creation All created beings are finite and contingent. Stars, oceans, animals, and even human cultures depend on physical processes and external conditions to exist and thrive. In stark contrast, God's self-existence guarantees eternal stability and unchanging perfection. His being is not limited by time or space, which means that while the cosmos may evolve or decay, God remains the constant foundation and sustainer of all reality.

16.2 Biblical Foundations

Old Testament Witness

1. **The "I AM" Revelation:** In Exodus 3:14, when Moses encounters the burning bush, God reveals Himself as "I AM WHO I AM." This declaration emphasizes that God's identity is self-determined—He simply is, independent of any other force. It is a bold

affirmation of His uncaused, eternal existence.

2. **Creation as a Manifestation of Aseity:** The Genesis account of creation demonstrates that God spoke the universe into existence. Unlike other ancient myths where gods emerge from chaos or struggle for power, the biblical God brings order by His own initiative. This creative act is not the result of external necessity but an expression of His infinite, self-sustaining will.

3. **Immeasurable Sovereignty:** Passages such as Isaiah 44:24 ("I am the LORD, who made all things, who alone stretched out the heavens...") and Psalm 90:2 ("Before the mountains were born or you brought forth the whole world, from everlasting to everlasting you are God") underline that God's existence and creative power extend beyond any temporal or spatial constraints.

New Testament Affirmations

1. **Christ as the Eternal Word:** The Gospel of John begins by stating, "In the beginning was the Word, and the Word was with God, and the Word was God" (John 1:1–2). This passage affirms that Jesus, as the incarnate Word, shares in the Father's eternal, self-existent nature. His life, ministry, and resurrection reveal a God who is both the Creator and the sustainer of all things, independent and unbound.

2. **Self-Sufficiency in Acts and Epistles:** In Acts 17:24–25, Paul declares that God "is not served by human hands, as though he needed anything, since he himself gives to all mankind life and breath." This statement encapsulates the idea that God's being is not contingent on external support—He is the source of all life, and everything depends on Him, not the other way around.

3. **The Image of the Invisible God:** Paul's description of Christ in Colossians 1:15–17— "the image of the invisible God… in him all things hold together"—emphasizes that the eternal, self-existent nature of God is the wellspring of creation's stability. Christ's role as the sustainer further demonstrates that God's independence is the foundation for every aspect of life.

16.3 Historical and Theological Perspectives

Early Church and Patristic Insights The Church Fathers, such as Athanasius and Augustine, laid the groundwork for understanding God's aseity. Athanasius defended the eternal nature of the Son against Arian claims, insisting that only a self-existent God could be truly divine. Augustine, in his writings, emphasized that all finite beings long for stability—a stability found only in the self-sufficient God. Their reflections reinforced that God's being is not derived from anything external; He is the ultimate, unchanging reality.

Medieval and Reformation Thought Medieval theologians like Thomas Aquinas further refined the doctrine by describing God as Ipsum Esse Subsistens—"Subsistent Being Itself."

Aquinas argued that all creatures are contingent and depend on God for their existence, whereas God, as the necessary being, exists by the very act of His nature. The Reformers, including Martin Luther and John Calvin, built on this tradition, emphasizing that salvation and divine grace stem solely from God's unchanging, self-existent nature.

Modern Perspectives In contemporary theology, debates continue regarding the interplay between God's self-existence and His relational involvement in the world. While process theologians sometimes suggest a dynamic, relational aspect, mainstream Christianity maintains that God's essence remains utterly self-sufficient, even as He engages lovingly with His creation. This doctrine remains central to orthodox Christian belief, underscoring that God's independence is not a barrier to intimate relationship but the source of all love and grace.

16.4 Practical Implications

Foundation for Faith Belief in God's self-existence assures believers that their hope rests on an unchanging, reliable foundation. In a world marked by instability, the knowledge that God "simply is" provides unwavering security. This conviction reassures Christians that no matter how circumstances change, the source of all life and truth remains constant.

Worship and Reverence Understanding that God's being is self-sufficient elevates worship from a transactional act to one of genuine adoration. Liturgical expressions and hymns often echo the truth that all creation flows from Him, and all life is sustained by His infinite resources. This perspective inspires humility, as believers recognize that everything they are and have originates from a God who lacks nothing.

Ethical Living and Responsibility Recognizing God's self-existence also shapes moral and ethical behavior. Since all finite things depend on God, believers are called to acknowledge their own limitations and vulnerability. This awareness fosters humility, encouraging individuals to live in a manner that reflects gratitude for God's unmerited provision. It also serves as a reminder that, unlike humans who require external validation, God's value is intrinsic—prompting us to pursue lives marked by integrity, generosity, and compassion.

Trust and Freedom from Manipulation A self-existent God cannot be manipulated or coerced. In ancient contexts, deities were often appeased with sacrifices because they needed nourishment or power. In contrast, the biblical God requires nothing from humanity—He simply gives. This truth shifts the believer's posture from anxiety and performance-based faith to one of trust and freedom. We worship a God who is not contingent on our efforts, and we find liberation in knowing that His favor is not earned but freely given.

In conclusion, the doctrine of divine self-existence—God's aseity—is a profound declaration that He is the uncaused, independent Source of all that exists. From the "I AM" of Exodus to the cosmic affirmations of John's Gospel, Scripture consistently reveals a God who needs nothing external to be; He is the eternal wellspring of life, wisdom, and love.

Historically, this belief has shaped Christian thought from the early Church through the medieval period and into modern theology. It provides a solid foundation for faith, assuring believers that despite the impermanence of creation, the One who sustains all things remains unchanging and wholly sufficient.

Practically, understanding God's self-existence transforms worship, ethical living, and our trust in His provision. It frees us from the burden of trying to earn His favor and inspires us to live with humility, knowing that our very existence is a gift from an infinitely self-sufficient God. In a world of constant change, the eternal, self-existent God stands as our secure, unshakable foundation—a truth that calls us to worship, trust, and live with profound gratitude.

May we continually reflect on and celebrate the reality that God, who "simply is," is the ultimate source of all that is good and true—a sovereign, self-existent King who lovingly sustains every moment of our lives.

Chapter 17: Self-Sufficient

God's self-sufficiency is one of the most humbling and awe-inspiring attributes of the Christian faith. It affirms that God depends on nothing outside Himself for His existence, purpose, or fulfillment. Unlike every created thing—from the smallest cell to the vast galaxies—that relies on external conditions to exist, God's being is entirely independent. His life, power, and wisdom arise from His own nature, and He is never in need. This chapter explores the biblical foundations of divine self-sufficiency, traces its development through historical theology, clarifies common misconceptions, and reflects on its practical implications for faith and worship.

17.1 Understanding Divine Self-Sufficiency

The Concept of Needing Nothing To say that God is self-sufficient means that He requires nothing beyond Himself. Unlike creatures that depend on food, water, love, or community for their existence and growth, God's being is complete in Himself. He neither lacks nor desires anything because His essence contains the fullness of life, power, and wisdom. This independence is not a sign of indifference; rather, it frees Him to act out of pure generosity and love. His ability to bless, sustain, and redeem flows not from a need to fill a void, but from an inexhaustible overflow of divine abundance.

Distinguishing Self-Sufficiency from Self-Existence While self-sufficiency (aseity) and self-existence both stress God's independence, they highlight different aspects. Self-existence emphasizes that God is uncaused and eternal—He simply is. Self-sufficiency, on the other hand, focuses on His ongoing ability to sustain Himself and accomplish His purposes without reliance on any external source. Together, they paint a picture of a God who not only exists from all eternity but also remains fully complete and empowered in every moment.

17.2 Biblical Foundations
Old Testament Indications

1. **The "I AM" Revelation:** In Exodus 3:14, when Moses encounters the burning bush, God declares, "I AM WHO I AM." This self-revelation underscores that God's identity is not derived from anything else—He exists by His own nature. This foundational moment distinguishes the biblical God from pagan deities who were thought to need sacrifices or offerings.

2. **Creation as a Manifestation of Self-Sufficiency:** The Genesis creation account powerfully illustrates God's self-sufficiency. God speaks the world into being, and every element—from light to humanity—is brought forth solely by His command. Unlike other ancient myths where deities are born from chaos or require sustenance, the biblical God acts from an unchanging, infinite reserve.

3. **Divine Ownership and Provision:** In Psalm 50:12, God declares, "If I were hungry, I would not tell you, for the world and its fullness are mine." Similarly, 1 Chronicles 29:14 reminds us that all things come from God and that our offerings are gifts we return to Him. These texts emphasize that God's resources are inexhaustible; He is never in want, regardless of human offerings.

New Testament Affirmations

1. **God's Independence in Christ:** The Gospel of John opens by affirming that "the Word was with God, and the Word was God" (John 1:1–2). This eternal Word, who becomes flesh in the person of Jesus Christ, demonstrates that the fullness of God's power and wisdom is self-generated. Jesus' teachings, miracles, and even His prayer life—such as in Matthew 6:8, where He reminds us that the Father already knows our needs—reveal a God who is never lacking.

2. **Divine Provision Through the Holy Spirit:** In Acts 17:24–25, Paul proclaims that God "is not served by human hands, as though he needed anything, since he himself gives to all mankind life and breath and everything." This statement underscores that God's capacity to provide is inherent, not dependent on external efforts or material sacrifices.

17.3 Historical and Theological Perspectives

Early Church Articulations Early Church Fathers such as Irenaeus and Tertullian emphasized that God, being completely self-sufficient, created the world out of pure generosity, not out of necessity. Their critiques of pagan gods, which were portrayed as needy or capricious, highlighted the unique independence of the Christian God.

Augustine and Scholastic Thought Augustine famously noted that every finite thing longs for the eternal stability found only in God—"alone art unto thyself." In the medieval period, Thomas Aquinas refined this idea by arguing that God is "pure act" (actus purus), meaning He has no unfulfilled potential and is utterly complete. This philosophical grounding reassured believers that God's self-sufficiency is not an abstract concept but the very foundation of His creative and redemptive work.

Reformation and Modern Theology The Reformers, including John Calvin, further emphasized that God's saving grace and sovereign rule stem from His independent, self-sufficient nature. In modern theology, while some debates explore whether God is affected by creation, mainstream Christian thought holds that God's self-sufficiency remains intact. He engages with the world freely, not out of need, but from an overflow of divine generosity.

17.4 Practical and Pastoral Implications

Confidence in God's Provision Believing in a self-sufficient God provides deep assurance. In times of personal crisis or global uncertainty, knowing that God "needs nothing" reinforces the truth that His power and presence are unshaken by external events. This truth encourages believers to trust Him, knowing that all resources come from an inexhaustible Source.

Freedom in Worship Recognizing God's self-sufficiency transforms worship. Since God is not dependent on human actions to sustain Him, worship becomes an act of genuine gratitude rather than a ritualistic duty to appease a needy deity. Our praise, then, acknowledges the overflowing abundance of a God who freely gives life and grace.

Ethical Generosity Understanding that God is completely self-sufficient frees believers to be generous. Since all we have is already a gift from a God who lacks nothing, we are encouraged to share freely—our time, resources, and compassion—without fear of scarcity. This attitude fosters a culture of stewardship and communal care, reflecting the limitless generosity of our Creator.

Assurance of Stability Amid Change In a world marked by rapid change and uncertainty, God's self-sufficiency is a bedrock of stability. While human institutions, relationships, and resources may falter, God's unchanging nature endures. This perspective offers hope that, regardless of life's fluctuations, our reliance on an independent, all-sufficient God is well-placed.

In conclusion, the doctrine of God's self-sufficiency—the conviction that He exists, acts, and sustains solely by virtue of His own nature—is a foundational truth that distinguishes the Creator from all creation. From the "I AM" declaration in Exodus to the testimony of the New Testament that God gives life and breath to all, Scripture reveals a God who is entirely independent, lacking nothing and needing nothing.

Historically, this belief has been championed by Church Fathers, medieval scholastics, and Reformers alike, each reinforcing that God's independence is not a barrier to intimate relationship but the source of all His generosity and grace. In practical terms, understanding God's self-sufficiency deepens our trust, transforms our worship, and inspires ethical living. It reassures us that our ultimate security and provision flow from a God who is unchanging, unbound by limitations, and free to bestow unmerited blessings.

As believers, we are invited to marvel at the truth that the One who created the cosmos does not depend on it for His existence, yet sustains every moment of our lives. This truth not only elevates our understanding of God's majesty but also liberates us to live with gratitude and confidence, knowing that our Creator is self-sufficient and abundantly generous. In a world of uncertainty, we find rest in the reality that all we are and have originates from a God who simply is—eternal, independent, and infinitely loving.

Chapter 18: Immutable (Unchanging)

God's immutability—His unchanging nature—is one of the most comforting and awe-inspiring truths in Christian theology. Unlike humans who evolve physically, mentally, and morally over time, God's essence remains constant. His character, purposes, and promises are fixed, providing a secure foundation for faith in a world that is constantly changing. This chapter explores the biblical foundations, historical and theological perspectives, and practical implications of God's immutability.

18.1 Understanding Divine Immutability

Defining "Immutable" To say that God is immutable means that His nature, attributes, and promises never change. His holiness, goodness, wisdom, and love are constant and reliable. This unchanging character forms the bedrock of biblical covenants; regardless of human failure, God remains the same. While He acts dynamically in history—dispensing grace, discipline, and mercy—these actions always flow from His unaltered divine nature.

Immutability Versus Inaction A common misconception is to equate immutability with passivity or emotional detachment. However, God's unchanging essence does not mean He is indifferent. Scripture portrays Him as actively engaging with His creation, expressing genuine compassion, righteous anger, and tender care. His responses may adapt to human circumstances, but the core of who He is remains constant.

18.2 Biblical Foundations

Old Testament Testimonies

1. **Covenantal Assurance:** Malachi 3:6 declares, "For I the LORD do not change; therefore you, O children of Jacob, are not consumed." Despite Israel's repeated disobedience, God's promises endure, anchoring the nation in hope. Similarly, Numbers 23:19 reminds us that "God is not a man, that he should lie, or a son of man, that he should

change his mind," contrasting the unreliability of humans with the steadfastness of God.

2. **Psalms of Unchanging Rulership:** Psalm 102:25–27 contrasts the fleeting nature of creation with the eternal stability of the Creator. The psalmist reflects that while the heavens and the earth may fade, God remains unaltered—a constant refuge for those in distress.

New Testament Reinforcements

1. **Christ's Consistency:** Hebrews 13:8 proclaims, "Jesus Christ is the same yesterday, today, and forever." Although Jesus experienced growth and human limitations, His divine nature remained unchanged. His teachings and miracles reveal a God whose compassion and righteousness do not vary with time.

2. **Divine Promises and Eternal Perspective:** James 1:17 states, "Every good gift and every perfect gift is from above, coming down from the Father of lights, with whom there is no variation or shadow due to change." This reinforces that God's provision and guidance are constant, offering believers unshakeable hope regardless of life's vicissitudes.

18.3 Historical and Theological Perspectives

Early Church Formulations The early Church distinguished the Christian God from the capricious deities of pagan cultures. Apologists like Justin Martyr and Irenaeus emphasized that, unlike gods who changed with human whims, the biblical God is steadfast. Augustine's reflections in his *Confessions* highlight that while all creation is transient, true stability is found only in God, who "alone art unto thyself."

Medieval and Reformation Thought Medieval theologians such as Thomas Aquinas argued that God is "pure act" (actus purus), meaning He is completely actualized without any potentiality or change. This view provided a philosophical basis for God's immutability, asserting that any change would imply imperfection. The Reformers, notably John Calvin, reinforced that salvation and divine grace rest on an unchanging God. They taught that while human actions may vary, God's sovereign will and moral perfection remain constant.

Modern Theological Developments Modern debates sometimes challenge classical immutability by suggesting that a loving God might be influenced by creation. However, mainstream theology maintains that while God interacts relationally with humanity, His essential nature is never altered. The Incarnation, where the eternal God entered history as Jesus Christ, shows that divine engagement does not compromise immutability; rather, it demonstrates that God's redemptive purpose is consistent across time.

18.4 Practical and Pastoral Implications

Stability in a Changing World In a world where everything—relationships, institutions, and even physical bodies—changes, the immutability of God provides a secure anchor for faith. Scriptures such as Hebrews 13:8 assure believers that God's character and promises are reliable. This unchanging nature offers comfort amid personal and societal upheaval, assuring us that no matter how transient our circumstances, our hope rests on an eternal, unwavering God.

Foundation for Trust Because God does not change, His promises are dependable. Believers can approach Him in prayer with confidence, knowing that His word is steadfast. This certainty encourages ethical living and a sense of responsibility, as we recognize that our actions take place before a God whose moral standard remains constant.

Worship and Devotional Life Worship gains depth when it is rooted in the knowledge that God is unchanging. Liturgical traditions, hymns, and prayers that extol God's eternal nature foster an atmosphere of reverence and awe. Congregations are united in the declaration that the One who has always been the same is worthy of endless praise—a truth that also inspires personal devotion and daily trust.

Ethical Consistency and Community Unity The unchanging nature of God also provides a universal moral standard. In an age of shifting values, believers look to God's immutable righteousness as the foundation for ethical behavior. This consistency fosters unity within the church, as all members share the common conviction that God's law and love are eternal, helping to bridge differences and promote mutual respect.

In conclusion, God's immutability—the truth that He remains constant in His being, character, and purposes—is a pillar of Christian hope. From the steadfast declarations of the Old Testament to the enduring witness of Christ in the New, Scripture reveals a God who does not change with time or circumstance. His unalterable nature ensures that His promises, guidance, and love are reliable anchors for all who trust in Him.

Historically, this doctrine has been a source of comfort and inspiration, distinguishing the Christian God from the mutable deities of other cultures. The teachings of Augustine, Aquinas, Calvin, and many others have affirmed that while the world may be in constant flux, our God remains the same—eternally perfect and unfalteringly just.

For believers today, the assurance of God's immutability transforms our approach to life. It invites us to trust Him amid uncertainty, to worship Him with reverence and joy, and to live out ethical principles rooted in eternal truth. As we navigate the challenges of a changing world, we find solace in the promise that God's nature never wavers. He is our rock, our constant guide, and the unchanging source of all grace.

Chapter 19: Just

God's justice is a foundational attribute of His nature—a perfect commitment to righteousness, equity, and moral order. In contrast to human justice, which is often marred by bias and error, divine justice is flawless and impartial, reflecting God's own unchanging moral character. This chapter explores the biblical basis for God's justice, examines its historical and theological development, and discusses its profound implications for personal faith and communal life.

19.1 Understanding Divine Justice

Defining Divine Justice Divine justice means that God administers judgment in a way that is perfectly aligned with His moral nature. Unlike human legal systems, which may falter due to partiality or incomplete evidence, God's justice is all-knowing and completely fair. His judgments are not arbitrary; they reflect an inherent righteousness. God's justice operates as both mercy and retribution—He provides a means of redemption through Christ while holding sin accountable.

Beyond Punishment: A Harmonious Blend In God, justice is intertwined with mercy and love. While human justice might focus solely on retribution, divine justice seeks to restore. God's judgments aim not only to punish wrongdoing but also to bring about repentance and transformation. In this way, His justice is a driving force for redemption and restoration, ensuring that moral order prevails while offering forgiveness through Christ.

19.2 Biblical Foundations

Old Testament Testimonies

1. **Covenantal Law and Righteousness:** From the early narratives, Scripture portrays God as the ultimate Judge. Abraham's plea in Genesis 18:25—"Shall not the Judge of all the earth do what is just?"—sets a standard that God's governance ensures moral order.

The Mosaic Law, with its instructions for fair treatment of the poor and honest dealings, reflects divine justice. Passages in Leviticus and Deuteronomy highlight that God's legal code is designed to protect the vulnerable and maintain social equity.

2. **Prophetic Warnings and Promises:** Prophets such as Amos, Micah, and Jeremiah denounce social injustice and call out corruption among the powerful. Amos' famous injunction, "Let justice roll down like waters, and righteousness like an ever-flowing stream" (Amos 5:24), underscores the expectation that divine justice must prevail. The prophets warn that persistent injustice will lead to judgment, yet they also emphasize that a repentant remnant can be restored through God's merciful intervention.

3. **Psalms of Assurance:** The Psalms frequently celebrate God's unwavering justice. For example, Psalm 89:14 declares that God's throne is established on "righteousness and justice." Such poetry reassures believers that, despite human failings and social injustice, God's judgments remain steadfast and trustworthy.

New Testament Revelations

1. **Jesus' Ministry as a Model of Justice:** In the Gospels, Jesus consistently challenges religious hypocrisy and the misuse of power. His confrontation with the Pharisees and His parables—such as the Good Samaritan and the Prodigal Son—reveal that true justice extends beyond mere legalism. Jesus teaches that righteousness must flow from the heart and that mercy is integral to fulfilling the law. His life exemplifies justice not through force but by transforming hearts through love.

2. **The Atonement and Redemption:** Paul's letters, especially in Romans 3:25–26, explain that God's justice was satisfied through the sacrificial death of Christ. In this act, God maintained His moral order by punishing sin while extending unmerited grace to the repentant. The cross unites divine justice with mercy, ensuring that while sin is condemned, redemption is made available.

3. **Eschatological Fulfillment:** The Book of Revelation portrays the ultimate vindication of divine justice, where God, as the final Judge, will right every wrong. In this future vision, the righteous are rewarded, and unrepentant evil faces eternal separation. This eschatological hope assures believers that God's justice will ultimately prevail over all injustice.

19.3 Historical and Theological Perspectives

Early Church and Patristic Insights Early Christian apologists contrasted the steadfast, moral governance of the biblical God with the fickle deities of pagan cultures. Church Fathers like Justin Martyr and Irenaeus emphasized that God's justice is rooted in His unchanging nature and that His judgments are part of a larger redemptive plan. Augustine, in his *City of God*, argued that even in the midst of human suffering, God's justice works toward the ultimate good—a perspective that has provided comfort throughout the centuries.

Medieval and Reformation Developments Medieval theologians such as Thomas Aquinas used Aristotelian philosophy to explain that God's law is eternal and unalterable. Aquinas asserted that divine justice flows from God's pure act—unchanged and complete. The Reformers, including Martin Luther and John Calvin, stressed that human sin is so profound that only God's perfect justice, satisfied in Christ, can reconcile us to Himself. Their teachings on penal substitution highlight that while sin warrants punishment, God's justice is ultimately redemptive.

Modern Discussions In modern times, theological debates continue on the nature of divine justice, particularly in light of the problem of evil. While some argue that the presence of injustice challenges the notion of a just God, mainstream Christian theology holds that God's justice, though sometimes delayed, will ultimately prevail. This perspective encourages believers to view present suffering within the broader framework of God's redemptive and eternal plan.

19.4 Practical and Pastoral Implications

Assurance and Hope Belief in God's perfect justice provides deep reassurance. Even when human courts fail and worldly systems falter, believers trust that every act of injustice will be accounted for by a just God. This promise, found in passages like Romans 8:28, serves as a source of hope and perseverance in the face of oppression or personal suffering.

Motivation for Ethical Living Understanding divine justice inspires moral conduct. Believers are called to live righteously—pursuing honesty, fairness, and compassion—knowing that they are accountable to a God who judges without partiality. This awareness helps foster ethical communities where truth and mercy guide relationships, rather than revenge or corruption.

Social Advocacy and Community Impact God's justice extends beyond individual morality to societal structures. Throughout history, Christians have drawn on the conviction of divine justice to challenge systems of exploitation and to advocate for the oppressed. Biblical mandates to "defend the rights of the poor" (Proverbs 31:9) motivate efforts in social justice, inspiring movements that seek to transform societies in line with God's eternal standards.

Worship and Devotional Life Worshiping a just God deepens our reverence. When believers praise God for His unchanging moral order, they acknowledge that His judgments are both righteous and redemptive. This understanding transforms worship into an act of trust and submission, as believers recognize that every aspect of life—joy, suffering, success, and failure—is held within God's just care.

In conclusion, God's justice is a vital dimension of His character—one that guarantees the righteous order of the universe and offers hope for ultimate redemption. From the covenantal laws of the Old Testament to the sacrificial love revealed in Christ's atonement, the Bible presents a God who judges sin fairly while extending mercy to the repentant. Historically, the church has upheld this doctrine as a source of comfort amid human injustice and as a call to live ethically and compassionately.

For the individual believer, the assurance that God is just means that no wrongdoing will go unnoticed and no virtue unacknowledged. It fosters trust in His redemptive plan and encourages perseverance even when earthly systems fail. In our communities, a commitment to divine justice challenges us to advocate for truth, extend forgiveness, and work tirelessly for the common good.

Ultimately, God's justice is not a cold, impersonal force but a dynamic expression of His perfect nature—a harmonious blend of righteousness, mercy, and grace. As we face the challenges of life, may we find solace and strength in the unshakeable promise that the just God will bring every wrong to account and every tear to an end. In doing so, we join in the divine mission of reflecting His justice in our own lives, ensuring that His eternal kingdom, founded on truth and love, continues to transform the world.

Chapter 20: Forgiving

God's forgiveness is a cornerstone of Christian hope and transformation. It reveals a Divine nature that not only recognizes sin and moral failure but also willingly removes guilt and restores relationships for those who truly repent. Far from a mere overlook of wrongdoing, divine forgiveness is the dynamic interplay of justice and mercy—a central theme of Scripture that finds its fullest expression in the atoning work of Christ. This chapter examines the biblical basis, theological significance, and practical impact of God's forgiveness.

20.1 Understanding Divine Forgiveness

Defining Divine Forgiveness In human relationships, forgiveness often means letting go of resentment after an offense. In contrast, divine forgiveness is an active, comprehensive process. It releases individuals from the full penalty of sin, not because sin is trivial, but because God, in His boundless mercy, chooses to restore rather than condemn. Unlike human forgiveness—often incomplete or tainted by lingering bitterness—God's forgiveness is pure, transformative, and definitive. It is rooted in His unchanging love and righteousness, ensuring that even as sin is acknowledged, its eternal consequences are removed for the repentant.

Justice and Mercy in Harmony A key tension arises from the coexistence of divine justice and forgiveness. Human understanding of justice suggests that wrongdoing deserves punishment. However, in God's economy, justice and mercy are not in opposition. The cross is the ultimate demonstration: Christ's sacrificial death satisfies the demands of justice while simultaneously extending unmerited grace. Through this act, God upholds moral order yet offers a pathway for restoration—a balance that transforms punishment into a gateway for reconciliation.

20.2 Biblical Foundations

Old Testament Insights

1. **Divine Compassion and Reconciliation:** The Hebrew Scriptures portray God as patient

and ready to forgive. In Exodus 34:6–7, God is described as "merciful and gracious, slow to anger, and abounding in steadfast love," establishing a standard for forgiveness even when Israel repeatedly strays. The sacrificial system and the Day of Atonement in Leviticus 16 provided structured means for cleansing sins, pointing forward to a more complete redemption.

2. **Psalms of Repentance:** Psalm 51, attributed to David after his grievous sin, exemplifies how sincere contrition invites God's cleansing. David's confident plea that "God, you do not delight in sacrifice; if I were to give a burnt offering, you would not be pleased" (Psalm 51:16) underscores that what matters most is a contrite heart—a principle that reaffirms God's readiness to forgive those who earnestly seek restoration.

New Testament Revelations

1. **Jesus' Ministry:** Jesus' life and parables vividly illustrate divine forgiveness. In the Prodigal Son (Luke 15:11–32), the father's joyous embrace of his repentant child models a forgiveness that is lavish and immediate. Similarly, Jesus' interactions with tax collectors and sinners demonstrate that He prioritizes restoration over condemnation. His teaching in the Lord's Prayer—"Forgive us our debts, as we also have forgiven our debtors" (Matthew 6:12)—links personal forgiveness with the receipt of divine pardon.

2. **The Atonement:** Central to the New Testament is the portrayal of Christ's death as the means by which God's justice is satisfied and forgiveness made possible. Romans 5:8 emphasizes that "while we were still sinners, Christ died for us," showing that forgiveness is offered as a free gift, not as a result of human merit. The apostolic teaching further underscores that the new covenant, sealed in Christ's blood, ensures that sins are not remembered, inviting believers into a life of renewed relationship with God.

20.3 Theological and Historical Perspectives

Early Church Reflections In the early church, theologians like Tertullian and Cyprian wrestled with the balance between discipline and grace. Their penitential practices sought to restore sinners rather than simply punish them, emphasizing that forgiveness, when genuine, leads to transformation. Augustine, in his *Confessions*, vividly recounts how God's mercy transformed his life, reinforcing that forgiveness is at the heart of salvation.

Medieval and Reformation Developments Medieval theologians, such as Thomas Aquinas, integrated Aristotelian thought with Scripture to show that divine forgiveness is both just and merciful. Aquinas argued that God's forgiveness is not a human concession but a necessary outflow of His perfect nature. The Reformers, notably Martin Luther and John Calvin, underscored that justification by faith alone rests on God's free forgiveness. They contended that salvation is entirely a work of divine grace—God's justice is met in Christ's sacrifice, not by human works.

Contemporary Views Modern theologians continue to affirm that God's forgiveness is transformative. Movements like liberation theology emphasize that forgiveness is crucial not only for individual healing but also for addressing systemic injustices. Regardless of cultural or philosophical shifts, the core biblical message remains: God's forgiveness is available to all who repent, and it is both a personal release from guilt and a call to live in renewed righteousness.

20.4 Addressing Misconceptions

License to Sin? One common error is the belief that divine forgiveness gives believers a license to sin. Paul counters this in Romans 6:1–2: "Shall we continue in sin that grace may abound? By no means!" True forgiveness is not a free pass to repeat wrongdoing; rather, it should lead to sincere repentance and a transformed life.

Instant Erasure of Consequences Another misconception is that forgiveness removes all consequences of sin. While God forgives sins and erases eternal guilt, earthly repercussions— such as broken relationships or legal penalties—might still require restoration. King David's experience after his transgressions illustrates that divine pardon does not always nullify every temporal outcome but does secure one's eternal standing before God.

God's Forgiveness as Weakness Some critics mistakenly view a forgiving God as weak or indecisive. However, the biblical portrayal of forgiveness, especially in the sacrifice of Christ, demonstrates that true strength is shown by overcoming sin and restoring relationships. God's willingness to forgive is not a sign of vulnerability but a powerful expression of love that upholds justice and transforms lives.

20.5 Pastoral and Practical Implications

Healing the Wounded Conscience For individuals burdened by guilt, God's forgiveness offers a path to emotional and spiritual healing. Pastoral care often emphasizes that confession and repentance lead not to condemnation but to renewal. The promise that God "remembers [our sins] no more" (Hebrews 8:12) provides relief from the weight of past mistakes, fostering personal growth and liberation.

Promoting Reconciliation in Community In interpersonal relationships, the call to forgive mirrors the divine example. Ephesians 4:32 instructs believers to "be kind and compassionate to one another, forgiving each other, just as in Christ God forgave you." This ethic of mutual forgiveness fosters unity and reconciliation, enabling communities to heal from conflicts and build stronger bonds.

Impact on Mission and Evangelism The message of forgiveness is central to the gospel. When missionaries proclaim that no sin is too great to be forgiven, they offer hope to those burdened by shame and regret. This liberating message invites people to experience transformation, as forgiveness opens the door to a renewed life in Christ. The cross becomes the ultimate emblem of forgiveness—where justice and mercy meet—challenging both individuals and societies to embrace reconciliation over retribution.

In conclusion, God's forgiveness is the heartbeat of the Christian gospel—a powerful testament to a God who, while upholding justice, offers unmerited grace. From the patience shown in the Old Testament to the radical redemption revealed in Christ's sacrifice, Scripture weaves a narrative where forgiveness restores and transforms.

Historically, the church has wrestled with the balance between discipline and grace, and the consistent lesson is that true forgiveness leads to genuine transformation. This doctrine is not an excuse for moral laxity but a call to sincere repentance, a renewed commitment to righteous living, and a humble recognition of our dependence on God's grace.

Practically, divine forgiveness provides deep comfort in personal struggles, inspires ethical behavior, and fosters a culture of reconciliation within communities. It challenges believers to extend the same grace they have received to others, breaking cycles of anger and retribution and paving the way for healing and unity.

Ultimately, God's forgiving nature reminds us that no sin is beyond redemption, no heart is too hardened to be softened, and no relationship is beyond repair. In a world often marred by unforgiving systems and relentless judgment, the promise of divine forgiveness stands as a beacon of hope. It invites each of us to experience the transformative power of God's love—a love that not only pardons but also renews, empowers, and calls us to a life of authentic, compassionate living.

May we embrace this truth, allowing it to shape our worship, guide our interactions, and fuel our mission, as we reflect the profound grace of a God who freely forgives and redeems all who come to Him in true repentance.

Chapter 21: Jealous

In Christian theology, the concept of a "jealous God" is both provocative and profoundly meaningful. Unlike human jealousy—which often stems from insecurity or selfishness—God's jealousy is rooted in His righteous zeal to preserve the exclusive, loving relationship He has established with His people. It reflects His deep commitment to protect the integrity of the covenant, ensuring that His people remain devoted solely to Him. This chapter explores the biblical foundations, theological nuances, and practical implications of divine jealousy, illustrating how it safeguards the true worship and well-being of His people.

21.1 Understanding Divine Jealousy

Holy Zeal versus Human Jealousy Human jealousy typically arises from fear of loss or feelings of inadequacy, leading to resentment or even manipulation. In contrast, God's jealousy is a protective and passionate response to any threat against His rightful claim over the devotion of His people. This "holy jealousy" is akin to a devoted spouse's protective instinct—it is not born out of insecurity but out of a deep desire for intimate, exclusive relationship. God's jealousy ensures that His people do not stray into idolatry or compromise their covenant allegiance.

Covenant Context At the core of divine jealousy is the covenant relationship. When God establishes a covenant—whether with Israel at Sinai or with the Church through Christ—He stakes a claim on the hearts of His people. Any act of worship directed toward other gods or the adoption of false allegiances is seen not merely as disobedience, but as a breach of a sacred, exclusive bond. Thus, divine jealousy is not arbitrary; it is a rightful demand for loyalty that reflects God's desire for His people to experience the fullness of His love and protection.

21.2 Biblical Foundations

Old Testament Perspectives

1. **Exodus and the Law:** In Exodus 34:14, God commands, "You shall worship no other god, for the LORD, whose name is Jealous, is a jealous God." This declaration follows the giving of the Law and serves as a stark reminder that God demands exclusive devotion. The covenant relationship established with Israel hinges on this commitment, and any deviation—such as idolatry—provokes divine jealousy as a form of corrective love.

2. **Prophetic Imagery:** The prophets frequently use marital and parental imagery to describe God's jealousy. Hosea, for example, portrays Israel's idolatry as spiritual adultery, emphasizing that God's jealousy is akin to a husband's protective love when his spouse is unfaithful. Such images underline that divine jealousy is not punitive for its own sake but aims to restore intimacy and faithfulness.

3. **Psalms of Assurance:** The Psalms echo this theme, portraying God as a vigilant guardian who defends the sanctity of worship. They remind believers that straying from God's path invites not just discipline, but the loss of the blessing that comes from an undivided heart.

New Testament Insights

1. **Jesus' Teachings:** While the term "jealous" is less frequent in the New Testament, its essence is evident in Jesus' call for wholehearted devotion. In Matthew 6:24, Jesus teaches, "No one can serve two masters," emphasizing that divided loyalties compromise our relationship with God. His cleansing of the temple (John 2:13–17) vividly demonstrates His zeal to protect sacred worship from corruption.

2. **Apostolic Warnings:** The apostles echoed this call to exclusive devotion. Paul warned the Corinthians against engaging in idolatrous practices that diluted their commitment to Christ (1 Corinthians 10:14–22). Moreover, the image of the Church as the Bride of Christ (Ephesians 5:25–27) underscores that genuine worship requires undivided loyalty—a reflection of the intimate, covenantal relationship God desires.

21.3 Theological and Historical Perspectives

Early Church and Patristic Thought In the early centuries, Christian apologists like Justin Martyr and Tertullian defended the exclusive worship of God against pagan practices. They argued that the biblical God's jealousy was not petty or self-serving but a necessary safeguard for the truth of His revelation. This jealousy was seen as a mark of divine honor—a demand for loyalty that distinguished the one true God from capricious deities.

Medieval Synthesis and Reformation Insights Medieval theologians such as Anselm and Aquinas integrated divine jealousy into their broader discussions of God's attributes, linking it to His absolute holiness and moral perfection. For them, God's jealousy was an expression of His unassailable worth, ensuring that no lesser power could share in His glory. The Reformers further emphasized that salvation by grace alone depends on an exclusive relationship with Christ. Figures like John Calvin stressed that any rival loyalty—be it to tradition, works, or worldly idols—undermines the pure gospel and the transformative power of God's forgiveness.

Modern Reflections Today, while some criticize the notion of a "jealous God" through the lens of human possessiveness, contemporary Christian apologetics clarify that divine jealousy arises from a righteous claim to exclusive devotion. It is not about controlling human hearts out of insecurity but about protecting the relationship that leads to true freedom and redemption.

21.4 Pastoral and Practical Implications

Guarding Against Idolatry For believers, understanding God's jealousy is a call to constant self-examination. Idols today may not be carved images but can include materialism, power, or even religious traditions that distract from the worship of Christ. Regular disciplines such as prayer, Scripture meditation, and accountable fellowship help maintain a singular focus on God and guard against the subtle drift into divided loyalties.

Strengthening Community and Unity Acknowledging God's jealous demand for exclusive devotion encourages communal unity. When congregations collectively affirm that God alone is worthy of worship, it fosters an environment where differences are minimized, and shared purpose is maximized. This unity becomes a powerful witness in a pluralistic world, reinforcing the idea that true spiritual fulfillment comes from undivided loyalty to the one true God.

Inspiration for Mission and Evangelism The message of divine jealousy carries an evangelistic impulse. Christians are called to proclaim that God's love and redemption are available only through exclusive faith in Him. This understanding challenges the pervasive cultural trend of religious pluralism and invites seekers to consider the transformative power of a God who passionately guards the covenant relationship with His people.

21.5 Addressing Common Misconceptions

Jealousy as Human Insecurity While human jealousy often stems from insecurity or envy, God's jealousy is rooted in His rightful claim to be the sole object of worship. It is not an emotional outburst but a protective zeal—a divine safeguard against any influence that would compromise the relationship between God and His people.

Conflict Between Jealousy and Love Some argue that jealousy contradicts love. However, in a covenant relationship, love must be exclusive to be genuine. Just as a loving parent may show a measure of jealousy to protect a child, God's jealousy is an expression of His deep commitment to His people. It ensures that they do not fall prey to false promises or idolatrous distractions that would ultimately harm them.

Tolerance Versus Exclusive Devotion In a multicultural world, the call for exclusive worship may seem intolerant. Yet divine jealousy is not about rejecting other cultures or ideas per se, but about maintaining the purity of the relationship with the true God. It is a call to prioritize what is eternally true over what is transiently appealing.

In Conclusion, the biblical portrayal of God's jealousy reveals a God who is passionately committed to the exclusive love and worship of His people. Far from a petty or insecure impulse, divine jealousy is a manifestation of God's righteous claim to be the sole recipient of worship—a safeguard that protects the covenant and fosters spiritual vitality. From the Old Testament's call to avoid idolatry to the New Testament's emphasis on the singular devotion exemplified by Christ and the early church, Scripture consistently portrays this attribute as essential for both personal faith and communal integrity.

Historically, Church Fathers and Reformers alike have stressed that God's jealousy is not a mark of divine insecurity but of divine honor. It is a protective measure that ensures His unchanging character is reflected in the lives of those who trust in Him. In practical terms, understanding God's jealousy compels believers to guard their hearts, cultivate unity in worship, and engage in missions that proclaim the transformative power of exclusive devotion to the one true God.

Ultimately, the doctrine of divine jealousy invites every believer to reexamine their priorities and renew their commitment to a relationship with God that is untainted by competing idols. In a world rife with distractions and divided loyalties, the call to exclusive worship stands as a testament to the unique, redemptive love of a God who cherishes His covenant people. As we embrace this truth, we are reminded that true freedom and flourishing come not from sharing our devotion among many, but from unreservedly aligning our hearts with the God who alone is worthy of all honor and praise.

Chapter 22: Wrathful

God's wrath is a central theme in Scripture, representing His unwavering opposition to sin and injustice. Unlike uncontrolled human anger, divine wrath is not vindictive or capricious; rather, it is a measured, righteous response rooted in God's holiness and commitment to uphold moral order. It safeguards the covenant relationship, ensuring that evil does not go unchecked while providing a pathway to redemption through repentance. This chapter explores the biblical foundations, theological significance, and practical implications of God's wrath, revealing how it both protects His people and calls them to a higher standard of righteousness.

22.1 Understanding Divine Wrath

Defining Divine Wrath In everyday language, "wrath" suggests furious anger or vengeful spite. In Scripture, however, God's wrath signifies His righteous indignation against sin and corruption. It arises from His holy nature—He cannot tolerate evil because it distorts the moral order He established. Divine wrath is not an outburst of impulsive emotion but a deliberate, measured response that balances justice with mercy. It acts to uphold truth and restore what has been broken, ensuring that sin is addressed while still offering the hope of reconciliation.

The Balance of Justice and Mercy God's wrath is inseparable from His justice and mercy. While His justice demands that sin be punished, His mercy provides a way for redemption. The cross is the ultimate demonstration: Christ's sacrifice absorbs the penalty for sin, satisfying divine justice while extending grace to the repentant. In this way, God's wrath is not an end in itself but a means to maintain moral order and invite transformation.

22.2 Biblical Foundations

Old Testament Perspectives

1. **Covenant and Warning:** In Exodus 34:14, God declares, "You shall worship no other god, for the LORD, whose name is Jealous, is a jealous God." This command

underscores that divine wrath is not arbitrary but arises when covenant loyalty is violated. Israel's history, including episodes like the golden calf (Exodus 32) and the recurring lure of idolatry, reveals that God's wrath is activated by persistent disobedience. The prophets, such as Amos and Micah, use vivid imagery to call out injustice and warn that unrepentant sin will inevitably bring judgment. Yet these warnings are always paired with an invitation to return to God's ways, highlighting that His wrath is ultimately restorative.

2. **Redemptive Discipline:** The flood narrative (Genesis 6–9) illustrates God's severe response to widespread corruption while also preserving Noah and his family. This dual focus on judgment and preservation shows that divine wrath functions to cleanse and renew, rather than simply to destroy.

New Testament Continuity

1. **Jesus' Teachings and Acts:** Although Jesus is renowned for His compassion, His teachings consistently affirm the seriousness of sin. Parables such as the wheat and the weeds (Matthew 13:24–30, 36–43) illustrate that judgment is an integral part of God's kingdom, separating the righteous from the unrepentant. Moreover, Jesus' cleansing of the temple (John 2:13–17) reveals a zeal for pure worship that mirrors Old Testament prophetic warnings against idolatry.

2. **Apostolic Exhortations:** Paul emphasizes in Romans 1:18 and Ephesians 5:6 that God's wrath is revealed against all unrighteousness and ungodliness. However, he also explains that through Christ, believers are delivered from the wrath to come (Romans 5:9). This duality reinforces that divine wrath is a response to sin that, while real and severe, is also met with the redeeming love of God.

3. **Apocalyptic Vision:** The Book of Revelation presents cosmic scenes of judgment, where God's wrath is directed toward those who persist in rebellion against Him. Although the imagery is dramatic, it serves to remind believers that God's moral order will ultimately prevail and that His righteous judgment will be executed in full measure.

22.3 Theological and Historical Perspectives

Early Church Thought Early Church Fathers like Tertullian and Irenaeus defended the concept of divine wrath against the backdrop of pagan deities known for erratic and self-serving anger. They argued that God's wrath, rooted in holiness, is a necessary response to sin—designed not to be destructive for its own sake but to restore the intended order of creation.

Medieval and Reformation Insights Medieval theologians, such as Thomas Aquinas, integrated divine wrath into a broader moral framework, arguing that God's judgment is essential for maintaining the perfect balance of justice and mercy. The Reformers, including Martin Luther and John Calvin, emphasized that while sin merits severe punishment, God's atoning work in Christ satisfies the demands of justice. This perspective highlights that divine wrath is not a symbol of divine cruelty but a reflection of the seriousness of sin, counterbalanced by the hope of redemption.

Modern Reflections Contemporary theologians continue to wrestle with the image of a wrathful God, especially in light of modern critiques that equate wrath with vindictiveness. However, mainstream Christian thought asserts that God's wrath is a necessary safeguard against evil—a moral boundary that protects the integrity of His creation while inviting repentance and transformation.

22.4 Practical and Pastoral Implications

Awakening Moral Conscience Awareness of divine wrath can jolt believers out of moral complacency. When individuals understand that sin provokes a righteous response from God, it fosters a healthy fear of sin—not in a terrorizing sense, but as a motivation for repentance and ethical living. This awareness helps maintain a sense of accountability and encourages a lifestyle aligned with God's standards.

Comfort for the Oppressed For those suffering injustice, the doctrine of divine wrath provides hope. The promise that God will one day right all wrongs assures believers that current suffering is neither overlooked nor eternal. This conviction comforts victims of oppression and fuels a commitment to seek justice, knowing that the final judgment belongs to a just God.

Encouraging Evangelism and Social Action The message of God's wrath, when understood in its proper context, is a call to evangelism and social advocacy. Believers are driven to share the gospel—not to incite fear, but to offer the liberating hope found in Christ's atonement. Social justice initiatives, inspired by the biblical mandate to care for the oppressed, reflect the transformative power of divine judgment coupled with mercy.

Balancing Justice with Grace in Ministry Pastoral care and community life benefit from a balanced understanding of God's wrath. While it reminds us of sin's gravity, it also reinforces the transformative power of forgiveness at the cross. This dual focus encourages ministries that hold individuals accountable while also extending the opportunity for restoration—a model that nurtures both discipline and compassion within the church.

In conclusion, the doctrine of divine wrath, when rightly understood, is not a portrayal of a vengeful or cruel deity but a declaration of God's unwavering commitment to justice and righteousness. From the Old Testament's calls to avoid idolatry to the New Testament's revelation of Christ's sacrificial atonement, Scripture presents a God whose wrath is inseparable from His love and holiness. Divine wrath is the necessary counterpart to sin; it upholds moral order and demands accountability while simultaneously paving the way for redemption through Christ.

Historically, this concept has been rigorously defended by early church fathers, refined by medieval theologians, and rearticulated during the Reformation. Modern Christian thought continues to affirm that God's righteous anger is aimed not at punishing for punishment's sake but at restoring a broken world. It calls believers to live with integrity, engage in social advocacy, and witness the transformative power of a God who confronts evil head-on while offering grace.

For the individual believer, the assurance of God's wrath means that no sin or injustice will ultimately go unaddressed. It encourages a life of repentance, moral vigilance, and compassionate outreach. In community, it fosters unity and inspires collective efforts to pursue justice while extending forgiveness. And in the broader world, it stands as a powerful testament against the acceptance of moral relativism and unchecked corruption.

Ultimately, divine wrath underscores that God's moral order is non-negotiable. It is a protective force ensuring that the holy, redemptive purposes of God are not compromised. As believers, we are called to embrace this truth, allowing it to shape our ethics, motivate our evangelism, and deepen our worship. In doing so, we join in the divine mission: to live under the banner of a just God who, through the cross, transforms wrath into the ultimate expression of love and redemption—a truth that promises restoration and hope for all of creation.

Chapter 23: Wise

God's wisdom is a foundational attribute of the Christian understanding of the Divine. It is not merely an accumulation of knowledge or raw intellectual power; rather, it represents the perfect application of insight, purpose, and moral clarity. Divine wisdom guides the orchestration of the cosmos and the unfolding of human history, ensuring that God's creative and redemptive purposes are fulfilled with precision and grace. This chapter examines the biblical foundations, theological reflections, and practical implications of God's wisdom, illustrating how it shapes Christian life and fosters ethical living.

23.1 The Nature of Divine Wisdom

More Than Knowledge Divine wisdom transcends simple information—it is the artful application of perfect knowledge in accordance with God's moral will. While humans might gather facts and make decisions based on limited understanding, God's wisdom is all-encompassing. It directs not only the physical laws of the universe but also the ethical dimensions of human relationships. In Scripture, wisdom is frequently personified (as in Proverbs 8), suggesting that it is active, relational, and even creative. This active wisdom is a reflection of God's own character, demonstrating that He is both the origin and the perfect administrator of all things.

Moral and Redemptive Dimensions At the core of divine wisdom is a commitment to righteousness and restoration. God's wisdom ensures that every decision and act contributes to the ultimate good, promoting justice, mercy, and reconciliation. Unlike human cunning, which can be misused for selfish ends, divine wisdom is redemptive—it seeks to restore broken relationships, renew creation, and guide individuals toward a life that reflects God's truth. This comprehensive view of wisdom fuses ethical excellence with profound insight, making it a dynamic force for transformation.

23.2 Biblical Foundations of Divine Wisdom

Old Testament Depictions

1. **Creation and Cosmic Order:** In the creation narratives of Genesis and the poetic language of the Psalms, God's wisdom is evident in the intricate order of the universe. Proverbs 8:22–31 personifies Wisdom as a master craftsman who was with God before creation began, suggesting that the entire cosmos rests on divine insight. This orderly design reflects a purposeful plan, where every element of nature operates according to a divine blueprint.

2. **Prophetic Insight:** The prophets frequently attest to God's surpassing wisdom. Isaiah 55:8–9 declares that "my thoughts are not your thoughts, neither are your ways my ways," emphasizing that God's understanding transcends human logic. Furthermore, the narrative of Joseph in Genesis 50:20—"You meant evil against me, but God meant it for good"—demonstrates how God's wise sovereignty can transform personal suffering into a means of salvation for many.

New Testament Revelation

1. **Christ as the Embodiment of Wisdom:** The New Testament presents Jesus as the living expression of divine wisdom. John 1:1–2 identifies Him as the eternal Word, the means by which all things were made. In His teachings and parables, Jesus reveals a wisdom that challenges conventional worldly values—such as turning the last into first or inviting the prodigal back with open arms. His life, culminating in the sacrificial act on the cross, embodies a wisdom that unites justice with mercy, offering redemption and new life.

2. **Apostolic Exhortations:** Paul's epistles highlight that while human wisdom is limited and flawed, God's wisdom is unsearchable. In 1 Corinthians 1:18–31, Paul contrasts the foolishness of the cross with the power and wisdom of God, showing that what appears weak to the world is, in fact, the very means of salvation. Likewise, Ephesians 3:10–19 speaks of the church as a platform where God's manifold wisdom is displayed—a wisdom that even the angels marvel at.

23.3 Theological and Historical Perspectives

Patristic Foundations Early Church Fathers like Justin Martyr and Irenaeus linked God's wisdom to the eternal Word, arguing that the divine logos was a reflection of the infinite intelligence behind creation. They saw Greek philosophical notions of "Reason" as a shadow of the wisdom now revealed in Christ, underscoring that God's wisdom is both transcendent and personal.

Medieval and Reformation Thought Medieval theologians such as Thomas Aquinas developed a systematic framework, arguing that God's wisdom orders the cosmos with an intrinsic purpose (telos) for every creature. For Aquinas, divine wisdom is the guiding principle that aligns all things with God's eternal plan. Reformers like Martin Luther and John Calvin further emphasized that human wisdom, marred by sin, pales in comparison to the unchanging wisdom of God, which is revealed fully through Christ's redemptive work.

Modern Reflections In contemporary theology, scholars continue to affirm that while human knowledge is ever-expanding, it remains finite compared to the infinite wisdom of God. Modern thinkers highlight that God's wisdom encompasses both the grandeur of the universe and the intimate details of personal lives. This holistic view encourages believers to approach both science and spirituality with humility and wonder.

23.4 Practical Implications for Christian Living

Trust in God's Providence Believing in God's wisdom provides a secure foundation in uncertain times. When faced with complex life challenges—whether personal loss, moral dilemmas, or global crises—believers can trust that God's wise plan is unfolding, even when it is beyond human understanding. Romans 8:28 reminds us that all things work together for good, a promise rooted in divine wisdom.

Guidance in Decision-Making Divine wisdom shapes how Christians make choices. Seeking God's counsel through prayer, Scripture, and wise community counsel is essential, for it aligns personal decisions with a higher, unchanging truth. This approach encourages thoughtful, ethical living that reflects God's orderly design.

Humility and Lifelong Learning Acknowledging that God's wisdom is infinite fosters humility. Humans are reminded that, despite our intellectual achievements, the fullness of truth lies beyond our grasp. This encourages continual learning, reflective study of Scripture, and an openness to new insights, all the while recognizing that ultimate wisdom comes from God.

Ethical and Social Engagement A commitment to divine wisdom motivates believers to act justly in society. Ethical decision-making, fair treatment of others, and responsible stewardship of creation all reflect the moral order that God has established. This perspective drives Christian involvement in social justice, environmental care, and advocacy, as believers seek to mirror the integrity and love of a wise Creator.

In conclusion, God's wisdom is not a mere attribute of intellect—it is the very foundation upon which the universe is ordered and human history is redeemed. From the orderly creation of the cosmos in Genesis to the redemptive teaching of Jesus in the New Testament, Scripture consistently reveals a God whose wisdom is perfect, unchanging, and all-encompassing.

Theologically, divine wisdom challenges us to reconcile human limitations with the infinite insight of God, urging us to seek His guidance in every aspect of life. Historically, the reflections of early Church Fathers, medieval scholars, and Reformers have enriched our understanding, reinforcing that while human wisdom is flawed, God's remains a reliable beacon of truth.

Practically, the assurance of God's wisdom instills trust in His providence, guiding ethical behavior and inspiring a lifelong pursuit of knowledge grounded in humility. It shapes worship that is both awe-inspired and intimately personal, as believers recognize that the One who governs the heavens also cares deeply about every detail of their lives.

Ultimately, embracing God's wisdom transforms our approach to life. It calls us to trust in His unerring plan, to seek alignment with His eternal purposes, and to live in a manner that reflects the moral and creative excellence of our Creator. In doing so, we find a source of hope, stability, and purpose that transcends the limits of human understanding—a truth that invites us into a deeper, more fulfilling relationship with the Divine.

Chapter 24: Perfect

God's perfection is a central, awe-inspiring attribute in Christian theology. To call God "perfect" means that He is complete, lacking no virtue or capability, and embodies the fullness of goodness, wisdom, and power. Unlike human notions of flawlessness, divine perfection encompasses both moral and ontological wholeness. It signifies a God who is unchanging in His character and consistently works for the ultimate good of creation. This chapter explores the biblical basis for divine perfection, examines historical and theological reflections, addresses common misconceptions, and considers its practical significance for personal faith and communal life.

24.1 Defining Divine Perfection

Beyond Flawlessness In everyday language, "perfect" often implies error-free performance or meeting specific expectations. When applied to God, however, perfection means complete and absolute excellence in every attribute. God's knowledge, power, love, and wisdom are infinite in degree and entirely integrated. He is morally pure—without sin or defect—and ontologically complete, possessing everything necessary for His nature without reliance on anything external. Divine perfection is not static or impersonal; rather, it is a dynamic, living quality that guides all of His creative and redemptive actions.

Perfection as Wholeness Biblical perfection connotes an all-encompassing wholeness. It means that God's being is unified and consistent, reflecting complete integrity in character and purpose. This holistic view implies that His actions, whether in judgment or redemption, always align with the highest moral standards. God's perfection serves as both a model and a standard for believers, who are called to strive for moral and spiritual maturity by reflecting His unchanging nature.

24.2 Biblical Foundations of Divine Perfection
Old Testament Witness

1. **Creation and Order:** The Genesis creation narrative paints a picture of a God whose work is "very good," highlighting the meticulous design and inherent beauty of the cosmos. This orderly creation reflects a Creator who is flawless in His planning and execution.

2. **Covenantal Integrity:** Deuteronomy 32:4 declares, "The Rock, His work is perfect, for all His ways are justice. A God of faithfulness and without iniquity, just and upright is He." Such texts emphasize that God's governance and laws are founded on His perfect character. Even when Israel falters, God's promises remain intact, underscoring His immutable moral order.

3. **Wisdom Literature:** Proverbs and Job illustrate that divine wisdom is intrinsically linked to perfection. Proverbs 8 personifies Wisdom as present with God before creation, reflecting the flawless nature of His counsel. Job 28, which contemplates the inaccessibility of true wisdom, ultimately points back to the perfect, all-knowing Creator.

New Testament Affirmations

1. **Christ as the Revelation of Perfection:** In Matthew 5:48, Jesus exhorts His followers, "Be perfect, as your heavenly Father is perfect." While this is an ideal that human beings can never fully attain, it highlights that God's perfection sets the benchmark for ethical and spiritual life.

2. **The Cross and Redemption:** The apostle Paul explains in 1 Corinthians 1:18–31 that what appears foolish to the world—the cross—is, in fact, the power and wisdom of God. Christ's sacrificial death and subsequent resurrection reveal that divine perfection is achieved not by avoiding sin but by overcoming it, satisfying both justice and mercy.

3. **Unchanging Character:** Passages such as James 1:17 and Hebrews 13:8 remind believers that "there is no variation or shadow due to change" in God. His gifts, guidance, and promises remain steadfast, providing an eternal foundation for faith and practice.

24.3 Historical and Theological Perspectives

Early Church and Patristic Thought Early Christian apologists like Justin Martyr and Irenaeus argued that the Christian God's perfection sharply contrasted with the mutable gods of pagan belief. They stressed that God's unchanging nature was a testament to His unique divinity. Augustine further emphasized that while all creation is transient, true stability and goodness are found only in God, whose perfection endures forever.

Medieval Scholasticism and the Reformation Medieval theologians such as Thomas Aquinas formulated the idea of God as "pure act" (actus purus), a being without any potentiality, fully actualized in every aspect. This metaphysical framework confirmed that God's nature is complete and unalterable. The Reformers, including Martin Luther and John Calvin, reinforced that salvation and divine grace are founded on a perfect God, whose righteousness and mercy remain constant regardless of human sinfulness.

Modern Dialogues In modern theology, debates continue regarding the nature of divine perfection, particularly as it intersects with contemporary understandings of science, ethics, and cultural relativity. Despite challenges from relativistic perspectives, the core Christian conviction remains: God's perfection is not a sterile abstraction but a vibrant reality that provides moral and spiritual certainty amid a shifting world.

24.4 Practical and Pastoral Implications

Assurance in Uncertainty Belief in a perfect God provides comfort and security in a world marked by imperfection and change. When life's challenges—whether personal, social, or environmental—seem overwhelming, the assurance that our Creator is complete and unchanging becomes a source of hope. This eternal constancy reminds believers that every trial is held within the unalterable purpose of God.

Transforming Worship Understanding God's perfection transforms worship from a mere ritual into a profound act of adoration. Congregations are encouraged to praise the One who is "the same yesterday, today, and forever" (Hebrews 13:8). In doing so, believers acknowledge that every good gift and every moment of grace originates from a God whose character is flawless and whose love is infinite.

Ethical Guidance and Personal Growth God's perfection sets a high moral standard that challenges believers to pursue holiness. While human beings remain imperfect, the call to reflect God's unblemished character motivates ethical living and continual personal growth. Spiritual disciplines—such as prayer, fasting, and community fellowship—are means through which believers seek to align their lives more closely with the divine example.

Community and Global Impact At a communal level, the recognition of divine perfection fosters unity. When church members collectively affirm that their foundation is a perfect, unchanging God, divisions and petty disagreements fade in light of the greater, eternal truth. This conviction also empowers believers to engage in social justice, knowing that moral integrity is anchored in an ultimate standard that transcends cultural and temporal boundaries.

In conclusion, the concept of God's perfection is central to the Christian worldview. It is far more than an assertion of flawlessness; it encompasses moral purity, complete knowledge, boundless power, and unwavering love. Scripture presents a God whose creative work is "very good," whose law is just, and whose redemptive plan in Christ transforms even the gravest sin into an opportunity for grace. From the wisdom literature of the Old Testament to the redemptive message of the New, divine perfection assures believers that the ultimate standard of truth and goodness is not subject to change.

Historically, the church has celebrated this doctrine, from the contemplations of Augustine and Aquinas to the reformative insights of Luther and Calvin. In every era, the belief in a perfect God has provided a stable foundation for hope, ethical living, and worship. In our own lives, this truth challenges us to trust in God's unchanging nature, to pursue moral excellence, and to worship Him with reverence and gratitude.

In a world rife with imperfection and shifting values, the eternal perfection of God stands as a beacon of stability and truth. It reminds us that every blessing, every moment of grace, and every step toward redemption originates from a God whose very nature is complete and unalterable. As we strive to mirror His character in our thoughts, actions, and relationships, we become living testaments to a God who is not only perfect in Himself but also graciously imparts His perfection to those who seek Him. May we, therefore, continually seek to align our lives with this divine standard, confident that in God's perfect presence, we find the fullness of life, hope, and eternal joy.

Chapter 25: Peaceful

God's peace is one of the most transformative and comforting aspects of the Divine. In Scripture, this peace is not merely the absence of conflict but the fullness of well-being, often expressed by the Hebrew word *shalom*. Divine peace signifies holistic harmony—spiritual, relational, and social—that originates from God and flows into every aspect of creation. This chapter explores the biblical foundations of God's peaceful nature, its theological and historical development, and its practical implications for personal devotion, community unity, and global engagement.

25.1 Understanding Divine Peace

The Meaning of Shalom In the Bible, *shalom* goes beyond a temporary truce or the absence of strife. It denotes completeness, prosperity, and overall well-being. God's peace is the state of wholeness that He bestows on creation—a peace that ensures proper order, healing, and justice. It is a dynamic, active force that nurtures right relationships among people, communities, and nations, offering both internal serenity and external harmony.

A Redemptive Reality Divine peace is not passive. It is a redemptive power that restores what has been fractured by sin. Throughout Scripture, God actively works to reestablish unity and order. His peace reverses the chaos of human conflict and offers a promise of renewal and reconciliation, culminating in the transformative work of Christ on the cross.

25.2 Biblical Foundations

Old Testament Foundations

1. **The God of Shalom:** In the Old Testament, God's character is frequently described in terms of *shalom*. For instance, in Judges 6:24, Gideon names God "Yahweh-Shalom," emphasizing that God is the source of well-being and security. The laws in the Torah—ranging from provisions for the poor to directives for fair social practices—were

intended to cultivate a society marked by justice and peace.

2. **Prophetic Visions:** The prophets envisioned a future where divine peace would transform societies. Isaiah 2:4 and Micah 4:3 foretell a time when nations will turn their swords into plowshares and live in lasting harmony. These visions highlight that God's peace is not a fleeting political arrangement but an eternal state that promises restoration on a cosmic scale.

New Testament Fulfillment

1. **Christ, the Prince of Peace:** The New Testament reveals Jesus Christ as the embodiment of God's peace. At His birth, angels proclaimed, "Glory to God in the highest, and on earth peace among those with whom he is pleased" (Luke 2:14). Jesus' ministry, characterized by healing, teaching, and the invitation to repent, demonstrated a peace that transcends mere absence of strife. In John 14:27, Jesus offers His disciples a peace "not as the world gives," underscoring a tranquility that surpasses worldly conditions.

2. **Redemption and Reconciliation:** Central to the gospel is the reconciliation achieved through Christ's sacrifice. The cross transforms wrath into peace, as God's redemptive work breaks the power of sin and restores broken relationships (Romans 5:1; Ephesians 2:14–17). Believers are thus invited to experience an inner peace that assures them of God's unchanging love and prepares them for eternal communion with Him.

25.3 Theological and Historical Perspectives

Early Church Insights Early Christians, facing persecution and cultural opposition, understood that true peace began in a right relationship with God. Church Fathers like Clement of Rome and Ignatius of Antioch emphasized that the peace of Christ should permeate both personal lives and communal worship. Their teachings underscored that God's peace was not an abstract concept but a tangible reality that upheld unity and moral integrity.

Medieval and Reformation Thought Medieval theologians such as Thomas Aquinas argued that peace results from the proper ordering of creation under God's sovereign rule. For Aquinas, a well-ordered society, reflecting divine justice and love, is a direct outgrowth of God's perfect design. The Reformers, including Martin Luther and John Calvin, stressed that true peace—"peace with God" (Romans 5:1)—comes solely through faith in Christ. They maintained that while earthly systems may fail, the peace offered by God remains unfaltering.

Modern Reflections Modern theologians continue to affirm that God's peace is a secure foundation amid cultural and societal turbulence. Amid global conflicts and social fragmentation, many Christians find that the biblical promise of *shalom*—a holistic, restorative peace—offers an enduring hope. This peace is not a passive acceptance of injustice but a call to active peacemaking and reconciliation.

25.4 Pastoral and Practical Implications

Inner Peace and Personal Resilience For individuals, the assurance of God's peace offers deep comfort during times of distress. Philippians 4:6–7 promises that by bringing our concerns to God, we receive a peace that transcends all understanding. This inner peace does not eliminate trials but provides a steadfast refuge amid life's storms. Practices such as contemplative prayer, meditation on Scripture, and retreats can help believers cultivate a personal awareness of God's calming presence.

Fostering Community Unity Within the church, a commitment to divine peace encourages unity and reconciliation. Believers are called to "make every effort to keep the unity of the Spirit through the bond of peace" (Ephesians 4:3). This involves not only forgiving one another but actively seeking to resolve conflicts and build a supportive, inclusive community. When churches model such unity, they become powerful witnesses to the transformative reality of God's peace.

Global and Social Engagement The biblical vision of peace extends to social and global dimensions. Many Christian organizations draw on the concept of *shalom* to guide initiatives in social justice, humanitarian aid, and conflict resolution. Whether through interfaith dialogue, community development projects, or advocacy for the oppressed, believers are motivated by the conviction that true peace is both a present reality and a future hope. This holistic peace challenges secular notions of compromise, calling for a restoration that respects human dignity and the integrity of creation.

Worship and Devotion Worship becomes enriched when it reflects on God's perfect peace. Hymns, liturgies, and prayers that focus on God as the "Prince of Peace" remind congregants that divine tranquility is not merely a desirable state but the essence of the One who sustains them. Such worship lifts hearts above the chaos of everyday life and reinforces the confidence that, in God, there is an unchanging source of hope and renewal.

In conclusion, God's peace, rooted in the biblical concept of *shalom*, is much more than the absence of conflict—it is the fullness of life and well-being that flows from a right relationship with Him. From the Old Testament's portrayal of a deliverer who establishes order to the New Testament revelation of Christ's redemptive work, Scripture presents a God whose peace restores, reconciles, and renews.

Throughout history, theologians from the early Church to the modern era have affirmed that this peace is both a personal gift and a communal calling. It offers believers the strength to endure hardship, the wisdom to resolve conflicts, and the courage to engage in acts of social justice. This enduring peace is not passive; it actively transforms lives, guiding individuals and communities toward the vision of a world where the divine reign brings lasting harmony.

For every believer, embracing God's peace means more than quieting inner anxiety—it means aligning oneself with a purpose that transcends the present, pursuing relationships marked by unity, and engaging the world with a spirit of hope and reconciliation. In a fractured and restless age, the promise of divine peace stands as a beacon of restoration. As we experience and share this peace, we testify to a God who not only calms the storms of life but also reorders chaos into a tapestry of grace, justice, and love.

May we continually seek and reflect the peace of God in our lives, knowing that in His presence, true *shalom*—the holistic well-being of body, mind, and spirit—is our birthright and our destiny.

Chapter 26: Personal

God's personal nature is a cornerstone of Christian faith. Unlike an abstract, impersonal force, the God of Scripture chooses to relate intimately with human beings—calling them by name, hearing their prayers, and guiding their lives with genuine care. This relational quality is not a mere metaphor but a dynamic reality that underpins covenant, redemption, and daily Christian experience.

26.1 The Meaning of God's Personal Nature

Moving Beyond Abstraction When many think of "God," they might picture an impersonal force or distant energy. However, Christian tradition reveals a God who is personal—possessing will, knowledge, and relational capacity. He communicates, forms covenants, and responds lovingly to our needs. This personal dimension means God is not a remote architect but an active, caring presence who desires a relationship with each individual.

Relationship at the Core The personal nature of God means that relationships are intrinsic to His being. The doctrine of the Trinity shows that even before creation, God existed in perfect, loving communion. This eternal relationality informs how God interacts with us: He calls us "Father, Son, and Holy Spirit," and invites us into a familial bond where we are cherished, guided, and redeemed. In Scripture, God's initiative in reaching out—to Abraham, Moses, Mary, and countless others—demonstrates that our search for meaning is answered by a God who actively seeks us.

26.2 Biblical Foundations

Old Testament Encounters

1. **Direct Interaction:** From the earliest stories in Genesis, God's personal involvement is evident. Adam and Eve experienced God walking in the garden (Genesis 3:8), suggesting an intimate connection before sin disrupted that fellowship. Throughout

the Old Testament, God speaks directly to individuals—whether in covenants with Noah, Abraham, and Moses or through prophetic messages that call Israel to repentance. These encounters are not distant commands but personal dialogues that shape the destiny of His people.

2. **Covenant Relationships:** The covenants God makes with His people are inherently personal. When God calls Abraham by name and promises him descendants and blessing (Genesis 12:1–3), He establishes a relationship built on mutual commitment. Similarly, Moses' encounters, notably at the burning bush (Exodus 3) and during the giving of the Law, reveal a God who not only commands but also cares deeply about the moral and spiritual welfare of His people.

New Testament Revelation

1. **The Incarnation:** The most profound revelation of God's personal nature is found in the Incarnation. The Gospel of John declares, "The Word became flesh and dwelt among us" (John 1:14), affirming that God entered human history in the person of Jesus Christ. Jesus lived, taught, and suffered among people, demonstrating divine compassion and accessibility. His interactions—whether healing the sick, engaging with outcasts, or dining with sinners—highlight that God values personal connection.

2. **Familial Intimacy:** Jesus often referred to God as "Father," a term that conveys intimacy and care. In Mark 14:36, He even addresses God as "Abba, Father," indicating a closeness that surpasses formal ritual. This familial language assures believers that God is not a distant authority but a loving parent who cares deeply about every aspect of our lives.

3. **Apostolic Affirmations:** The letters of the New Testament reinforce this personal bond. Believers are called "children of God" (1 John 3:1) and co-heirs with Christ (Romans 8:17), emphasizing that our identity is intimately connected with the Divine. Through personal prayer and community fellowship, Christians experience God's nearness, which transforms worship from a duty into a heartfelt conversation.

26.3 Theological Perspectives

Patristic Insights Early church fathers such as Justin Martyr and Irenaeus argued that the personal God of Scripture is distinct from the impersonal "unmoved mover" of Greek philosophy. They emphasized that the Christian God not only created the universe but also entered into human history through revelation and covenant. Their writings stress that God's personal interaction with humanity is a testament to His love and relational nature.

Medieval and Reformation Reflections Medieval mystics like Julian of Norwich and Bernard of Clairvaux described God's closeness in deeply emotional and poetic terms, encouraging believers to seek intimate communion through prayer and contemplation. During the

Reformation, figures such as Martin Luther and John Calvin reasserted that faith is a personal trust in God's promises. Their teachings underscored that salvation comes through an intimate, unmediated relationship with a God who is both transcendent and near.

Modern Discourse Contemporary theologians continue to affirm God's personal nature. Karl Barth, for example, argued that God reveals Himself in the person of Christ, emphasizing a relational dynamic that transcends mere abstraction. Modern Christian thought encourages believers to cultivate personal devotion, integrating spiritual disciplines that foster a deeper sense of God's nearness in everyday life.

26.4 Practical Implications

Transforming Prayer and Worship Believing in a personal God transforms prayer from a ritualistic recitation into a dynamic conversation. When we call God "Father," we affirm that He is approachable, caring, and intimately involved in our lives. This intimate dialogue nurtures trust and encourages honesty—allowing us to share our deepest struggles, joys, and aspirations. Worship, too, becomes a communal celebration of God's loving presence, uniting believers as a family bound by shared experience and mutual care.

Strengthening Personal Relationships Understanding that God is personal motivates believers to cultivate genuine relationships. Since the Creator knows each of us by name and cares about our individual stories, we are called to mirror that same attentiveness in our relationships. This may involve practicing forgiveness, offering empathy, and building community where each person feels seen and valued.

Impact on Ethical Living God's personal nature implies that ethical behavior is not simply about following rules, but about fostering relationships that reflect divine love and care. Believers are encouraged to pursue justice, kindness, and compassion, understanding that these virtues flow from a relationship with a God who is actively involved in the world. Our actions, both in private and public spheres, are meant to echo the personal care that God extends to us.

Global and Interpersonal Outreach The relational aspect of God's nature has far-reaching implications for mission and evangelism. In sharing the gospel, Christians proclaim a God who seeks personal connection—one who desires to know and be known by each individual. This message resonates across cultures and helps break down barriers of alienation. Whether in one-on-one ministry or through global humanitarian efforts, the call is to reflect a God who values every human life and extends His love personally and inclusively.

In conclusion, the personal nature of God is not an abstract theological concept; it is a vibrant reality that shapes every dimension of Christian faith and practice. Scripture repeatedly reveals a God who reaches out, calls individuals by name, and enters into deep, transformative relationships. From the intimate dialogues with Abraham and Moses to the incarnation of Jesus and the apostolic affirmation that we are God's children, the Bible presents a God who is relational, accessible, and loving.

Historically, this understanding has set Christianity apart from impersonal philosophies and pagan traditions. The early church, medieval mystics, and Reformation reformers all emphasized that a personal God is at the heart of salvation and spiritual growth. Modern theology continues to stress that God's personal nature invites us into a living, ongoing relationship—one marked by prayer, worship, ethical living, and compassionate outreach.

For every believer, embracing the personal nature of God means discovering that He is not a distant authority but a loving Friend, Shepherd, and Father. This truth transforms prayer into conversation, worship into an intimate celebration, and ethical decisions into expressions of divine love. In our daily lives, it provides comfort in times of distress and hope amid uncertainty. It calls us to build communities of mutual support and to extend the same compassion and care that we receive from God.

Ultimately, acknowledging that God is personal invites us to experience a relationship where we are known, cherished, and guided by the very Creator of the universe. It assures us that our lives are not governed by impersonal forces, but by a God who seeks to walk with us— transforming our weaknesses, celebrating our joys, and drawing us ever closer into His eternal, loving embrace.

Chapter 27: Triune

Christian theology uniquely proclaims that God is Triune—one God in three distinct Persons: Father, Son, and Holy Spirit. This doctrine affirms both the oneness of God and an eternal, relational unity within the Godhead. Though the term "Trinity" is not found verbatim in Scripture, the biblical narrative consistently reveals this mystery through the interwoven roles of the Father, Son, and Spirit. This chapter examines the biblical foundations, historical development, theological significance, and practical implications of the Triune God.

27.1 Understanding the Trinity

Oneness and Threeness The biblical assertion "There is one God" (Deuteronomy 6:4) stands side by side with numerous New Testament passages that reveal God's presence in three Persons. In this mystery, the Father, Son, and Holy Spirit share one divine essence without dividing God into separate deities. Instead, each Person fully embodies the one divine nature while maintaining personal distinctions. The Father is not the Son, nor is the Spirit a mere mode of the Father; rather, they exist in a dynamic, eternal communion of love and purpose.

Relational Essence The very nature of God is relational. The doctrine of the Trinity teaches that before creation, God existed in perfect fellowship among the Father, Son, and Holy Spirit. This eternal relationship is the wellspring of all divine activity—God's creative power, redemptive work, and sustaining presence all flow from this inner communion. Thus, the Trinity is not an abstract puzzle but a profound revelation that love, self-giving, and relationality are at the core of God's being.

27.2 Biblical Foundations

Old Testament Echoes While the Old Testament affirms strict monotheism, it also contains hints of a complex unity within God:

- **Creation Dialogue:** In Genesis 1:26, God says, "Let us make man in our image," suggesting a plural conversation that foreshadows a relational nature.

- **Divine Attributes:** The wisdom literature, such as Proverbs 8, personifies wisdom in a way that implies an intimate aspect of God's creative work.

- **Covenantal Language:** God's dealings with Israel, characterized by personal engagement and covenant promises, set the stage for understanding His relational nature.

New Testament Revelation The New Testament provides clearer expressions of the Trinity:

- **Christ's Identity:** The Gospel of John opens with the assertion that "the Word was with God, and the Word was God" (John 1:1–2). Jesus' own claims, such as "Before Abraham was, I am" (John 8:58), reveal His eternal, divine nature.

- **Baptism and Commission:** In Matthew 3:16–17, the baptism of Jesus presents a vivid triune scene: as Jesus is baptized, the Spirit descends like a dove and the Father's voice declares His approval. Later, Jesus commissions His disciples to baptize "in the name of the Father and of the Son and of the Holy Spirit" (Matthew 28:19), affirming the unity of the Godhead.

- **Apostolic Teaching:** Paul and other apostles routinely bless believers "by the grace of the Lord Jesus Christ and the love of God and the fellowship of the Holy Spirit" (2 Corinthians 13:14), reinforcing the triune nature of God.

27.3 Historical Development

Early Church Formulations In the post-apostolic era, early Christians confronted the challenge of expressing a three-in-one God without slipping into polytheism. The debates against Arianism and Modalism led to the formulation of key doctrinal terms like *homoousios* (of the same essence) at the First Council of Nicaea (AD 325) and later, the full articulation of the Trinity at the Council of Constantinople (AD 381). These councils affirmed that the Father, Son, and Spirit are coequal, coeternal, and consubstantial, preserving both the oneness and the threeness of God.

Medieval and Reformation Insights Medieval theologians like Augustine and Thomas Aquinas further refined Trinitarian doctrine. Augustine's reflections on the internal life of God highlighted that the eternal love shared among the divine Persons is the basis for all creation and redemption. The Reformers, including Luther and Calvin, maintained that salvation rests on the one true God revealed in a personal, triune relationship, underscoring that true faith is an intimate communion with Father, Son, and Spirit.

Modern Theological Perspectives Today, while some question the coherence of the Trinity, mainstream Christian theology continues to uphold it as a revealed mystery. Modern theologians emphasize that the Trinity is not a human invention but a biblical truth that shapes our understanding of divine love, mission, and community. This relational model of God offers a robust framework for engaging both spiritual and cultural challenges.

27.4 Practical Implications

Worship and Prayer Recognizing the Triune nature of God transforms worship. Believers are invited to approach God in a relational manner—addressing Him as Father, through the mediation of Christ, and under the guidance of the Holy Spirit. This tri-personal structure enriches prayer, making it a dynamic dialogue rather than a one-sided plea. Liturgical practices, such as the doxology "Glory be to the Father, and to the Son, and to the Holy Spirit," remind congregations of the unity and distinctiveness of God's revelation.

Community and Unity The relational essence of the Trinity provides a blueprint for Christian community. Just as the Father, Son, and Spirit coexist in perfect harmony, so should believers foster unity despite their differences. This understanding encourages churches to embrace diversity while maintaining a shared commitment to the gospel, thus strengthening bonds and promoting mutual accountability.

Ethical Living and Mission A Trinitarian perspective underpins a holistic view of ethics and mission. The self-giving love among the divine Persons calls believers to act with generosity, compassion, and justice in every sphere of life. Evangelism, social justice, and community service are seen as extensions of the divine relationality, urging Christians to share the gospel and work for the common good with the same love that flows within the Godhead.

Interfaith Engagement The doctrine of the Trinity, while unique, also offers opportunities for respectful dialogue with other faiths. By explaining that the Trinity is not a form of polytheism but a revelation of one God in a perfect relational unity, Christians can bridge understanding with those who view ultimate reality differently. This conversation can foster mutual respect and deepen the search for truth across cultures and traditions.

In conclusion, the doctrine of the Trinity—God as one essence in three coequal Persons—is central to Christian faith. It reveals a God who is not an abstract force but a dynamic, relational Being who creates, redeems, and sustains with profound love. From the subtle plural hints of the Old Testament to the explicit revelations in the New Testament, Scripture presents a God who exists in eternal communion with Himself, inviting humanity into that same intimate relationship.

Historically, the church's formulation of the Trinity has been vital in distinguishing the Christian God from the capricious deities of paganism, as well as in shaping doctrines of salvation, worship, and ethical living. The early Church, medieval theologians, and Reformers all contributed to a rich tradition that celebrates both the unity and the relational diversity of the Godhead.

Practically, embracing the Trinity transforms every aspect of Christian life. Worship becomes a dynamic, communal celebration of God's multifaceted nature. Prayer deepens into a personal conversation with a loving Father, through the intercession of Christ, and under the guidance of the Spirit. Communities thrive in unity, and ethical living is enriched by the example of divine relationality. Even in interfaith contexts, the distinctiveness of the Trinity can open doors to meaningful dialogue and mutual understanding.

Ultimately, the triune God is not merely an abstract mystery to be debated but a living reality that invites every believer into a deep, personal relationship. As we reflect on the eternal fellowship within the Godhead, we are inspired to mirror that same self-giving love in our lives—pursuing unity, justice, and compassion. In a world often divided by differences and conflicts, the revelation of a Triune God offers a vision of true, transformative community—a community where the Father, Son, and Holy Spirit work in perfect harmony, inviting us all to share in the fullness of divine love and eternal fellowship.

Chapter 28: True

The assertion that God is "true" forms a cornerstone of Christian belief. In Scripture, divine truth goes far beyond factual accuracy—it embodies God's unchanging character, moral integrity, and reliable promises. Because God is truth itself, every word He speaks and every act He performs reflects absolute honesty and fidelity. This chapter explores the biblical basis for God's truthfulness, its historical and theological development, and its practical implications for Christian life, worship, and ethics.

28.1 Understanding Divine Truth

More Than Factual Correctness When we say God is true, we affirm that His nature is the standard of truth. His truth is not merely about being factually correct; it is about a complete and unwavering commitment to what is real, right, and good. Unlike human statements, which can be partial or misleading, God's words and actions are entirely reliable. His truth encompasses both the objective realities of the world and the moral dimensions of love, justice, and mercy.

Truth as Relational and Revealing Divine truth is also relational. It shows that God is not a distant, impersonal force but a God who speaks, loves, and interacts with humanity. The Bible portrays God as knowing each person intimately and inviting us into a genuine relationship based on His flawless, unchanging nature. Because His truth is revealed through covenant, prophecy, and ultimately in the person of Jesus Christ, believers are called to live with honesty, integrity, and faithfulness.

28.2 Biblical Foundations

Old Testament Testimony

1. **Covenant Fidelity:** Throughout the Old Testament, God's truth is closely linked with His covenant promises. Psalm 18:30 declares, "God's way is perfect; the word of the

131

LORD proves true." Whether promising descendants to Abraham or deliverance to Moses, God's declarations are never empty. His consistent fulfillment of these promises demonstrates that His word is a firm foundation for trust.

2. **Prophetic Revelation:** The prophets repeatedly affirmed that God's judgments and promises are rooted in absolute truth. In Isaiah 46:9–11, God's foreknowledge and unchanging purposes are emphasized, showing that nothing can thwart His plan. These passages assure the people that divine truth remains constant, even when human circumstances seem chaotic.

New Testament Revelation

1. **Christ, the Embodiment of Truth:** The New Testament brings a clear focus on truth through Jesus. John 14:6 famously states, "I am the way, and the truth, and the life," positioning Christ as the ultimate revelation of God's truth. In His life, teachings, and sacrificial death, Jesus displays a truth that transforms lives, providing a model of integrity and love that believers are called to follow.

2. **The Authority of Scripture:** The New Testament affirms that the words inspired by God are reliable. James 1:17 reminds us that every good gift comes from the Father, who does not change or waver. This underscores that the revelation of truth in Scripture is grounded in God's immutable nature and provides a trustworthy guide for life.

3. **Eschatological Assurance:** In Revelation, the final victory of truth is vividly portrayed. Christ's return brings an end to all deception, establishing a new order where the truth of God reigns supreme and every falsehood is vanquished.

28.3 Historical and Theological Perspectives

Early Church Insights Early Christian apologists such as Justin Martyr and Irenaeus emphasized that the biblical God is fundamentally different from the capricious deities of pagan traditions. They argued that God's truth—manifest in His consistent revelation and redemptive work—provides the sure foundation for Christian faith. The early church saw divine truth as a counterpoint to the shifting, unreliable values of the surrounding cultures.

Medieval and Reformation Thought Medieval theologians like Thomas Aquinas argued that all truth ultimately derives from God, who is the measure of all reality. Aquinas maintained that God's nature is the standard against which all human knowledge and morality are judged. During the Reformation, figures such as Martin Luther and John Calvin reinforced the idea that the Bible's revelation of God's truth is absolute. They insisted that true faith rests on the assurance that God's promises are irrevocable—a truth that transforms personal lives and ecclesial communities.

Modern Reflections Modern theology continues to affirm that God's truth is unchanging, even as cultural and scientific paradigms shift. While some contemporary thinkers question absolute truth, mainstream Christian thought holds that the integrity of God's word remains a vital anchor in a relativistic age. This ongoing dialogue encourages believers to engage critically with new ideas while trusting in the timeless truth of Scripture.

28.4 Practical and Pastoral Implications

Assurance and Stability For believers, the truthfulness of God provides deep comfort and assurance. In a world of uncertainty and shifting values, knowing that God's word is unalterable offers a secure foundation. Verses like Hebrews 13:8 ("Jesus Christ is the same yesterday, today, and forever") remind us that our faith rests on a God who does not change.

Ethical Living and Integrity Believers are called to reflect God's truth in their own lives. If God is the ultimate standard of truth, then honesty, integrity, and authenticity become essential virtues. In personal relationships, in business, and in public life, Christians are encouraged to act transparently and justly, mirroring the unwavering truth of their Creator.

Worship and Community Life Understanding that God is truth enriches worship. When congregations praise God, they are not only acknowledging His mighty acts but also affirming His unchanging character. This truth unites believers, providing a common foundation that transcends cultural and personal differences. As a "pillar of truth," the church is called to promote transparency, accountability, and ethical behavior within the community.

Evangelism and Cultural Engagement The proclamation of divine truth is central to the gospel message. In sharing the message of Christ, believers testify that God's truth is not a human construct but a revealed reality that brings light to a dark world. This conviction challenges cultural relativism and encourages engagement in social justice, education, and public discourse. When Christians speak truth with love, they offer a compelling alternative to the fragmented narratives prevalent in today's society.

In conclusion, the doctrine of divine truth undergirds all of Christian theology. It is not merely a set of correct facts, but the very nature of God—immutable, reliable, and wholly good. From the steadfast promises of the Old Testament to the revelatory ministry of Jesus in the New, Scripture consistently portrays a God whose word is the ultimate standard of truth. Historically, the church has defended and celebrated this truth against the shifting sands of human opinion and philosophical skepticism.

For believers, embracing God's truth means living with the assurance that every promise of Scripture is reliable. It compels Christians to lead lives marked by honesty, integrity, and ethical responsibility. In worship, the acknowledgment of God's unchanging truth lifts hearts beyond fleeting concerns, inviting communal and personal encounters with a God who is as constant as He is loving.

In a world that often contends with deception, relativism, and moral ambiguity, the conviction that God is true provides a beacon of hope and stability. It calls us to reflect that same truth in our interactions, our communities, and our global engagement. As we anchor our lives in the unwavering truth of God's word, we find not only the foundation for faith but also the power to transform our world with justice, mercy, and love.

May we continually seek, embrace, and reflect the truth of God, confident that His unchanging word and character guide us into a future defined by hope, integrity, and eternal light.

Chapter 29: Transcendent

God's transcendence is one of the most awe-inspiring aspects of the Christian vision. It declares that God exists far above and beyond all created things, surpassing every measure and limitation. While His immanence assures us of His intimate involvement in the world, His transcendence highlights His supreme majesty, holiness, and infinite wisdom. This chapter explores the biblical foundations, historical developments, theological reflections, and practical implications of God's transcendence.

29.1 Unpacking Divine Transcendence

Beyond Mere Distance Transcendence is often misunderstood as simply God being "far away" in a physical sense. However, biblical transcendence speaks to God's nature and infinite superiority over creation. Isaiah 55:8–9 reminds us, "For my thoughts are not your thoughts, neither are your ways my ways... as the heavens are higher than the earth, so are my ways higher than your ways." This verse emphasizes that God's wisdom and methods are utterly beyond human comprehension—not because He is distant, but because He is infinitely greater than every finite measure.

Majesty, Holiness, and Infinity Scripture portrays God as exalted and holy. Passages like Psalm 47:8 and Isaiah 6 vividly depict God enthroned in glory, radiating perfect righteousness and unending power. His holiness ensures moral purity and sets a standard for justice that no earthly ruler can match. Moreover, God's infinite nature means He is not limited by time or space; His existence is eternal, and His power and wisdom are boundless. Together, these elements reveal a God whose transcendence is not cold detachment but a profound, majestic presence that underpins all of creation.

29.2 Biblical Foundations
Old Testament Revelations

1. **Creation as a Testament:** In Genesis 1, God speaks the universe into existence with effortless authority. Unlike other ancient myths filled with conflict among gods, the Bible presents Yahweh as the sole Creator whose commands bring forth light, life, and order. This creative act establishes God's transcendence—His power and authority are not derived from anything external.

2. **Revelatory Encounters at Sinai:** The dramatic manifestations at Mount Sinai (Exodus 19:16–19) reveal a God whose presence is both intimately near and overwhelmingly exalted. While the people tremble at His appearance, Moses alone is permitted closer communion, underscoring that God's transcendence does not exclude personal engagement but elevates it.

3. **Prophetic Visions:** Prophets like Isaiah and Ezekiel depict God as reigning above the earth (Isaiah 40:22; Ezekiel 37:26). Their visions of a majestic, all-powerful God who orchestrates nations and events affirm that no human force or worldly institution can constrain His divine plan.

New Testament Expansion

1. **Christ's Dual Revelation:** Jesus Christ embodies both immanence and transcendence. While He walks among us—healing, teaching, and engaging with individuals—He also declares His unity with the Father (John 10:29) and speaks of being one with God. His incarnation demonstrates that God, though transcendent, chooses to enter human history. This union is best captured in John 1:1–14, where the eternal Word becomes flesh, revealing divine truth and glory in a personal way.

2. **Apostolic Testimony:** Paul emphasizes in Ephesians 1:20–23 that God's power raised Christ and set Him far above every rule and authority. Likewise, Revelation's vivid imagery of God seated on a throne (Revelation 4–5) portrays a transcendent King whose dominion is unassailable. These texts affirm that while God's ways remain inscrutable to human minds, His rule is perfect and ultimately redemptive.

29.3 Historical and Theological Perspectives

Early Church Emphasis Early Christians distinguished the transcendent God from the capricious deities of pagan traditions. Apologists such as Justin Martyr argued that unlike gods who were subject to human-like passions and conflicts, the Christian God is supreme and unchanging. Tertullian and Irenaeus highlighted that the divine revelation in Christ reveals a God who is both infinitely above and deeply involved with humanity.

Medieval and Reformation Insights Medieval theologians like Thomas Aquinas used philosophical reasoning to explain God's transcendence. Aquinas argued that God is a "necessary being" whose essence is beyond all finite limitations—a truth that confirms His supreme authority and perfect order. During the Reformation, theologians such as Martin

Luther and John Calvin reaffirmed that, despite the fallibility of human institutions, the gospel rests on a transcendent God who remains constant through all ages.

Modern Dialogue Modern debates sometimes question the notion of transcendence, suggesting that God might be primarily immanent. However, mainstream Christian theology holds that while God is intimately involved in creation, His nature remains infinitely above and beyond it. This tension between transcendence and immanence does not diminish God's accessibility; rather, it magnifies the wonder that the infinite can choose to be near the finite.

29.4 Practical and Pastoral Implications

Worship and Reverence The recognition of God's transcendence inspires profound worship. When believers acknowledge that they serve a God whose ways are higher than ours, worship becomes an act of both humility and awe. Liturgical practices—such as hymns, prayers, and doxologies—often draw upon images of heavenly thrones and cosmic order to remind congregations of the majesty of God's rule. This cultivates a deep respect that elevates personal devotion and communal prayer.

Assurance in Uncertainty God's transcendence offers comfort amid life's uncertainties. In moments of personal crisis or global turmoil, believers can find stability in the knowledge that the Almighty's wisdom and power extend beyond the temporal and the visible. The assurance that God's plans are unbounded and perfect provides a firm foundation for hope, even when human circumstances seem chaotic or unjust.

Ethical and Social Engagement A commitment to the transcendent nature of God reinforces ethical living. Since God's standards are not limited by human cultural biases, believers are called to pursue justice, truth, and compassion that reflect an eternal, unchanging moral order. This perspective can motivate social justice initiatives, environmental stewardship, and efforts to promote human dignity—all seen as expressions of a higher, divine order that governs society.

Interfaith and Cultural Dialogue In a pluralistic world, understanding God's transcendence can enrich interfaith discussions. Christians can share how the biblical God is both above and yet actively engaged with creation—a reality that contrasts with impersonal deities or purely naturalistic explanations. This approach fosters respectful dialogue by demonstrating that transcendent truths are not distant abstractions but are revealed in history and human experience.

In conclusion, the doctrine of divine transcendence is central to Christian faith. It proclaims that God is not confined by the limitations of space, time, or human understanding. From the orderly creation of Genesis to the triumphant visions in Revelation, Scripture presents a God whose nature is both awe-inspiringly exalted and intimately involved with His creation.

Historically, the church has defended this truth against competing worldviews, from pagan polytheism to modern secularism, continually affirming that the infinite majesty of God remains the ultimate source of wisdom, power, and moral order. The theological insights of early Church Fathers, medieval scholastics, and Reformation reformers have all contributed to a rich tradition that holds God as transcendent yet accessible—a balance that fuels both reverence and personal relationship.

Practically, embracing God's transcendence transforms worship, fortifies hope in times of uncertainty, and guides ethical and social actions. Believers are called to live in a way that reflects the order and justice of a transcendent Creator while engaging meaningfully with a world that is both flawed and beautiful.

In our daily lives, the promise of God's transcendent presence encourages us to seek truth, practice justice, and pursue peace, knowing that the One who reigns above all is both infinitely majestic and intimately compassionate. As we continue to explore the depths of divine transcendence, we are invited to marvel at a God whose glory not only eclipses our finite understanding but also draws us into a loving, transformative relationship—a relationship that unites heaven and earth in eternal harmony.

Chapter 30: Immanent

In contrast to God's transcendence—which proclaims His infinite majesty—divine immanence emphasizes that God is actively present and intimately involved in His creation. Rather than being a distant ruler, He is a loving, attentive presence who walks with us through every circumstance. This chapter examines the biblical foundations, theological significance, and practical implications of God's immanence, revealing how His nearness transforms personal devotion, community life, and global engagement.

30.1 Understanding Divine Immanence

The Essence of Immanence Divine immanence means that God is not removed from creation but permeates every part of it. His presence is not confined to a distant heaven but is actively involved in our daily lives. Unlike human concepts of distance, immanence speaks to both the quality and the relational depth of God's presence. He listens to our prayers, comforts us in sorrow, and guides us through every challenge, showing that His care is both constant and personal.

Complementary to Transcendence While transcendence highlights God's supreme majesty and power beyond human limits, immanence assures us of His nearness. Imagine a light so vast that it fills every corner of a room—the source remains exalted, yet its glow is experienced intimately. In a similar way, God's transcendence and immanence work together: His infinite greatness does not keep Him aloof but allows Him to be deeply involved in every aspect of creation.

30.2 Biblical Foundations

Old Testament Revelations

1. **Presence in Creation:** From the very beginning, Genesis portrays God as the active Creator whose word brings the universe into being. The creative acts are imbued with

His Spirit, suggesting that every part of creation reflects His presence. Psalm 139 vividly declares, "Where can I go from your Spirit? ... If I ascend to heaven, you are there; if I make my bed in Sheol, you are there" (Psalm 139:7–8), affirming that no place is beyond His reach.

2. **Covenant Relationships:** God's intimate relationship with His people is evident in His covenants. When He calls Abraham, Moses, and others by name, it is a personal invitation into a lasting relationship. The tabernacle and later the temple were designed as visible reminders that God dwells among His people. Even during exile and hardship, the prophets assured Israel that God remained near, guiding and restoring them.

New Testament Fulfillment

1. **The Incarnation:** The pinnacle of divine immanence is revealed in the Incarnation. John 1:14 states, "The Word became flesh and dwelt among us." In Jesus, God enters into human experience fully—sharing our joys, sorrows, and struggles. His ministry, marked by healing, teaching, and compassionate engagement with individuals, demonstrates that God is not a remote force but a present and personal Savior.

2. **The Holy Spirit:** After Christ's ascension, the promise of the Holy Spirit ensures that God remains present in the lives of believers. At Pentecost, the Spirit descended powerfully, transforming a frightened group of disciples into bold witnesses (Acts 2). Today, the indwelling Spirit continues to guide, convict, and comfort, assuring believers that God's presence is not limited by time or place.

30.3 Theological Perspectives

Relationship as Divine Nature The doctrine of immanence is inseparable from God's relational character. The Trinity itself—Father, Son, and Holy Spirit in eternal communion— demonstrates that relationship is at the very heart of God's being. This eternal fellowship within the Godhead sets the template for how God interacts with humanity. Because God is relational, He is not an impersonal force but a loving Friend, Counselor, and Shepherd who seeks to draw us into His embrace.

The Incarnation's Paradox The Incarnation encapsulates the mystery of immanence and transcendence. While God remains infinitely above all, He chooses to step into our finite world as Jesus. This union of divine and human does not diminish His majesty but reveals the depth of His love. Through Christ, God's transcendence is made accessible, inviting believers to experience divine intimacy even as they recognize His supreme authority.

30.4 Practical and Pastoral Implications

Transforming Prayer and Worship Knowing that God is immanent transforms prayer into a true conversation. Believers are encouraged to approach God not as a distant deity but as a near, loving presence. When we pray, we are not merely reciting formulas; we are engaging in dialogue with a God who listens and responds. Liturgical practices—such as the recurring declaration "Behold, the Lord is near"—reinforce this intimate relationship, deepening our sense of security and trust in His ongoing care.

Strength in Times of Trouble In moments of crisis—whether personal, familial, or communal—the assurance of God's immanence brings profound comfort. When facing uncertainty, loss, or injustice, believers can find solace in the promise that God is present. Pastoral counseling often emphasizes that even in the darkest valleys, the Creator remains a constant companion, offering guidance, healing, and hope.

Fostering Community and Ethical Living Church communities that embrace God's immanence tend to exhibit genuine fellowship. When members recognize that God is present in every interaction, they are more likely to engage with each other in honest, supportive ways. This deep sense of shared presence fosters unity, accountability, and mutual care. Moreover, knowing that God is actively involved in our lives compels us to live ethically—extending compassion, seeking justice, and working to resolve conflicts in ways that honor His close, transformative presence.

Global and Interpersonal Outreach The belief in an immanent God has significant implications for mission and social engagement. Missionaries and humanitarian workers are driven by the conviction that every person bears the image of a God who is near and loving. This understanding dissolves cultural and social barriers, encouraging believers to view every individual as worthy of care and respect. Whether in local neighborhoods or on the global stage, the immanent presence of God inspires actions that promote healing, reconciliation, and justice.

In conclusion, the doctrine of divine immanence reveals a God who is not distant or detached but is intimately involved in every aspect of creation. From the early chapters of Genesis to the life of Jesus and the ongoing work of the Holy Spirit, Scripture consistently portrays a God who is near—actively present in our struggles, joys, and daily routines.

Historically, the church has celebrated this attribute as it contrasted the biblical God with impersonal deities and embraced a relational faith that transformed worship, ethics, and community. The realization that God is immanent encourages believers to cultivate a vibrant prayer life, engage deeply with their communities, and extend love and justice in all areas of life.

In a rapidly changing world where isolation and dislocation often prevail, the promise of God's nearness offers enduring hope. Whether through quiet personal devotion or dynamic communal action, the awareness that God dwells with us brings comfort and strength. It challenges us to live in a way that reflects His care—treating each person with dignity, pursuing reconciliation, and working toward a more just society.

Ultimately, embracing divine immanence is an invitation to intimate communion with the Creator—a relationship marked by constant care, active guidance, and transformative love. As we acknowledge that God is not far off but present in every moment and every place, we are empowered to live boldly, love deeply, and engage the world with the assurance that the One who created the stars also walks beside us every day.

Chapter 31: Gentle

God's gentle nature is a profound and transformative attribute that sets Him apart from worldly power, which is often linked to harshness or coercion. In Scripture, divine gentleness is not weakness but a demonstration of strength exercised with love, compassion, and wisdom. This quality reassures the oppressed, comforts the weary, and heals the broken. It shapes how believers relate to God, to one another, and to the world around them

31.1 Understanding Divine Gentleness

Defining God's Gentleness In biblical terms, to say God is gentle means that He uses His strength with tenderness. Divine gentleness involves:

- **Measured Strength:** It is not a passive or timid force, but a controlled and compassionate power.

- **Restorative Action:** God corrects and guides without harshness, aiming to restore rather than to dominate.

- **Relational Engagement:** His gentle touch is evident in how He cares for the vulnerable and responds to human need.

While gentleness in human relationships can sometimes be misinterpreted as weakness, in God it reflects the perfect balance of might and mercy. This divine quality is evident when God calms storms, heals the sick, and forgives sins—all acts that demonstrate strength coupled with tenderness.

Gentleness versus Weakness Human gentleness can be seen as a lack of assertiveness, but God's gentleness is different. It is an active, deliberate choice to express power in a way that nurtures, transforms, and restores. For instance, when Jesus heals the sick or forgives sinners, He does so gently—addressing the pain without inflicting additional harm. Thus, divine gentleness is a model of strength perfected in humility and compassion.

31.2 Biblical Foundations

Old Testament Images The Old Testament offers rich imagery that portrays God as gentle:

- **Shepherd Imagery:** Isaiah 40:11 describes God as one who "tends his flock like a shepherd; he gathers the lambs in his arms and carries them in his bosom." This vivid picture conveys intimacy, care, and a protective presence.

- **Covenant Love:** In passages like Psalm 103, God is described as "merciful and gracious, slow to anger and abounding in steadfast love," suggesting that His gentle character is intertwined with His willingness to forgive and restore.

- **Guiding Presence:** God's interaction with His people, such as His direct communication with Abraham and Moses, demonstrates that even in judgment, His approach is aimed at redemption rather than mere retribution.

New Testament Revelation The New Testament magnifies God's gentle nature through the life and ministry of Jesus:

- **Christ's Ministry:** Jesus frequently invited the "wearied and heavy-laden" to find rest in Him (Matthew 11:29). His compassionate interactions—with the woman caught in adultery, with the lepers, and with the outcasts—exemplify how divine gentleness transforms lives.

- **The Incarnation:** By becoming flesh, God entered into human suffering and joy. Jesus' gentle approach—marked by empathy, healing, and forgiveness—shows that divine gentleness is not distant but intimately involved in our struggles.

- **The Holy Spirit:** The indwelling Spirit continues this gentle presence, guiding, comforting, and empowering believers. The Spirit's work in sanctification and community-building assures Christians that God's tender care is a daily reality.

31.3 Theological Reflections

Interplay with Justice and Mercy God's gentleness works in harmony with His justice and mercy. While His justice demands that sin be addressed, His gentleness ensures that correction is administered in a way that heals and restores. For example, prophetic warnings in the Old Testament often come with a promise of restoration—a gentle call to repentance that preserves the covenant relationship. The cross epitomizes this balance: Christ absorbs the penalty for sin while extending grace, demonstrating that true correction is rooted in love.

The Incarnation as the Ultimate Expression The incarnation of Jesus stands as the pinnacle of divine gentleness. Though God is infinitely powerful, He chose to enter human history in the form of a vulnerable, compassionate servant. Philippians 2:5–8 describes how Jesus, though divine, humbled Himself by taking on human nature. His gentle life—teaching, healing, and forgiving—models for all believers how power can be expressed with tenderness and how even the mightiest God can relate to our fragile condition.

Balance of Transcendence and Immanence While God is transcendent in His majesty, His immanence assures us of His nearness. This balance means that although He is infinitely above creation, He is also personally involved in every human life. In this dual reality, His gentleness becomes all the more significant—it is the channel through which the transcendent God reaches out to the finite, offering comfort and hope.

31.4 Misconceptions About Divine Gentleness

Gentleness Is Not Passivity Some mistakenly equate gentleness with a lack of decisive action. However, biblical gentleness is the use of power with restraint. When Jesus calmed the storm (Mark 4:35–41), His gentle command over nature demonstrated that true power can be both assertive and compassionate.

Gentleness Does Not Excuse Sin Another misconception is that a gentle God might be overly lenient toward sin. In truth, divine gentleness always accompanies a call to repentance. It provides an opportunity for restoration without compromising the seriousness of sin. For example, the gentle warning of the prophet Jonah to the people of Nineveh led them to repentance, thereby averting judgment.

Gentleness Is Not Weakness Some critics argue that gentleness suggests an absence of strength. However, the biblical God exemplifies that real power is expressed in love and compassion. True strength lies in the ability to forgive, heal, and transform without resorting to forceful domination.

31.5 Pastoral and Practical Implications

Inner Healing and Personal Growth Belief in God's gentle nature brings profound comfort to those burdened by guilt, sorrow, or fear. Knowing that God cares for the vulnerable, as illustrated in Isaiah 40:11, encourages individuals to seek healing through prayer, confession, and spiritual counseling. This inner peace fosters resilience and nurtures a spirit of hope.

Cultivating Harmonious Communities Churches that embrace divine gentleness naturally cultivate environments of reconciliation and unity. When members treat one another with the same care and compassion that God shows, conflicts are resolved more gracefully. Practical steps such as small group meetings, pastoral counseling, and community service projects can help create a culture where gentleness prevails over division.

Ethical Leadership and Social Justice A commitment to gentleness in leadership challenges both personal and institutional approaches to power. Leaders who exemplify gentleness inspire ethical decision-making and foster a culture of empathy and cooperation. In social justice efforts, the gentle pursuit of reconciliation and restorative justice reflects a commitment to transforming rather than simply punishing. This approach can influence policies and community actions that prioritize healing over retribution.

Global Outreach and Interfaith Dialogue The message of God's gentle nature also has global significance. Missionaries and peacemakers use the example of Christ's gentle ministry to bridge cultural and religious divides. By emphasizing that true strength is expressed through love and compassion, Christians can engage in interfaith dialogue and global humanitarian work that promote lasting peace and mutual respect.

In conclusion, the gentle nature of God offers a transformative vision for Christian faith and practice. Far from indicating weakness, divine gentleness is the refined expression of true power—a power that heals, restores, and unites. From the tender shepherd imagery of Isaiah to the compassionate ministry of Jesus, Scripture consistently presents a God who meets humanity with love and care.

Historically, the church has celebrated this quality as a counterpoint to the harshness often seen in worldly power, and it has inspired movements for peace, reconciliation, and social justice. Today, God's gentleness invites believers to approach prayer as a heartfelt conversation, to engage in ethical and compassionate leadership, and to foster communities characterized by empathy and unity.

In a world frequently marked by conflict and cruelty, the gentle character of God offers a beacon of hope—a reminder that real strength lies in kindness and that true power transforms hearts without resorting to domination. As we embrace and reflect this divine gentleness in our lives, we participate in a broader mission: to heal, reconcile, and bring about a more compassionate society that mirrors the heart of our Creator.

May our lives be a testament to the gentle power of God, influencing every relationship, community, and culture with the hope and healing that flow from His tender, unyielding love.

Chapter 32: Incomprehensible

The Bible teaches that God is incomprehensible—beyond the full grasp of our finite minds. While He graciously reveals Himself through creation, Scripture, and ultimately in Christ, His complete nature, wisdom, and power remain a divine mystery. This chapter explores the biblical foundations, theological reflections, and practical implications of God's incomprehensibility, inviting believers to approach Him with humility, trust, and awe.

32.1 Understanding Divine Incomprehensibility

The Nature of the Infinite When Scripture declares that God is incomprehensible, it emphasizes that His essence, wisdom, and ways surpass human understanding. Verses like Isaiah 55:8–9 and Romans 11:33 remind us that God's thoughts and judgments are far higher than ours. Just as the unfathomable depths of an ocean cannot be measured by a shallow container, so too does the infinite nature of God exceed our language and logic.

Revelation Amid Mystery Although we cannot fully grasp all of God's attributes, He chooses to reveal Himself to us. Through creation, He displays order and beauty; through Scripture, He communicates His character; and through Jesus Christ, He offers a personal encounter with the truth. This partial revelation is not a failure on God's part but an invitation for us to trust Him even when our understanding is limited.

The Role of Faith Because God's full nature is beyond our comprehension, faith becomes our bridge to the Infinite. Hebrews 11:1 defines faith as "the assurance of things hoped for, the conviction of things not seen." Trusting in God means accepting that while we see only a glimpse of His reality, His revealed truth is reliable and transformative.

32.2 Biblical Foundations

Old Testament Witness The Old Testament consistently portrays God's greatness and mystery. In Job 11:7–9, questions about the limits of God's wisdom remind us that no human effort can fathom His power. Likewise, Psalm 145 declares that "His greatness is unsearchable," underscoring that even the most inspired worship cannot capture the fullness of God's nature. In creation narratives and prophetic literature, God's acts—from bringing forth the universe in Genesis to the assurances of His eternal purpose in Isaiah—reveal a being who is both imminently real and forever beyond complete human understanding.

New Testament Revelation The New Testament deepens our insight into divine incomprehensibility. The Gospel of John introduces Jesus as the "Word" who became flesh (John 1:1, 14), a mystery that unveils God's nature in human form while preserving its infinite depth. Jesus' teachings, such as those found in John 6 and 14, illustrate that while He reveals the Father's will, the totality of divine wisdom remains beyond full disclosure. Paul reinforces this idea in 1 Corinthians 2:9–10, where he explains that God's plans are beyond what the human heart can imagine, revealed only through the Spirit.

32.3 Theological Reflections

Embracing Divine Mystery Theologically, God's incomprehensibility is not a flaw or an invitation to despair; it is an expression of His infinite nature. As finite beings, our language and concepts are inadequate to describe the fullness of the Divine. This mystery calls us to a posture of humility, encouraging us to seek God through faith rather than through exhaustive rational analysis. The mystery of God's nature invites continual wonder and worship—a realization that each encounter with Him is a glimpse into a reality far greater than we can fully articulate.

Revelation and the Limits of Knowledge God has chosen to reveal key aspects of His character without disclosing every detail of His infinite nature. This selective revelation is purposeful; it provides us with enough truth to know Him, while preserving an element of mystery that invites deeper exploration. Our understanding is always partial, yet it is sufficient for salvation and daily living. As we study Scripture and experience God's presence in prayer, we learn to appreciate the tension between what is revealed and what remains hidden, and to trust that His unseen depths are a source of continuous growth.

Faith in the Face of Uncertainty Since God's full essence is beyond human grasp, faith becomes the necessary response. Believers are encouraged to trust in the revealed truth, even as they acknowledge their limited understanding. This reliance on faith fosters spiritual maturity and humility, allowing us to live with hope and assurance despite unanswered questions.

32.4 Practical and Pastoral Implications

Comfort Amid Uncertainty The truth that God is incomprehensible can be a profound comfort in times of crisis. When events defy human explanation, knowing that an eternal, all-wise God governs all things provides a stable foundation for hope. Pastoral care often emphasizes that while we may not understand every trial, we can trust in God's unchanging nature and perfect plan.

Transforming Worship Recognizing the mystery of God inspires a worship that is both reverent and dynamic. Congregations that celebrate God's incomprehensible nature do so with a blend of adoration, confession, and thanksgiving—acknowledging that although our knowledge is limited, His revealed truth is enough to transform our hearts. Liturgical expressions, from hymns that speak of "unsearchable riches" to moments of silent contemplation, invite believers to rest in the awe of God's eternal presence.

Ethical Living and Integrity A commitment to divine truth calls believers to live with honesty and integrity. Since God's nature is the ultimate standard of truth, our actions, relationships, and decisions should reflect that same unwavering commitment. This moral framework challenges us to seek transparency in our dealings, to confess our shortcomings, and to pursue a life that aligns with the unchanging goodness of God.

Community and Mutual Support Within the church, the acknowledgment of God's incomprehensibility fosters a culture of humility and mutual encouragement. Small groups, Bible studies, and communal prayers provide opportunities for sharing personal experiences of God's mysterious yet comforting presence. In such settings, believers are reminded that while they may not understand everything about God, they can still experience His transforming love and support in tangible ways.

Global and Interfaith Engagement The doctrine of divine incomprehensibility also has implications for engaging with other cultures and religious traditions. In interfaith dialogues, Christians can explain that while God's full nature remains a mystery, His revealed truth in Scripture and in Christ offers a reliable foundation for faith. This approach encourages respectful conversation, fostering mutual understanding and cooperation, even as differences persist.

In conclusion, the concept of divine incomprehensibility challenges and humbles us. God's nature—His wisdom, power, and love—is so vast that it defies complete human understanding. Yet, He graciously reveals enough of Himself through creation, Scripture, and the person of Jesus Christ so that we may know, trust, and worship Him.

Historically, this doctrine has inspired both profound theological reflection and practical spiritual living. From the poetic declarations of the Old Testament to the transformative teachings of the New, believers have learned to embrace mystery as an integral part of faith. This acknowledgment invites us to a life of humble inquiry, where we seek God not as a solved puzzle but as an ever-unfolding mystery that continually draws us deeper into His love.

In practical terms, the awareness of God's incomprehensibility offers comfort in uncertainty, transforms worship into a heartfelt encounter with the divine, and calls us to live ethically with integrity and honesty. It encourages communal support, as we share our experiences of God's unsearchable depths, and it challenges us to engage with the world—intellectually and spiritually—knowing that some truths are beyond our grasp but fully accessible through faith.

Ultimately, God's incomprehensible nature is not a barrier to relationship but the very reason that relationship is so precious. It reminds us that while we may never fully understand the infinite, we can rest in the assurance that His revealed truth is sufficient to guide, comfort, and transform our lives. As we continue to seek Him, may we do so with wonder, humility, and a deep, abiding trust in the One who is eternally greater than our understanding yet intimately involved in our every day.

Chapter 33: Glorious

God's glory is the radiant expression of His perfect nature—a harmonious blend of beauty, honor, and divine excellence. It is far more than dazzling light or superficial splendor; it is the inherent manifestation of God's holiness, power, wisdom, and love. Throughout Scripture, God's glory is revealed in creation, covenant, and redemption, inviting believers into a life of awe, ethical integrity, and transformative worship.

33.1 Understanding Divine Glory

Defining Divine Glory When we call God "glorious," we affirm that every aspect of His being—His character, actions, and revelations—radiates with complete perfection. Divine glory encompasses:

- **Holistic Excellence:** Not limited to outward splendor, it integrates moral purity, infinite wisdom, and boundless love.

- **Intrinsic Worth:** God's glory is inherent in His very nature and is the standard by which all true beauty and honor are measured.

- **Revelatory Presence:** His glory is both an intrinsic quality and something He makes known through creation and revelation.

Radiance and Splendor Scriptural imagery often employs light to describe God's glory. The burning bush, the pillar of fire, and the luminous presence in the temple testify to a God whose majesty overcomes darkness. In the New Testament, the transfiguration of Jesus reveals His divine radiance, confirming His identity as the Son of God whose glory surpasses all earthly measure.

33.2 Biblical Foundations

Old Testament Witness The Old Testament lays a strong foundation for understanding God's glory:

- **Creation:** In Genesis, God speaks the universe into existence. Every command—"Let there be…"—demonstrates His unmatched power and artistry.

- **Covenant and Worship:** In 1 Kings 8, Solomon's prayer at the temple dedication proclaims that even the highest heavens cannot contain God. Such passages affirm that His glory fills all of creation and invites total devotion.

- **Prophetic Imagery:** The prophets, like Isaiah, remind us that God's ways are higher than ours, and His wisdom—manifested in His glory—remains unsearchable.

New Testament Revelation The New Testament deepens our understanding of divine glory:

- **The Incarnation:** John 1:14 declares, "And the Word became flesh and dwelt among us," showing that Jesus is the visible manifestation of God's glory.

- **Christ's Ministry:** Through His teachings, miracles, and sacrificial love, Jesus reveals a glory that is both transcendent and intimate. His transfiguration offers a glimpse of divine splendor.

- **Eschatological Vision:** Revelation describes a future New Jerusalem, bathed in the unceasing light of God's presence—a promise that divine glory will ultimately redeem and transform all creation.

33.3 Theological Perspectives

The Nature of Divine Glory God's glory is not an incidental quality but the very essence of who He is. It:

- **Integrates All Attributes:** His justice, mercy, love, wisdom, and power are all expressed in perfect unity.

- **Embodies Holiness:** Divine glory reflects the moral perfection of God, serving as the ultimate standard for all truth and beauty.

- **Inspires Worship:** The overwhelming majesty of God's glory calls for reverence and adoration, drawing believers into deep, transformative communion.

The Incarnation as the Pinnacle of Glory The incarnation of Christ reveals divine glory in a unique way. By becoming human, God did not diminish His glory; rather, He made it accessible:

- **Empathetic Engagement:** Jesus experienced human suffering and joy, proving that divine power can be expressed with humility and tenderness.

- **Redemptive Power:** The cross transforms judgment into reconciliation—sin's penalty is borne by Christ, paving the way for eternal restoration.

- **Resurrected Glory:** Christ's resurrection and ascension validate that divine glory endures and overcomes all darkness.

33.4 Common Misconceptions

Glory as Mere Ostentation Some mistakenly view glory as flashy display or superficial beauty. In reality, biblical glory is a profound, all-encompassing reflection of God's perfect nature, not limited to physical splendor but expressed in His moral and spiritual excellence.

Human Glory vs. Divine Glory Human achievements are fleeting and marred by pride. In contrast, God's glory is eternal and flawless, stemming from His very essence. While human glory is transient, divine glory is the ultimate, immutable standard that all creation is meant to mirror.

Exclusivity of Glory Another error is to assume that emphasizing God's glory excludes other forms of good. However, all true beauty and virtue in the world reflect, in part, God's glory. Every act of kindness, every moment of genuine justice, serves as a small echo of the Creator's boundless perfection.

33.5 Pastoral and Practical Implications

Transforming Worship and Devotion Understanding that God is gloriously perfect elevates worship from routine to profound encounter. When believers reflect on His majesty, they are moved to offer heartfelt praise and live lives marked by integrity and beauty. This perspective shapes both corporate liturgy and personal prayer, inviting a deep, reverent intimacy.

Inspiring Ethical Living Recognizing that our lives are to mirror God's glory has ethical implications. Believers are called to pursue righteousness, fairness, and compassion in every sphere of life. This commitment to ethical excellence challenges us to reject deceit and injustice, striving instead to live transparently and lovingly.

Building Unified Communities Church communities that celebrate God's glory foster unity and mutual encouragement. When congregants acknowledge that each person is created in the image of a glorious God, differences fade, and genuine relationships form. This shared vision promotes a culture of support and accountability, making the church a living testimony to divine excellence.

Global and Cultural Impact On a wider scale, the doctrine of divine glory has profound cultural and missional significance. In a world often preoccupied with transient accolades, proclaiming God's eternal glory offers a counter-narrative that values lasting truth over superficial success. It inspires Christians to engage in social justice, advocate for human dignity, and build bridges across cultural divides—testifying that all creation finds its meaning in the ultimate, unchanging source of beauty and honor.

33.6 Embracing Divine Glory in Daily Life

Cultivating Personal Reflection Believers are encouraged to reflect on God's glory in everyday moments—through nature, art, and personal experiences. Journaling, meditation, and contemplative prayer can help deepen one's awareness of the divine presence, transforming mundane routines into opportunities for worship.

Expressing Glory Through Service Ethical living and compassionate service are practical expressions of divine glory. By working for justice, caring for the vulnerable, and promoting peace, Christians mirror the Creator's perfection in tangible ways. Such acts serve as a testimony to a higher standard that transcends cultural trends and personal ambitions.

Witnessing to the World When Christians live lives that reflect God's glory—marked by integrity, love, and beauty—they become beacons of hope in a fragmented world. Their example challenges societal norms that prioritize fleeting success over enduring virtue, inviting others to experience the transformative power of a life aligned with divine purpose.

In conclusion, the glory of God is a multifaceted reality that transcends mere visual splendor. It encompasses the full spectrum of His perfect nature—His holiness, wisdom, justice, love, and creative power—and is revealed through creation, Scripture, and ultimately in the person of Jesus Christ. Biblical narratives, from the majestic scenes of the Old Testament to the radiant transfiguration and redemptive work of Christ, testify to a God whose glory is both inherent and revealed.

This divine glory sets an eternal standard of excellence and offers profound comfort and direction. It transforms worship into an encounter with the infinite, inspires ethical living that reflects truth and beauty, and unites believers in a shared vision of a world redeemed by the Creator's splendor. While human glory is transient and often marred by pride, God's glory is everlasting—providing a beacon of hope in a chaotic world and a model for how we are to live in integrity and love.

As we contemplate and proclaim the glory of God, we are invited into a deeper relationship with the One who is the ultimate source of all that is good and true. May our lives be a constant reflection of His radiant perfection, drawing others into the light of His eternal and transformative presence.

Chapter 34: Long-Suffering

In Christian theology, **long-suffering** is not a passive endurance but an active, redemptive quality—a divine capacity to bear with human weakness, repeated sin, and error over time without forsaking the commitment to restore and redeem. Far from being indifferent, God's long-suffering is a steady expression of His love that continually invites repentance and transformation, spanning generations and life's many failures.

34.1 Defining Divine Long-Suffering

Enduring with Hope Long-suffering means enduring hardship and injustice over extended periods while withholding immediate judgment. It is the patient, generous restraint that allows time for genuine repentance and growth. God's long-suffering is active: rather than ignoring sin, He consistently calls His people back to Him, offering renewal through His unfailing love. This enduring patience reflects not weakness but the strength of a God who is deeply invested in human restoration.

A Process, Not an Instant Fix Unlike the notion of instant forgiveness, long-suffering acknowledges that transformation is often gradual. It involves repeated opportunities for change. God's delay in judgment is not a sign of indulgence but a deliberate strategy aimed at nurturing lasting spiritual maturity and moral renewal.

34.2 Biblical Foundations

Old Testament Witness The Old Testament frequently displays God's long-suffering with His people. Despite Israel's recurring cycles of rebellion and idol worship, God renews His covenant and calls them back.

- **Exodus & Prophetic Warnings:** After the golden calf incident, God's anger is evident, yet He renews His covenant with Israel rather than destroying them. Prophets like Hosea and Isaiah vividly portray God's tender grief over Israel's unfaithfulness, emphasizing that His patience is intended to lead to repentance (e.g., Isaiah 30:18).

- **Psalms of Assurance:** Psalm 103 praises God for being "merciful and gracious, slow to anger and abounding in steadfast love," underscoring that His long-suffering is a foundation for forgiveness and restoration.

New Testament Revelation In the New Testament, the theme of long-suffering reaches its fullest expression in the life and work of Jesus Christ.

- **The Parable of the Prodigal Son:** In Luke 15, the father's patient waiting for his wayward son illustrates divine long-suffering—a love that endures despite repeated disobedience.

- **Christ's Ministry:** Jesus consistently shows compassion toward sinners and outcasts. His gentle corrections and healing acts reveal a God who is not quick to condemn but works to bring about genuine change.

- **Paul's Exhortation:** In 2 Peter 3:9, Paul explains that the Lord is patient, "not wishing that any should perish, but that all should reach repentance." This underscores that divine long-suffering is aimed at redemption, not mere tolerance of sin.

34.3 Theological Reflections

Long-Suffering as a Moral Exemplar God's patience is a model for human behavior. Believers are called to forgive and bear with one another, mirroring divine forbearance. As Ephesians 4:2 urges, we are to be humble and patient, bearing with one another in love—a practical outworking of the same grace that God extends.

Interplay of Wrath and Long-Suffering A notable tension in Scripture is the balance between God's righteous wrath and His long-suffering. While divine wrath underscores the seriousness of sin, God's long-suffering reflects His desire for repentance and restoration. The cross embodies this balance: Christ's sacrifice satisfies the demands of justice while opening the door to forgiveness.

The Mystery of Redemption Long-suffering is intertwined with God's redemptive plan. Even as sin incurs rightful judgment, God's patient delay is designed to allow time for transformation. This mystery—where every setback becomes a chance for renewal—offers hope that no sin is beyond redemption if met with genuine contrition.

34.4 Common Misconceptions

Not Indifference Some mistakenly view long-suffering as indifference or passivity. In truth, God's patient endurance is a proactive, compassionate engagement with a broken world—it is the deliberate choice to allow room for change.

No License for Sin Long-suffering does not mean that sin is excused. While God delays judgment to allow repentance, He also warns that unrepentant sin will eventually meet its due consequence. This dual aspect upholds moral accountability while extending mercy.

Avoiding Complacency Believers are cautioned not to misuse God's patience as an excuse to remain in sin. Divine long-suffering is meant to inspire sincere repentance and moral growth—not to foster a false sense of security that justifies continual wrongdoing.

34.5 Pastoral and Practical Implications

Comfort in Personal Failure For individuals burdened by recurring sin or personal failure, the doctrine of long-suffering provides deep comfort. It assures believers that God's love is unwavering—even when they fall short, He continually offers a path back to restoration and renewal.

Cultivating a Spirit of Forgiveness In community life, the call to emulate divine long-suffering fosters an environment of forgiveness and reconciliation. By actively choosing to forgive and patiently work through conflicts, believers build stronger, more compassionate relationships that reflect God's own redemptive love.

Encouraging Ethical and Social Transformation Long-suffering has significant implications for social justice. Recognizing that change often requires time, Christian activists and community leaders are inspired to pursue gradual, sustained reforms. This approach—rooted in persistent, compassionate advocacy—challenges systems of injustice while nurturing reconciliation and healing.

Strengthening Spiritual Resilience In times of crisis, the assurance of God's patient care strengthens believers' resolve. Knowing that God's timing is perfect, even when His judgment appears delayed, allows Christians to persevere through hardships with hope and trust.

Enhancing Worship and Prayer Acknowledging that God's love endures through long-suffering transforms prayer into a heartfelt dialogue with a compassionate Father. Worship becomes an expression of gratitude not only for God's mercy but also for His steadfast commitment to bring about redemption and healing.

34.6 Global and Cultural Impact

Promoting a Culture of Reconciliation On a broader scale, the principle of divine long-suffering challenges societies to adopt a more restorative approach to conflict and injustice. Whether in addressing systemic issues like racial discrimination or environmental degradation, a long-suffering perspective encourages persistent efforts toward reconciliation and healing.

A Beacon of Hope in a Turbulent World In regions plagued by prolonged conflict or social upheaval, the promise of divine long-suffering offers hope. It reassures communities that even entrenched injustices can be overcome through enduring patience, persistent advocacy, and the transformative power of forgiveness.

Personal Transformation Understanding and internalizing God's long-suffering inspires believers to cultivate resilience and humility. Engaging in spiritual disciplines—such as regular prayer, reflective journaling, and meditation on Scripture—helps individuals experience personal renewal. This ongoing process of repentance and restoration strengthens their capacity to forgive, learn, and grow.

Building Healthy Communities Church communities that embody long-suffering create environments of mutual care and open dialogue. Through practices like conflict resolution, restorative justice, and small group fellowship, believers can model the patient, redemptive love of God, thus fostering unity and compassion.

Witnessing to the World When Christians live out a commitment to long-suffering, they become powerful witnesses to a higher standard of love and forgiveness. Whether through personal acts of kindness or broader social initiatives, their example offers a countercultural message: lasting transformation is achieved through persistent, patient grace rather than through immediate, punitive measures.

In conclusion, the doctrine of divine long-suffering reveals a God who endures with unwavering compassion and active commitment to redemption. Far from suggesting passivity, it is a dynamic, life-giving quality that balances righteous judgment with patient mercy. From the cycles of rebuke and restoration in the Old Testament to the redemptive work of Christ and the enduring encouragement in Paul's letters, Scripture presents a God whose patience is both profound and purposeful.

This long-suffering nature provides deep comfort to individuals, encourages communities to practice forgiveness, and inspires social efforts toward reconciliation and justice. It calls believers to embrace transformation through humble repentance and to reflect divine patience in all relationships. By understanding that God's enduring love is designed to bring about genuine change—even through repeated failures—Christians are empowered to live with hope, resilience, and a commitment to building a more compassionate world.

In a turbulent, often unforgiving world, the truth of divine long-suffering stands as a beacon of hope. It invites us to recognize that no matter our shortcomings, God's love remains steadfast, offering us endless opportunities for renewal. Embracing this truth transforms our prayer, our relationships, and our social engagements, guiding us toward a future where grace and redemption triumph over sin. Ultimately, the call of long-suffering is an invitation to participate in God's redemptive work—a journey of healing, restoration, and profound love that endures through all generations.

Chapter 35: Majestic

The majesty of God expresses His supreme splendor, authority, and beauty—qualities that inspire awe and reverence. In Christian thought, God's glory is not mere ostentation; it is the intrinsic expression of His perfect character, manifest in His creation, covenant, and redemptive work. This chapter explores the meaning of divine majesty, its biblical foundations, theological significance, common misconceptions, and practical implications for personal worship, ethical living, and cultural expression.

35.1 Understanding Divine Majesty

Defining Majesty: To call God "majestic" is to recognize that His very being embodies power, authority, and beauty in a way that surpasses all earthly comparisons. Divine majesty means that God's nature is complete and perfect—He is both supremely powerful and perfectly gracious. His majesty reflects not only raw strength but also moral excellence, as seen in His justice, mercy, and wisdom.

Regal Authority and Beauty: Biblical majesty portrays God as the King of kings whose rule encompasses the entire universe. Verses such as 1 Chronicles 29:11 and Psalm 29:4 declare that all that is in heaven and earth belongs to Him, attesting to His absolute sovereignty. This authority is coupled with an inherent beauty: His commands bring order from chaos, His laws promote justice and compassion, and His creative work reveals an artistry that transforms even the mundane into something extraordinary.

35.2 Biblical Foundations

Old Testament Witness: The Old Testament lays a strong foundation for understanding divine majesty.

- **Creation Narratives:** In Genesis 1, God's creative command "Let there be…" brings forth a cosmos that is ordered and "very good," reflecting His flawless design and authority.

- **Covenantal Imagery:** At Mount Sinai and in Solomon's temple dedication (1 Kings 8:27), God's presence is depicted as so magnificent that even the heavens cannot contain Him.

- **Psalms and Prophets:** Psalm 8 marvels at the dignity of creation as a reflection of God's glory, while prophets like Isaiah proclaim that God's ways are higher than human ways (Isaiah 55:8–9).

New Testament Revelation: The New Testament deepens our understanding of divine majesty through Jesus Christ.

- **Incarnation:** John 1:14 declares, "And the Word became flesh and dwelt among us," revealing that God's glory entered human history through Christ, who embodied both divine power and humble love.

- **Transfiguration:** In the Transfiguration (Matthew 17:1–9), Jesus' radiant appearance confirms His divine authority and the splendor of His nature.

- **Apostolic Teachings:** Paul, in Ephesians 1:18–23, prays that believers may grasp the hope and riches of God's glorious inheritance, emphasizing that the same power that raised Christ now sustains the church.

- **Eschatological Vision:** Revelation portrays the New Jerusalem bathed in perpetual light, a future reality where God's majestic presence fills every corner, signifying the ultimate fulfillment of His reign.

35.3 Theological Perspectives

Majesty as an Expression of Divine Nature: God's majesty is inseparable from His essence. Unlike earthly kings who may falter, God's perfection is absolute—His justice, mercy, and love are perfectly united in His being. The doctrine of divine simplicity teaches that His attributes are not parts but aspects of one indivisible nature.

Interplay with Holiness: Divine majesty reaches its fullest expression when paired with holiness. Isaiah 6's vision of God's unapproachable light and the seraphim's cry of "Holy, holy, holy" remind us that God's majesty is both magnificent and morally pure. His majestic rule is founded on unchanging righteousness that commands respect and inspires moral transformation.

Redemptive Majesty: The redemptive work of Christ is the pinnacle of divine majesty. The cross transforms an instrument of suffering into a symbol of victorious love. Through His sacrificial death and resurrection, Jesus displays a majesty that redeems, reconciling humanity to God and promising a future where divine glory is fully realized.

35.4 Addressing Common Misconceptions

Not Mere Flashiness: Divine majesty is often mistakenly seen as superficial display. However, biblical majesty is the inherent excellence of God's nature. It is not about ostentation or mere visual splendor but about the perfection of His character—truth, justice, mercy, and love—that transforms lives.

Divine vs. Human Glory: Human glory is fleeting and earned through achievements, often marred by pride. In contrast, God's glory is intrinsic and eternal. It does not depend on external accomplishments but flows from His unchanging essence as Creator and Sustainer.

Approachability of the Majestic God: Some fear that a majestic God is distant and unapproachable. Yet Scripture consistently portrays God as both exalted and intimately involved. The same God who sits on a heavenly throne also invites believers to commune with Him in prayer, revealing His nearness through Christ and the indwelling Holy Spirit.

35.5 Pastoral and Practical Implications

Transforming Worship: A proper understanding of God's majesty should transform worship from a routine act into an encounter filled with awe and gratitude. Congregations that meditate on His splendor—through majestic hymns, reverent liturgy, and reflective prayer—experience a deep sense of humility and inspiration, recognizing that every star and every life reflects His divine excellence.

Ethical Living: Belief in divine majesty challenges believers to live with integrity and purpose. When Christians see their lives as part of a grand divine design, they are motivated to pursue justice, kindness, and moral excellence. Their decisions and actions are measured against an eternal standard of perfection, fostering a culture of accountability and service.

Community and Global Impact: Churches that embrace God's majesty build communities marked by unity and mutual respect. This shared vision of divine excellence encourages collaborative ministry, social justice, and advocacy for the marginalized. On a global scale, proclaiming God's glory unites diverse cultures under a common standard of truth and beauty, inspiring efforts that transcend national and ethnic boundaries.

Witness Through Creativity: Throughout history, the arts have been inspired by the majesty of God—from the soaring cathedrals of the Middle Ages to contemporary expressions in music and visual art. These creative endeavors do not capture the full glory of God but serve as humble homages that invite viewers and listeners to reflect on the infinite beauty of the divine.

35.6 Embracing the Eternal Vision

Living with an Eternal Perspective: Understanding God's majesty reorients our priorities. In the light of divine perfection, temporary setbacks and superficial achievements lose their hold. Believers are called to invest their time, talents, and resources in pursuits that reflect eternal values—acts of service, creative expression, and ethical leadership that honor God's unchanging standard.

Personal Transformation: Encountering the majesty of God transforms lives. It inspires personal growth, fosters resilience in the face of hardship, and ignites a desire to emulate His virtues. When individuals recognize that their Creator is supremely glorious, they are compelled to live in a way that reflects His beauty and integrity, becoming beacons of hope and testimony in a fractured world.

Global and Cultural Witness: The proclamation of God's majesty offers a unifying message in a diverse world. It challenges cultural norms that prize fleeting accolades over lasting virtue. By embracing and sharing the truth of a glorious God, Christians contribute to a global narrative of hope, promoting social justice and reconciliation that mirrors divine excellence.

In conclusion, divine majesty encapsulates the supreme beauty, power, and perfection of God—qualities that manifest in His creation, covenant, and redemptive work. From the majestic creation account in Genesis to the revelatory moments of Christ's transfiguration and the eternal hope depicted in Revelation, Scripture reveals a God whose glory is both inherent and revealed. This glory is not merely about dazzling light or impressive power; it is the reflection of God's unchanging character—His justice, mercy, and love.

Recognizing God's majesty transforms worship, ethical living, and community engagement. It challenges believers to seek an eternal standard in all aspects of life, fosters unity across diverse cultures, and inspires personal transformation through the pursuit of true excellence. As we contemplate the grandeur of our Creator, we are invited to live with reverence and humility, aware that every moment and every act can reflect the radiant beauty of the One who is supremely glorious.

In a world often mired in mediocrity and transient achievements, the majesty of God stands as a timeless beacon, urging us to look beyond the ordinary and to embrace a life of purpose, integrity, and awe. May we continually be inspired to worship, serve, and bear witness to a God whose glory transforms all of creation and endures forever.

Chapter 36: Infallible

In Christian theology, divine infallibility means that God's wisdom, judgments, and works are without error. Unlike fallible human beings, whose limited perspective can lead to mistakes, God operates in perfect alignment with His nature. His decrees, promises, and actions never deviate from truth, providing a foundation of certainty and hope for believers.

36.1 Understanding Divine Infallibility

Inherent Perfection: Divine infallibility signifies that God is incapable of error because His nature is perfectly wise and morally pure. Every act of creation, every command, and every promise reflects His unerring character. This assurance means that when God speaks or acts, His words are a reliable guide to truth, and His plans will inevitably come to fruition as intended.

Reliable Revelation: Because God is infallible, all Scripture and divine revelation are trustworthy. His messages, delivered through prophets, the person of Jesus Christ, and the inspiration of the Holy Spirit, form an unchanging standard. Believers can depend on God's word as the ultimate measure of reality and morality, even when human reasoning falls short.

Divine Wisdom in Action: God's creative acts—manifested in the intricacy of nature and the orderly universe—demonstrate His flawless wisdom. Likewise, the unfolding of salvation history, from the call of Abraham to the redemptive work of Christ, proceeds with absolute precision. Even when events appear mysterious or delayed, they are part of a sovereign plan that is free from error.

36.2 Biblical Foundations

Old Testament Testimony: The Old Testament frequently emphasizes God's infallibility as the source of perfect guidance:

- **Psalm 18:30** states, "As for God, his way is perfect; the word of the LORD proves true," affirming that divine governance is without flaw.

- **Isaiah 46:9–10** declares, "I am God, and there is no other; I am God, and there is none like me, declaring the end from the beginning and from ancient times things not yet done." This highlights that God not only foresees the future but establishes it according to His perfect plan.

- Throughout Israel's history, even in moments of rebellion, God's steadfast fulfillment of His covenants demonstrates that His promises are unwavering.

New Testament Revelation: The New Testament builds on this foundation by revealing God's infallibility through Jesus Christ:

- **John 1:1, 14** presents Jesus as the incarnate Word, embodying divine truth in human form. His life and teachings confirm that God's truth is not abstract but lived out perfectly.

- **John 14:6** records Jesus proclaiming, "I am the way, and the truth, and the life," emphasizing that truth is not merely a concept but is embodied in Him.

- **Romans 8:28** assures believers that "all things work together for good" for those who love God, grounded in the confidence that His plan is error-free.

- The consistent witness of the Holy Spirit in guiding and transforming lives further confirms that divine revelation remains unfailing.

36.3 Theological Reflections

Divine Perfection and Infallibility: In classical theology, God is the epitome of perfection. His nature is entirely good, wise, and just—attributes that ensure His actions are without fault. Divine infallibility is inseparable from this perfection; if God were capable of error, His moral character would be compromised. Instead, His flawless nature guarantees that every judgment and act is aligned with ultimate truth.

Human Limitations: Our finite minds can only grasp a fraction of God's infinite wisdom. While God's word is complete and trustworthy, our understanding remains partial. This recognition calls for humility: we are encouraged to trust in God's perfect revelation rather than rely solely on our limited perspective. In doing so, our faith becomes an ongoing journey of learning and dependence on divine guidance.

Providence and Unerring Plan: God's infallibility assures us that every event, whether joyous or painful, fits into a larger, flawless divine plan. Even when circumstances appear chaotic, the reality is that nothing happens outside the scope of His perfect will. This truth provides deep comfort: our struggles are temporary, and in the end, every injustice will be rectified as God's plan unfolds with impeccable precision.

36.4 Addressing Common Misconceptions

Divine Fallibility vs. Human Error: A common mistake is to project human error onto God. Humans err because our knowledge is limited and our judgments are influenced by personal biases. In contrast, God's infinite wisdom and moral perfection ensure that His actions are always right. Recognizing this fundamental difference helps us avoid the trap of equating divine actions with human shortcomings.

Delays as Deliberate Wisdom: Sometimes, God's timing may seem slow or mysterious. Critics might interpret delays as mistakes, but these delays are part of His intentional, providential plan. What appears as a postponement is, in fact, a measured process that allows for repentance, growth, and the eventual fulfillment of His promises. As Romans 8:28 assures, even when the outcome is not immediately apparent, all things work together for good under God's unerring guidance.

Infallibility and the Problem of Suffering: Some argue that if God's plans are infallible, then human suffering must be justified or predetermined. However, divine infallibility does not eliminate the consequences of free will or the effects of sin. Instead, it guarantees that even amidst suffering, God is working for a greater good. The cross and resurrection exemplify how God transforms pain and injustice into the ultimate victory over sin and death.

36.5 Pastoral and Practical Implications

Assurance in Uncertainty: Believers find comfort in knowing that God's word and plans are infallible. This assurance enables them to face life's uncertainties with confidence. In times of personal crisis or doubt, the unchanging truth of God's promises provides a secure foundation for hope and perseverance.

Cultivating Humility and Dependence: Recognizing our limited understanding encourages a humble reliance on divine wisdom. Believers are urged to seek God's guidance through prayer, Scripture, and communal discernment. This dependence on God fosters spiritual growth, as we learn to trust that His perfect plan will guide us even when our own judgments falter.

Ethical Living and Integrity: The infallibility of God sets an absolute standard for morality. Believers are called to model their lives on His unerring truth, cultivating integrity, honesty, and fairness in every aspect of their lives. This ethical framework challenges Christians to reject deception and moral compromise, reflecting a commitment to live according to the flawless standard of their Creator.

Community Formation and Witness: Church communities that embrace divine infallibility develop strong bonds based on mutual trust and a shared commitment to God's truth. Such communities become powerful witnesses in a world rife with moral ambiguity, as their collective adherence to unchanging divine principles fosters unity, accountability, and love. Through worship, teaching, and disciplined practice, these communities demonstrate that God's word is a reliable foundation for life.

36.6 Global and Cultural Reflections

Influencing Global Apologetics: In a pluralistic world, the doctrine of divine infallibility stands as a testament to the reliability of God's revelation. Christian apologists assert that while human wisdom is fallible, God's truth remains absolute. This conviction challenges relativistic worldviews and provides a stable foundation for interfaith dialogue, encouraging mutual respect while affirming the ultimate truth found in Scripture.

Cultural Impact of Absolute Truth: The belief in God's infallibility influences cultural values by promoting transparency, accountability, and justice. In societies where truth is often seen as subjective, the Christian conviction that God's standards are unchanging offers a counter-narrative that supports ethical behavior and social reforms. This moral anchor has historically inspired movements for civil rights, educational reform, and legal integrity, as communities strive to reflect the unblemished nature of divine truth.

36.7 Personal Transformation and Community Building

Spiritual Maturity: Embracing divine infallibility nurtures personal transformation. When individuals understand that God's word is flawless, they are motivated to examine their lives, repent, and align their actions with His truth. This ongoing process of spiritual growth leads to greater resilience, compassion, and moral clarity, as believers learn to rely on God's perfect wisdom rather than their own limited insight.

Living as Ambassadors of Truth: Believers are called to embody the unchanging standard of God's truth in every area of life. By modeling integrity, ethical conduct, and honesty, Christians become ambassadors of divine truth, offering a credible witness to a world often marred by deception and moral relativism. Whether in personal relationships, business dealings, or public service, living according to God's infallible standards invites others to experience the transformative power of His grace.

In conclusion, the doctrine of divine infallibility proclaims that God's wisdom, judgments, and works are utterly reliable. Rooted in Scripture—from the unshakeable declarations of Psalm 18:30 and Isaiah 46:9–10 to the redemptive power of Christ as attested in the New Testament—this truth provides a steadfast foundation for Christian faith. It assures believers that even when human understanding is limited or circumstances seem chaotic, God's perfect plan prevails.

This unerring nature of God invites us into a relationship marked by unwavering trust, humility, and ethical integrity. As we rely on His flawless word, we are transformed—our personal lives enriched by hope and our communities strengthened by mutual accountability and shared purpose. Globally, the belief in an infallible God challenges cultural relativism and inspires movements for justice, transparency, and moral renewal.

Ultimately, divine infallibility is not an abstract theological concept but a dynamic reality that shapes every facet of our lives. It compels us to live in light of eternal truth, to pursue righteousness with conviction, and to confidently bear witness to a God whose promises never fail. In this assurance, we find the courage to face uncertainty, the motivation to grow in holiness, and the strength to build a world that reflects the unchanging, perfect nature of our Creator.

Chapter 37: Unsearchable

The attribute of God's unsearchability reveals that His ways, wisdom, and purposes are so vast that no human mind can fully grasp them. Scripture tells us that God's understanding is "unsearchable" (Psalm 145:3; Isaiah 40:28), pointing to a divine mystery that both comforts and challenges us. While God graciously reveals parts of Himself through creation, Scripture, and the person of Jesus Christ, His full nature remains beyond complete human comprehension. This chapter explores what it means for God's wisdom and purposes to be unsearchable, examines its biblical foundations and theological significance, addresses common misconceptions, and considers its practical impact on our spiritual lives.

37.1 Understanding Divine Unsearchability

The Nature of Incomprehensibility: To say that God is unsearchable means that His infinite wisdom, power, and love exceed every limit of human thought and language. Our finite minds can only glimpse a fraction of His reality. Passages like Isaiah 55:8–9 and Romans 11:33 remind us that while God has graciously revealed Himself, the fullness of His being remains a mystery. This does not imply that God is unknowable; rather, He has chosen to disclose what is necessary for our salvation and growth, leaving the rest as an invitation to wonder and trust.

Revelation Versus Mystery: God's self-disclosure through Scripture, nature, and the person of Jesus provides us with reliable truths about His character, even as many aspects remain hidden. The tension between what is revealed and what remains mysterious calls us to a humble, trusting faith. We learn to appreciate that every revelation is a gift while accepting that the totality of God's glory is forever beyond our grasp. In this way, divine unsearchability fosters awe and continuous inquiry without the pressure to achieve complete understanding.

Accessibility Amid Mystery: Although God's wisdom is unsearchable, He is not distant. On the contrary, He is accessible to all who seek Him. Our limited understanding does not hinder our relationship with God; instead, it invites us to trust in His character and lean on His revealed word. The paradox is that while His essence is infinite, He remains intimately involved in our lives, guiding and sustaining us through the work of the Holy Spirit.

37.2 Biblical Foundations

Old Testament Witnesses: The Old Testament abounds with imagery and declarations that underscore the unsearchable nature of God.

- **Job's Inquiry:** In Job 11:7–9, we are challenged to fathom the mysteries of God—a humbling reminder of our limitations compared to His infinite wisdom.

- **Psalms of Praise:** Psalm 145:3 proclaims that God's greatness is unsearchable, inviting worshipers to trust in a God whose power and knowledge far exceed human capacity.

- **Creation Narratives:** In Genesis, God's command "Let there be…" not only creates order from chaos but also reveals a design so intricate that it defies full explanation. These texts call us to trust that while we receive enough revelation to live rightly, the depth of His wisdom remains beyond our complete understanding.

New Testament Revelation: The New Testament builds upon this foundation, centering the ultimate revelation of God's unsearchable nature in Jesus Christ.

- **The Incarnation:** John 1:1–14 tells us that the Word became flesh, making the infinite nature of God partially accessible to us through the person of Jesus. Although Christ reveals much about God's character, His teachings (e.g., John 6:38) and actions also hint that the full extent of God's plan remains a divine mystery.

- **Paul's Epistles:** In 1 Corinthians 2:9–10, Paul affirms that no eye has seen nor ear heard the riches of God's plans. This underscores that even as God reveals His will through the Spirit, the complete tapestry of His wisdom remains unfathomable.

- **Eschatological Promise:** Revelation offers a vision of a future where God's glory and truth are fully manifest, assuring believers that despite our present limitations, His ultimate purposes are perfect and eternal.

37.3 Theological Reflections

Embracing Divine Mystery: Theologically, God's unsearchability invites a posture of humility and awe. The mystery of His infinite nature challenges us to recognize the limits of our understanding and to trust in His greater wisdom. Renowned theologians, such as Karl Barth, have taught that divine revelation is a gift that transcends our ability to fully comprehend, compelling us to live in faith and wonder.

Revelation and Faith: Since complete knowledge of God is unattainable, faith becomes the bridge between our finite minds and His infinite reality. Hebrews 11:1 describes faith as "the assurance of things hoped for, the conviction of things not seen." Believers are called to trust in a God whose truth is revealed in part but whose whole essence remains a mystery—an invitation to ongoing spiritual growth.

Balancing Revelation and Incompleteness: This balance between what God has revealed and what remains hidden is central to Christian spirituality. It encourages us to value every insight as a step toward deeper understanding while acknowledging that the divine mystery is an eternal, unending journey. This perspective fosters a continuous reliance on God's grace and a commitment to worship Him not only for what we know but also for the mystery that inspires us to seek more.

37.4 Common Misconceptions and Clarifications

Inaccessibility Misunderstood: Some mistakenly believe that if God's ways are unsearchable, then He is distant or indifferent. However, Scripture consistently shows that while His wisdom is infinite, God remains actively involved in creation and human affairs. His mystery does not equal remoteness; it calls us to trust and to approach Him with humility.

Over-Intellectualization: There is a risk of reducing divine mystery to mere abstract speculation. While rigorous theology is valuable, over-intellectualizing can strip the mystery of its relational and redemptive power. God's unsearchable nature is meant to inspire worship and trust, not to be solved like a puzzle. We are invited to embrace the mystery as a gift that deepens our relationship with Him.

Absolute Truth Amid Mystery: Another misconception is that if God is incomprehensible, then truth becomes relative. Yet, the biblical witness affirms that while our understanding is limited, God's nature remains absolutely true. The unsearchable aspects of His wisdom do not imply that truth is malleable; instead, they underscore that God's eternal reality stands firm regardless of our limited perceptions.

37.5 Pastoral and Practical Implications

Comfort in Uncertainty: Believers find solace in the truth that God's wisdom and plans, though unsearchable, are perfect and unchanging. In moments of crisis or confusion, the assurance that God's greater plan is beyond our understanding provides a stable foundation for hope. Pastoral care often emphasizes that even when we cannot grasp all the reasons behind our struggles, we can trust in a God who is both faithful and infinitely wise.

Encouraging Humility and Continuous Learning: Recognizing our limited capacity to understand the divine fosters humility. This awareness encourages a lifelong pursuit of learning and spiritual growth. Church communities can support one another through Bible studies, mentorship, and reflective prayer, cultivating an environment where questions are welcomed, and every revelation is cherished as a stepping stone toward deeper faith.

Transforming Worship: Worship that embraces the mystery of God's unsearchable nature transcends routine ritual. When believers acknowledge that they are encountering a God whose wisdom and power are infinite, their worship becomes an act of both adoration and surrender. Hymns and liturgies that reflect on God's unfathomable majesty inspire awe and deepen the communal experience of His presence.

Ethical Living: Understanding that God's truth and moral order are derived from an infinite source calls believers to a higher standard of integrity. As we recognize that our grasp of God's wisdom is partial, we are urged to live with honesty, fairness, and compassion. This ethical framework, anchored in divine truth, challenges us to pursue justice and kindness in our personal and communal lives.

Global and Cultural Impact: On a broader scale, the acknowledgment of God's unsearchable nature can foster interfaith dialogue and cultural humility. In a world where multiple perspectives vie for truth, the Christian claim that God's wisdom surpasses all human understanding invites respectful conversation. This perspective also challenges cultural relativism, reminding us that while human knowledge is fragmented, the divine reality is coherent and eternal.

37.6 Personal and Communal Formation

Spiritual Formation: Embracing God's unsearchable nature nurtures a spirit of wonder and humility. Practices such as contemplative prayer, meditation, and journaling help believers experience the divine mystery personally, transforming everyday life into a continuous encounter with God's infinite love and wisdom.

Community Building: Churches that appreciate the mystery of God create spaces where questions are encouraged, and growth is celebrated. By sharing personal testimonies of encountering God's unfathomable grace, congregations build a collective narrative that reinforces mutual support and spiritual renewal. This communal bond not only strengthens individual faith but also fosters a dynamic, vibrant church culture.

In conclusion, the doctrine of divine unsearchability teaches us that while God graciously reveals aspects of His character, the totality of His wisdom, power, and love remains beyond human comprehension. From the poetic declarations of the Old Testament to the profound revelations in the New Testament—especially in the person of Jesus Christ—Scripture consistently portrays a God whose nature is infinite and mysterious.

This mystery is not a barrier to relationship but an invitation to trust, worship, and grow. Believers are called to approach God with humility, embracing the partial truths revealed in Scripture while acknowledging that the fullness of His glory will forever remain a divine mystery. In doing so, we find comfort amid uncertainty, ethical guidance for our lives, and a continuous inspiration to seek deeper communion with the Almighty.

Chapter 38: Benevolent

God's benevolence is a core aspect of His character, revealing His active desire to do good for all creation. It is more than mere kindness—it is a dynamic, redemptive force that sustains, protects, and restores. Unlike created things that depend on external resources, God's nature is the source of all good, and His benevolence flows freely from His abundant love. This chapter explores the meaning of divine benevolence, its biblical foundations, theological implications, common misconceptions, and practical effects on personal and community life.

38.1 Understanding Divine Benevolence

Active Love and Care: To say God is benevolent means that His heart is wholly oriented toward the well-being of His creation. He not only sustains life but continually works to improve and restore it. Divine benevolence is an active commitment—it reaches out to heal the broken, protect the vulnerable, and guide His people toward flourishing. Unlike passive tolerance, God's benevolence is marked by intentional acts of mercy and redemptive love.

Holistic Well-Being: The biblical concept of "shalom"—complete peace and wholeness—captures the essence of God's benevolence. It is not limited to material blessings but encompasses physical, emotional, and spiritual restoration. God's benevolence is evident in the natural order, in human history, and ultimately in the person of Jesus Christ, who embodies and extends God's gracious care.

Moral and Relational Dimensions: Divine benevolence is rooted in God's moral nature. His goodness is not accidental or arbitrary; it is the natural expression of His holiness, justice, and love. This benevolence creates a moral framework where caring for the marginalized and upholding justice become reflections of God's own character. In every act of compassion and mercy, God invites His people to mirror His love.

38.2 Biblical Foundations

Old Testament Witness: Scripture frequently portrays God's benevolence as His active care for creation and His people.

- **Psalm 145:9** proclaims, "The LORD is good to all, and his mercy is over all that he has made," emphasizing the inclusivity of His goodness.

- In **Deuteronomy 10:18**, God is described as one who defends the fatherless and widows, underscoring His commitment to protect the vulnerable.

- Israel's history, even after episodes of rebellion like the golden calf incident, reveals a God who renews His covenant and extends mercy, as seen in His calls for repentance and restoration through the prophets (e.g., Isaiah 54:10).

New Testament Revelation: The New Testament deepens our understanding of divine benevolence through the life and ministry of Jesus Christ.

- **Jesus' Ministry:** In Matthew 5:45, Jesus teaches that God "makes his sun rise on the evil and on the good," illustrating that His blessings are given without discrimination. Jesus' acts of healing, feeding, and forgiving highlight a heart moved by compassion.

- **The Incarnation:** John 1:14 reveals that "the Word became flesh and dwelt among us," showing that God's benevolence is made tangible in Christ's life. His gentle interactions and sacrificial death provide the ultimate example of unmerited love.

- **The Holy Spirit:** At Pentecost, the indwelling of the Holy Spirit continues this benevolent presence, empowering believers to exhibit the fruits of love, kindness, and generosity (Galatians 5:22–23).

38.3 Theological Reflections

Benevolence as a Reflection of God's Nature: Divine benevolence is not an optional quality but is intrinsic to God's character. As the source of all that is good, God's actions—creating, sustaining, and redeeming—flow from His own fullness. His benevolence serves as a moral compass, guiding human conduct toward love, justice, and reconciliation.

Unmerited Favor and Redemption: A central theme is that God's benevolence is freely given, not earned. This unmerited favor is best exemplified in the atoning work of Christ. The cross transforms sin's penalty into a gateway for redemption, assuring believers that every good gift comes from God's overflowing grace.

Interplay with Justice: Benevolence and justice are inseparable in God's dealings. His compassionate restraint in administering judgment—allowing space for repentance—demonstrates that true justice is always tempered by mercy. This balance ensures that while sin is not ignored, every person has the opportunity for restoration.

38.4 Addressing Misconceptions

Benevolence is Not Weakness: Some mistakenly view benevolence as a sign of weakness or passivity. In contrast, divine benevolence is the expression of strength perfected by love. God's gentle care does not prevent decisive action; rather, it transforms judgment into restorative discipline, as seen in the prophetic calls for repentance and the redemptive work of Christ.

Not a License for Complacency: Divine benevolence does not imply that sin is excused or overlooked. Instead, it calls for a response of sincere repentance and ethical living. God's generosity encourages us to live in gratitude and to share our blessings, without using His mercy as an excuse for ongoing wrongdoing.

Inclusive, Not Exclusive: Some fear that emphasizing God's benevolence might suggest that all moral actions are acceptable. However, His goodness is a standard that calls believers to pursue justice and compassion. Divine benevolence is not a softening of moral rigor but a powerful impetus for ethical behavior that reflects God's character.

38.5 Pastoral and Practical Implications

Transforming Personal Lives: Recognizing God's benevolence offers immense comfort to individuals burdened by guilt, despair, or hardship. Knowing that every blessing comes from a loving, generous Creator can renew one's self-worth and purpose. Personal prayer, reflection, and meditation on God's kindness help transform feelings of failure into hope and resilience.

Cultivating a Lifestyle of Generosity: Believers are called to mirror God's benevolence in their daily lives. This means sharing resources, offering compassion, and actively working for the well-being of others. Acts of kindness, community service, and charitable giving become tangible expressions of the divine goodness that flows from God.

Fostering Community Unity: Churches that embrace the doctrine of divine benevolence build vibrant, supportive communities. When congregants recognize that God's mercy extends to all, it breaks down barriers of judgment and exclusion. A culture of mutual care, open dialogue, and restorative justice helps forge deep, lasting bonds within the community, reflecting the holistic peace of God's kingdom.

Inspiring Social Justice: Divine benevolence also motivates broader social engagement. Recognizing that all people are recipients of God's unmerited favor challenges us to address systemic injustices—whether in poverty, discrimination, or environmental degradation. Many Christian movements, from local outreach programs to global humanitarian initiatives, are inspired by the call to extend God's benevolence, thereby transforming society with compassion and justice.

Global Impact and Interfaith Dialogue: The message of God's benevolence resonates across cultures and borders. In interfaith contexts, Christians can share how God's inclusive love and mercy offer hope and healing in a world divided by conflict and inequality. This universal message fosters mutual respect and dialogue, encouraging collaborative efforts toward peace and justice worldwide.

38.6 Living Out Divine Benevolence

Personal Transformation: Encountering God's benevolence transforms the individual. It encourages a renewed commitment to forgiveness, humility, and service. As believers internalize that every good gift is a sign of God's loving nature, they develop a heart that seeks to extend that same grace to others, breaking cycles of bitterness and fostering lasting change.

Everyday Acts of Kindness: Divine benevolence is best manifested in the small, everyday actions that express genuine care. Whether it's lending a listening ear, offering a meal, or simply showing compassion to someone in need, these acts reflect the heart of God's goodness. They build a culture of kindness that, over time, transforms communities.

Worship and Gratitude: Personal and corporate worship that centers on God's benevolence is marked by profound gratitude and adoration. When believers reflect on His boundless mercy, their worship becomes a vibrant testimony of hope and transformation. This adoration not only deepens one's relationship with God but also inspires others to seek His redeeming love.

In conclusion, divine benevolence is the outpouring of God's active, unmerited love—a love that sustains, restores, and transforms. From the Old Testament's calls for justice and care to the New Testament revelation of Christ's sacrificial love, Scripture portrays a God who is deeply committed to the well-being of all creation. His benevolence is evident in every act of creation, every redemptive gesture, and every ongoing provision of grace.

For believers, this truth is both a source of personal comfort and a powerful ethical call. Recognizing that all blessings come from a benevolent God inspires gratitude, generosity, and a commitment to justice. It encourages us to build communities marked by unity and mutual care and challenges us to engage with the world in ways that reflect His compassionate heart.

Ultimately, the call to embody divine benevolence invites us to mirror the loving nature of our Creator. By extending kindness, practicing forgiveness, and advocating for justice, we participate in God's redemptive work in the world. In doing so, we not only transform our own lives but also become beacons of hope and instruments of change in a world in need of genuine love.

May our lives, both individually and collectively, reflect the enduring, transformative power of divine benevolence—a power that continually invites us into deeper fellowship with God and with one another, and that promises a future where every heart is nurtured and every need is met by the generous love of our Creator.

Chapter 39: Provider

In Christian theology, God as Provider means that He actively supplies every need of His creation with wisdom, abundance, and care. This attribute, exemplified by the name Jehovah Jireh ("The LORD will provide") in Genesis 22 and affirmed in Philippians 4:19, is not limited to material blessings but encompasses spiritual, emotional, and relational sustenance. God's provision is a dynamic expression of His love, ensuring that nothing is overlooked and that every aspect of life is nurtured.

39.1 Understanding Divine Provision

Comprehensive Care: To call God our Provider is to recognize that He is the source of every blessing. His provision goes beyond merely dispensing food or shelter; it also involves comforting our sorrows, guiding our decisions, and renewing our spirits. God's care is holistic—sustaining physical life, nurturing emotional well-being, and enriching spiritual growth.

Active and Ongoing: Divine provision is not sporadic or accidental. It is an active, continuous process that undergirds creation. The regular cycles of nature and the constant care shown in human history reflect a God who anticipates needs and responds with perfect timing. Even in our darkest moments, His faithful presence reassures us that our every need is seen and met.

Relational and Covenant-Based: God's role as Provider is deeply relational. He establishes covenant relationships with His people, promising both immediate care and eternal blessings. These covenants—seen in the lives of Abraham, Moses, and ultimately through Jesus—underscore that God's provision is both a present reality and a promise for the future.

39.2 Biblical Foundations for Divine Provision

Old Testament Witness: The Old Testament is replete with examples of God's provision:

- **Jehovah Jireh (Genesis 22):** In the test of Abraham's faith, God provides a ram as a substitute for Isaac, demonstrating that even in the most desperate moments, He supplies an alternative.

- **Psalm 145:9:** "The LORD is good to all, and his mercy is over all that he has made," affirms that God's goodness extends universally.

- **Covenant Relationships:** The Mosaic covenant and the temple's symbolism show that God dwells among His people, offering guidance, discipline, and blessing even when they falter.

New Testament Revelation: In the New Testament, the theme of divine provision is deepened through Jesus Christ:

- **Incarnation and Miracles:** Jesus' life demonstrates God's provision as He heals, feeds, and forgives, embodying compassion and care. His actions reveal that divine provision is personal and transformative.

- **Paul's Assurance (Philippians 4:19):** "My God will supply every need of yours according to his riches in glory in Christ Jesus," provides a concrete promise that believers' needs are met by God's abundant resources.

- **Redemptive Provision:** Christ's sacrificial death and resurrection illustrate the ultimate provision—salvation. Through the cross, God supplies forgiveness and eternal life, confirming that His provision extends far beyond the material.

The Work of the Holy Spirit: After Christ's ascension, the Holy Spirit continues to work within believers. The Spirit's indwelling presence guides, comforts, and empowers the church, ensuring that God's provision is experienced daily in personal growth and communal unity.

39.3 Theological Reflections

Infallible Wisdom and Abundance: God's provision flows from His infinite wisdom and perfect nature. Unlike human efforts, which are prone to error, His plans are flawless. Every blessing is a deliberate act of divine generosity, revealing that nothing happens by chance. As James 1:17 reminds us, "Every good gift and every perfect gift is from above," affirming that God's abundance is intentional and reliable.

Providence and Free Will: Divine provision works in tandem with human freedom. While God supplies every need, He also invites us to steward these gifts wisely. His provision empowers us to make choices that lead to flourishing, balancing divine initiative with personal responsibility.

Redemptive Purpose: The provision of God is fundamentally redemptive. Even when our lives are marred by failure or suffering, God's care offers a pathway to restoration. The incarnation of Christ, His sacrificial death, and the ongoing work of the Holy Spirit all demonstrate that divine provision transforms brokenness into hope and renewal.

39.4 Common Misconceptions

Not Mere Chance or Luck: Some mistakenly equate divine provision with randomness or luck. However, biblical teaching shows that God's provision is purposeful—a reflection of His loving nature rather than the result of a lottery. While human effort plays a role, it is ultimately God's sovereign hand that directs all circumstances.

Beyond Material Wealth: God as Provider is often misconstrued as a guarantee of wealth. In truth, His provision encompasses far more than material abundance; it includes spiritual nourishment, emotional healing, and relational support. The promise in Philippians 4:19 assures believers that their needs will be met in ways that align with God's ultimate purposes, not necessarily in terms of worldly riches.

Active Engagement, Not Passive Dispensation: Some critics suggest that if God provides, He is passive. Yet Scripture reveals a God who is actively involved in every detail of creation. From natural laws sustaining life to miraculous interventions in history, His provision is dynamic and responsive. God is not a distant benefactor but an ever-present guide who works continually on behalf of His people.

39.5 Pastoral and Practical Implications

Security in Uncertainty: Believers find immense comfort in knowing that God is their Provider. In times of financial strain, illness, or emotional distress, the assurance that God supplies every need offers a firm foundation for hope. This security comes from trusting in His unchanging nature and His faithful promises, which remain reliable even in the midst of uncertainty.

Cultivating Trust and Gratitude: Embracing God as Provider fosters a spirit of gratitude. Recognizing that every blessing is a gift from a loving Creator encourages believers to live generously, share with others, and steward resources wisely. Gratitude transforms anxiety into peace, as individuals learn to rely on God's continual care rather than on their own limited means.

Empowering Ethical Living: The knowledge that God's provision is both abundant and purposeful compels believers to live ethically. When we understand that every need is met by a benevolent God, we are motivated to reflect His character by treating others with kindness, honesty, and compassion. This ethical framework influences personal relationships, business practices, and public policies, promoting justice and mercy in all spheres of life.

Community Building: Church communities that internalize the truth of divine provision become hubs of mutual support. Shared testimonies of God's provision strengthen communal bonds, as members encourage one another through acts of charity, prayer, and service. This collective reliance on God's care creates resilient, compassionate communities that mirror His generosity and grace.

Missional Impact: The message that God provides for every need is a powerful tool for evangelism and social justice. When believers experience His provision, they are compelled to share that hope with a world in distress. This missional impulse drives Christian outreach—whether through local food banks, international humanitarian work, or advocacy for systemic change—demonstrating that the love of God transforms lives and communities.

39.6 Global and Cultural Reflections

Universal Relevance: God's provision is not confined by culture, nation, or time—it is universal. The biblical promise that "every need" will be met applies to all people. This universality fosters interfaith dialogue and global cooperation, as diverse communities recognize that true care comes from a Creator who is impartial and abundantly generous.

Shaping Societal Values: The belief in divine provision influences societal ethics by challenging cultures that prioritize self-reliance and greed. When communities acknowledge that all blessings stem from God, there is a natural impetus toward sharing, fairness, and justice. This can lead to reforms in education, healthcare, and economic policy that align with the principles of generosity and communal well-being.

39.7 Personal Transformation and Community Life

Transforming the Heart: Encountering God's provision can radically change an individual's perspective. Personal testimonies abound of lives turned around by the realization that God cares deeply—even in the most desperate circumstances. This transformation, marked by increased gratitude, hope, and trust, propels believers to extend that same care to others, breaking cycles of fear and isolation.

A Lifestyle of Generosity: When believers internalize the truth that God is their Provider, they are inspired to live generously. This extends beyond financial giving to include acts of kindness, mentorship, and service. A generous lifestyle reflects the character of God and transforms personal relationships and community dynamics, creating a culture where resources are shared and no one is left in need.

Ambassadors of Provision: Living as beneficiaries of God's provision equips believers to be effective witnesses in their communities. By modeling trust, gratitude, and ethical behavior, they demonstrate that God's care is reliable and transformative. This living testimony challenges cultural norms that equate success with self-reliance and inspires others to seek a deeper, more sustaining relationship with the divine.

In conclusion, the doctrine of divine provision proclaims that God actively supplies every need—physical, emotional, spiritual, and relational—with wisdom and abundance. Rooted in Scripture, from the promise of Jehovah Jireh in Genesis to Paul's assurance in Philippians, this attribute reveals a God who is intimately involved in every detail of creation. His provision is purposeful, ensuring that every blessing is a deliberate act of love designed to nurture, restore, and sustain life.

Understanding God as Provider transforms our lives: it offers security in uncertainty, fosters gratitude and ethical living, and builds communities marked by compassion and shared purpose. Globally, the promise of divine provision challenges societies to value generosity and justice over greed and individualism, inspiring reforms and humanitarian efforts that reflect the Creator's boundless care.

Ultimately, embracing the truth that God is our Provider invites us into a dynamic relationship of trust and dependence. As we live out this truth, we become channels of divine grace, sharing our blessings and extending hope to a world in need. In every sunrise, every act of kindness, and every moment of care, we witness the radiant, transformative love of the One who provides for all—now and for eternity.

Chapter 40: Attentive

In Christian theology, God's attentiveness reveals a deeply personal, engaged, and responsive Creator. Far from being distant or indifferent, God listens to every cry, watches over each heart, and responds with perfect wisdom and care. This attribute assures believers that nothing escapes His notice and that every prayer is valued. As Psalm 34:17 states, "When the righteous cry for help, the LORD hears and delivers them," and 1 Peter 3:12 confirms, "The eyes of the Lord are on the righteous, and His ears are open to their prayer."

40.1 Defining Divine Attentiveness

Active Listening and Response: To say God is attentive means He not only hears but also actively responds to our needs. His attentiveness is deliberate and relational. Unlike an impersonal force, God listens intently—even to our unspoken thoughts—and answers according to His perfect will. His care spans every aspect of life: physical, emotional, spiritual, and relational.

Relational Engagement: Divine attentiveness highlights that God is not aloof; He is a loving Father who interacts with us personally. His readiness to listen transforms prayer from a mere ritual into an intimate conversation, where believers can share their joys, struggles, and hopes, confident that their Creator is always present.

40.2 Biblical Foundations

Old Testament Witness: The Old Testament is rich with examples of God's attentiveness. For instance, Psalm 34:17 assures that God hears the prayers of the righteous and delivers them from trouble. In Exodus, God responds to Moses' pleas for the Israelites, providing manna, water, and guidance even amid their recurring failures. Prophets like Daniel and Isaiah illustrate that God grants wisdom and insight to those who seek Him, underscoring that no need is too small to escape His notice.

New Testament Revelation: The New Testament amplifies this theme through Jesus Christ. His ministry is filled with compassionate acts: He heals the sick, comforts the sorrowful, and listens to those marginalized by society. In John 4, Jesus engages personally with the Samaritan woman, offering life-changing conversation and hope. His promise in Matthew 6:8 that "Your Father knows what you need before you ask" assures believers of His constant care. Furthermore, the Holy Spirit continues this work by indwelling believers, guiding and empowering them daily, proving that divine attentiveness endures beyond Christ's earthly ministry.

40.3 Theological Reflections

Attentiveness as an Expression of Love: God's attentiveness flows from His deep, unconditional love. It reflects a relational nature where every individual is cherished. This attribute assures us that God is not a remote judge but a compassionate Father who cares for our smallest concerns and our greatest challenges alike.

Prayer as Dynamic Relationship: Divine attentiveness transforms prayer into a dynamic relationship. As we converse with God, our prayers are met with thoughtful, often life-changing responses. Whether through gentle nudges, profound insights in Scripture, or miraculous interventions, God's replies are always tailored for our ultimate good, even when His timing differs from our expectations.

The Balance of Mystery and Clarity: While God's ways are beyond complete human understanding, His attentiveness provides clarity and reassurance. This balance invites us to trust Him even when we cannot see the full picture, fostering humility and continuous spiritual growth.

40.4 Common Misconceptions

Inconsistency vs. Divine Timing: Some may perceive delays in answers to prayer as inconsistency. However, God's responses follow His perfect wisdom and timing. What might seem like silence is often a period of preparation or refinement, ensuring that His eventual answer aligns with a greater, redemptive plan.

Over-Personalization: While it is comforting to think God listens exactly as we desire, His responses are not mere reflections of our wishes but are guided by His perfect understanding. His answers may differ from our expectations, always aiming for our deepest good—even if it requires a path we did not choose.

Manipulation vs. Relationship: Critics sometimes argue that if God is always listening, prayer becomes a tool for manipulation. In reality, prayer is not transactional but relational. God's attentiveness is a gift of His grace, inviting us into a transformative dialogue that is not based on our merit but on His unwavering love.

40.5 Pastoral and Practical Implications

Personal Comfort and Security: Believers find deep comfort in knowing that God is always listening. In times of distress—whether facing illness, loss, or emotional turmoil—this assurance replaces feelings of isolation with the promise of divine companionship. Pastoral care often emphasizes that even in silence, God is at work, guiding us toward healing and restoration.

Encouraging Persistent Prayer: Understanding God's constant attentiveness motivates a persistent prayer life. Believers are encouraged to pray continually, knowing that every heartfelt cry is heard. This persistence nurtures patience, resilience, and a deeper trust in God's providence, even when answers come gradually.

Transforming Relationships: The principle of divine attentiveness calls believers to mirror this care in their interactions. In families, workplaces, and communities, active, empathetic listening fosters understanding and reconciliation. When we truly hear one another, we reflect God's attentive nature and build bonds of mutual respect and compassion.

Empowering Community Worship: Church communities that embrace God's attentiveness cultivate environments of genuine support and unity. When congregants share their experiences of answered prayers and divine guidance, they reinforce the collective faith. This shared testimony of God's caring nature strengthens the community and serves as a powerful witness to the world.

Missional Impact: Belief in a God who is attentive to every need inspires global and local mission work. When Christians recognize that God hears even the faintest cry for help, they are moved to act on behalf of those who are voiceless. This commitment to social justice, humanitarian aid, and interfaith dialogue reflects the assurance that divine care extends to every corner of the world.

40.6 Global and Cultural Reflections

Universal Relevance: God's attentiveness is a truth that transcends cultural and national boundaries. The promise that He listens to every cry for help unites believers worldwide and offers hope to all who suffer. This universal care fosters interfaith dialogue and global cooperation, as diverse communities recognize the value of a loving, responsive Creator.

Shaping Societal Values: The idea that every need is noticed by God challenges societies to value empathy and accountability. When communities understand that no plea is too small, they are more likely to promote justice, transparency, and support for the vulnerable. This cultural shift encourages policies and practices that mirror divine care, emphasizing collective well-being over individual gain.

40.7 Personal and Community Transformation

Spiritual Maturity and Inner Healing: Experiencing God's attentiveness leads to profound personal transformation. As believers encounter divine care in moments of crisis and joy, they develop deeper resilience and gratitude. Spiritual disciplines such as prayer, meditation, and journaling foster an ongoing dialogue with God, encouraging continual growth and healing.

Cultivating a Lifestyle of Reflective Listening: Learning to listen to God's voice enhances our ability to listen to others. This practice transforms interpersonal relationships, fostering a culture of empathy and mutual support. Whether in family settings or church groups, active, compassionate listening builds trust and deepens community bonds.

Ambassadors of Divine Care: Living out the truth of God's attentiveness makes believers powerful witnesses. When our lives reflect the care and guidance of a loving God, others are drawn to the hope we embody. This testimony—through acts of kindness, ethical leadership, and unwavering faith—demonstrates that divine attentiveness is not abstract but is actively transforming lives.

In conclusion, the doctrine of divine attentiveness reveals a God who is intimately involved in every detail of creation. Far from being an indifferent force, He listens to every prayer, sees every need, and responds with wisdom, compassion, and grace. From the comforting assurances of Psalm 34:17 to the apostolic promises in 1 Peter 3:12, Scripture paints a portrait of a God whose attentive care is the bedrock of our hope and trust.

Understanding that God is always listening transforms our prayer life into a dynamic conversation with a loving Father. It reshapes our relationships, inspiring us to listen and respond with empathy, and it empowers communities to build supportive, united environments that reflect His care. Globally, this truth challenges cultures to value compassion and justice, inviting believers to engage in mission and social initiatives that uplift the vulnerable.

Ultimately, embracing divine attentiveness encourages us to live boldly, with integrity and hope. As we trust in the One who hears every cry and responds with perfect wisdom, we are transformed from within and become channels of His love in a world that so desperately needs to be heard. In this profound assurance, we find the courage to face every challenge, knowing that our God is always near, always caring, and always attentive to our every need.

Chapter 41: Intimate

The intimate nature of God reveals a relationship where He is not merely an abstract power but is deeply involved in every aspect of our lives. Scripture shows that God not only observes us from afar but knows our innermost thoughts and feelings and engages with us in a personal, compassionate way. This truth transforms our prayer, worship, and everyday interactions.

41.1 Understanding Divine Intimacy

Defining Divine Intimacy Divine intimacy means that God is not distant or impersonal; He is actively involved in every detail of our lives. It signifies that God is aware of our joys, sorrows, and even our unspoken needs. Unlike an impersonal force, God invites us into a genuine relationship. He listens, comforts, and guides us through all circumstances. This relational closeness is evident in how God speaks to us, as seen in Psalm 139, where the psalmist marvels, "You have searched me, LORD, and you know me."

The Depth of God's Knowledge God's knowledge is all-encompassing. He understands our thoughts and emotions completely and without error. This deep familiarity reassures us that nothing is hidden from Him. When Jesus said, "I know my own and my own know me" (John 10:14–15), He affirmed a relationship of mutual knowledge. God's intimate awareness invites us to trust Him with every part of our lives.

A Two-Way Relationship Divine intimacy is not one-sided; it is a dynamic, reciprocal relationship. God reveals Himself through creation, Scripture, and especially through Jesus Christ. In turn, He calls us to know Him more deeply through prayer, worship, and obedience. Our relationship with God grows as we learn to listen to His voice and respond with trust and love.

41.2 Biblical Foundations

Intimacy in the Old Testament The Old Testament provides many examples of God's intimate engagement with His people. God's personal relationship with Abraham, Moses, and the prophets shows that He desires closeness. For instance, when God called Abraham, He established a covenant filled with promise and personal dialogue. Likewise, Moses' encounter at the burning bush (Exodus 3) reveals a God who speaks directly, inviting personal transformation. Psalm 139 vividly portrays that God is present at every moment of our lives, from our waking hours to our quiet, private moments.

The Incarnation as Ultimate Revelation The New Testament reveals the fullest expression of divine intimacy in the Incarnation. In John 1:14, "the Word became flesh and dwelt among us" demonstrates that God chose to enter human experience in the person of Jesus. Throughout His ministry, Jesus showed compassion, healed the sick, and forgave sins, exemplifying a God who is deeply engaged with humanity. His interactions—whether with the Samaritan woman at the well or the outcast and the sinner—demonstrate that God values every individual enough to enter into their story.

The Indwelling of the Holy Spirit After Christ's ascension, the Holy Spirit continues to manifest God's intimate presence in believers' lives. The Spirit dwells within us, guiding, comforting, and empowering us for daily living and service. This ongoing indwelling assures us that divine intimacy is not confined to isolated moments but is a constant, nurturing reality.

41.3 Theological Reflections

Immaculate Knowledge and Love God's intimate knowledge is perfectly paired with His love. Unlike human knowledge, which is partial and flawed, God's understanding is complete and unconditional. This perfect insight enables Him to love us fully—even our hidden fears and struggles. Knowing that God sees and cares for every detail of our lives encourages us to live transparently and trustingly.

Mystery and Relationship While the fullness of God's nature remains a mystery, He still reveals Himself personally. This paradox—being both infinitely beyond our grasp and intimately near—invites a humble, ongoing quest for deeper relationship with Him. Our finite minds cannot capture all of His glory, but we are continually invited to experience His love and guidance.

The Role of Vulnerability True intimacy requires vulnerability. God's intimate engagement calls us to be honest about our weaknesses and open to His transforming love. When we share our inner struggles with God, we experience His compassionate response, which leads to healing and growth. Vulnerability is not a sign of weakness but a pathway to deeper spiritual transformation.

41.4 Common Misconceptions

Over-Familiarity vs. Reverence Some worry that describing God as intimate might lead to taking Him for granted. However, genuine intimacy deepens our reverence. Recognizing that God is so close to us should inspire heartfelt worship and disciplined devotion, not casual familiarity.

Self-Centeredness While God knows us intimately, His care extends to all creation. Divine intimacy invites us to value others equally, preventing a self-centered view. Our relationship with God encourages us to love our neighbors as ourselves, fostering a balanced and generous community.

Privacy and Divine Presence Another misconception is that God's intimacy means He invades our privacy. Instead, God respects our autonomy while offering His presence as a supportive companion. His intimate involvement is a gracious gift, freely given without compromising our personal space.

41.5 Pastoral and Practical Implications

Enriching Prayer and Worship Knowing that God is intimately involved in our lives transforms our prayer life into a genuine conversation. We can share our deepest concerns and joys with confidence that God listens and responds. Worship, then, becomes a time of both adoration and honest dialogue with our loving Father.

Healing and Restoration Divine intimacy provides profound comfort during personal crises. When we allow ourselves to be vulnerable before God, His loving care brings healing to broken hearts and mends fractured relationships. Pastoral counseling often emphasizes that no matter how deep our wounds, God's intimate presence offers hope and restoration.

Strengthening Community Church communities that embrace divine intimacy cultivate genuine fellowship. When members experience God's personal care, they are inspired to support one another through small groups, fellowship meals, and shared testimonies. This environment of mutual care fosters a resilient, compassionate community that reflects the heart of God.

Missional Impact Believers who encounter divine intimacy are compelled to share that transformative relationship with others. Mission work—both locally and globally—is driven by the desire to invite others into the same deep, personal connection with God. The testimony of a life touched by divine intimacy becomes a powerful witness to a loving and caring Creator.

41.6 Global and Cultural Dimensions

Universal Invitation to Intimacy God's intimate nature is a message for all people. Across cultures, the desire for a personal relationship with the divine is universal. This common ground encourages interfaith dialogue and mutual respect, as believers and others alike explore what it means to experience a loving, personal God.

Cultural Expressions of Divine Intimacy Art, music, and literature often capture the beauty of divine intimacy. Whether through reflective hymns, evocative poetry, or inspiring visual art, these cultural expressions remind us of God's nearness. They serve to deepen our appreciation for a God who is both transcendent in majesty and personal in care.

41.7 Personal and Communal Transformation

The Journey to Vulnerable Trust Embracing divine intimacy requires openness and vulnerability. As we share our true selves with God, we learn to trust Him more deeply. This journey transforms our inner life, leading to spiritual maturity and authentic relationships with others.

Living Authentically Knowing that God sees and loves every aspect of our being encourages us to live genuinely. Without pretense, we can embrace our flaws and strengths, and in doing so, reflect God's authentic care in our relationships.

Building a Supportive Community A church that values divine intimacy nurtures a culture of honest communication and mutual support. When individuals feel truly known and loved, they are more likely to extend that care to others, creating a ripple effect of healing and unity in the broader community.

In conclusion, the attribute of divine intimacy reveals a God who is deeply involved in every detail of our lives. Far from being a distant or indifferent force, God's personal nature is expressed in His comprehensive knowledge of us, His loving responses to our prayers, and His constant presence in our daily journey. From Psalm 139's intimate portrayal of God's all-encompassing awareness to Jesus' heartfelt interactions and the indwelling of the Holy Spirit, Scripture invites us into a relationship marked by vulnerability, trust, and transformative grace.

This intimate relationship reassures us in our moments of joy and sorrow, encourages us to live authentically, and calls us to extend that same love to others. It enriches our prayer life, deepens our worship, and strengthens our communities. Globally, the message of divine intimacy unites diverse cultures and offers hope for a world in need of compassionate connection.

As we journey through life, may we embrace the profound truth that God is intimately involved in every moment. In doing so, we find comfort, inspiration, and the courage to live authentically—reflecting the love of a God who knows us completely and cherishes us beyond measure.

Chapter 42: Victorious

The attribute of God as Victorious proclaims His complete triumph over sin, death, and every force of evil. This victory is not a temporary military win but an eternal conquest, securing our salvation and promising ultimate restoration. As 1 Corinthians 15:54–57 declares that "death is swallowed up in victory" and Revelation 19:11–16 portrays Christ's final, glorious defeat of wickedness, we understand that no adversary—visible or unseen—can ultimately prevail against God's redemptive plan.

42.1 Understanding Divine Victory

Defining Divine Victory To say God is victorious means that His power overcomes every enemy and all forms of evil with absolute certainty. His victory is the culmination of a cosmic battle against sin and death—a battle fought with perfect wisdom, justice, and love. Unlike human efforts, which can falter under pressure, God's triumph is complete, ensuring that chaos is transformed into order, despair into hope, and death into eternal life.

Overcoming Evil Divine victory is not merely about defeating evil; it is about redeeming and transforming it. God's triumph rescues and renews creation, turning every setback into an opportunity for redemption. Whether in historical events or our personal struggles, His victory reassures us that every moment of suffering is part of a larger, unerring plan that leads to ultimate restoration.

42.2 Biblical Foundations

Victory in 1 Corinthians 15:54–57 Paul's declaration in 1 Corinthians 15 captures the essence of divine victory. He teaches that when the perishable is clothed with the imperishable, death is defeated, and the power of sin is nullified. This passage assures believers that the resurrection of Christ is not only a past event but a present reality that empowers us to live boldly and hope confidently.

The Vision of Revelation 19 Revelation 19 vividly presents Jesus as the triumphant King riding a white horse. His eyes blaze with divine fire, and His word is like a sharp sword, symbolizing the decisive defeat of all opposition. This apocalyptic imagery serves as both a promise of future judgment against evil and a source of hope for the faithful, assuring us that no force can thwart God's eternal plan.

Victory Through the Incarnation and Resurrection The life, death, and resurrection of Jesus Christ are the ultimate demonstration of divine victory. Through His sacrificial death, Jesus bore the penalty of sin, and through His resurrection, He conquered death. This redemptive act is the foundation of Christian hope—confirming that every trial is temporary under the protective shadow of a victorious Savior.

42.3 Theological Reflections

The Nature of Divine Power Divine victory is rooted in God's infinite, unassailable power. Unlike human strength, which is often limited and unpredictable, God's power is perfect and all-encompassing. This power undergirds all acts of creation and redemption, ensuring that every event, no matter how chaotic it may seem, is part of a flawless divine design.

Interplay of Victory and Redemption God's triumph over evil is inseparable from His redemptive plan. The cross and resurrection of Christ reveal that divine victory is not an isolated act of force but a transformative process that redeems, restores, and reconciles. In this way, divine victory converts judgment into grace—ensuring that every defeat of evil brings forth renewed life and hope.

The Moral Imperative Understanding that God is victorious challenges believers to live in a way that reflects this truth. We are called to stand firm against sin, to embody moral courage, and to actively participate in God's redemptive work. Our lives should be a testimony to the power that overcomes every obstacle, transforming both personal struggles and societal injustices.

42.4 Addressing Common Misconceptions

Victory as a One-Time Event A common error is to view divine victory as confined solely to Christ's resurrection. However, the victory of God is ongoing—empowering believers to overcome daily challenges and continuously triumphing over sin. Christ's resurrection is the definitive act, yet its transformative power remains active in every aspect of our lives.

Misunderstanding Victory as Political or National Some mistakenly equate divine victory with political success or national triumph. Yet, God's victory is comprehensive—it encompasses spiritual, moral, and physical realms, transcending human divisions. It is a victory over all evil that unites believers from every culture and background.

The Danger of Complacency Another pitfall is the belief that divine victory removes the need for personal effort. Far from fostering passivity, the assurance of God's triumph should inspire us to pursue righteousness with determination. Knowing that God has overcome every enemy encourages us to actively resist sin and engage in transformative works in our communities.

42.5 Pastoral and Practical Implications

Finding Hope in God's Triumph For believers, the promise of divine victory offers profound comfort. In moments of personal crisis or collective injustice, the assurance that "death is swallowed up in victory" transforms despair into hope. This hope is not mere wishful thinking—it is rooted in the historical reality of Christ's resurrection and the ongoing power of God at work in our lives.

Empowering Daily Living The victorious nature of God equips us to face daily battles with courage. It provides the strength to resist temptation, overcome setbacks, and stand up for justice. When we trust in the same power that raised Christ from the dead, our personal struggles are met with divine support, inspiring resilience and moral clarity.

Transforming Communities Church communities that embrace the truth of God's victory become beacons of hope and renewal. They foster environments where members support one another in faith, work collectively against injustice, and embody the transformative power of the gospel. Such communities not only inspire individual confidence but also serve as powerful testimonies to the world that the forces of darkness are ultimately powerless before the light of Christ.

Global Impact The message of divine victory transcends cultural and national boundaries. In a world marked by conflict and despair, the promise that God overcomes every enemy inspires international humanitarian efforts, social justice movements, and interfaith dialogues. This global vision of victory offers a counter-narrative to prevailing ideologies of defeat, challenging us to work together for a future defined by peace, reconciliation, and the triumph of good over evil.

42.6 Personal Transformation and the Call to Victory

The Journey to Spiritual Renewal Embracing divine victory is a transformative journey that reshapes our character and fortifies our faith. Recognizing that the power that defeated sin and death is at work within us inspires a mindset of hope and perseverance. This internal transformation leads us to overcome personal weaknesses, resist destructive patterns, and cultivate a spirit of gratitude for God's unending care.

Living as Ambassadors of Victory Believers are called to be living testimonies of God's victorious power. This means actively engaging in acts of kindness, ethical leadership, and social advocacy that reflect the redemptive work of Christ. As ambassadors of victory, our lives become a powerful witness that, no matter the challenge, God's triumph brings healing, justice, and renewal.

A Call to Active Participation The promise of divine victory is not a passive assurance but a dynamic call to action. It invites us to contribute to God's redemptive work in every sphere—be it in our families, workplaces, or communities. By living with the confidence that God's plan is unfailing, we are motivated to pursue righteousness, support the vulnerable, and work for a society that mirrors the values of God's kingdom.

In conclusion, the attribute of God as Victorious stands as a cornerstone of Christian hope and identity. Scripture—from 1 Corinthians 15's triumphant declaration to Revelation's vivid portrayal of Christ's final victory—confirms that no enemy or force of evil can thwart God's redemptive plan. This eternal victory empowers us to face life's struggles with courage, inspires us to live ethically, and transforms our communities into bastions of hope.

For the individual believer, the assurance of divine victory provides comfort and strength in the midst of adversity. It reminds us that every trial is temporary and that the same power that raised Christ from the dead is at work within us, turning setbacks into opportunities for growth. In community, this truth fosters unity and collective action, encouraging us to support one another and advocate for justice and reconciliation.

Globally, the message of God's victory challenges prevailing narratives of defeat and despair, inviting us to work together for a just and compassionate world. As we live in the light of divine victory, our lives become a living testimony of the transformative power of God—a power that overcomes sin, redeems the broken, and ushers in an eternal future of peace and glory.

May we, therefore, embrace the call to live victoriously, confident in the promise that our God reigns supreme, and let our lives reflect the indomitable hope that comes from knowing that, in every battle, the Lord is triumphant forevermore.

Chapter 43: Protector

Scripture assures us that God is our steadfast Protector—a shield who guards us against every danger and uncertainty. From the psalmist's declaration, "The LORD is my rock and my fortress" (Psalm 18:2), to the promise in Proverbs 18:10 that "The name of the LORD is a strong tower; the righteous run into it and are safe," we learn that God's protection covers not only our physical safety but our spiritual, emotional, and relational well-being. This chapter examines the biblical, theological, and practical dimensions of God's protective care, addressing common misconceptions and exploring how embracing this truth transforms personal faith and community life.

43.1 Understanding Divine Protection

The Essence of Divine Protection God's protection means more than keeping physical harm at bay—it is a comprehensive guardianship that sustains and restores. He actively shields His people from both visible and unseen threats through a commitment rooted in His unchanging covenant. His protection offers believers a secure refuge in the midst of life's battles, assuring them that they never face adversity alone.

A Shield for Every Sphere of Life God's protective care spans every aspect of existence. Whether confronting external dangers like warfare or internal struggles such as despair and moral failure, His safeguarding reaches into every area of life. The imagery of a "fortress" and "strong tower" illustrates that in every crisis—be it personal, familial, or societal—believers can run to God for safety and deliverance.

43.2 Biblical Foundations of Divine Protection

Old Testament Foundations The Old Testament consistently presents God as a protector. Psalm 18:2 portrays Him as an unmovable rock and a deliverer who rescues His people from overwhelming foes. Similarly, Proverbs 18:10 highlights that God's name itself is a reliable refuge. Throughout Israel's history—from the dramatic deliverance at the Red Sea to His guidance in the wilderness—God's intervention demonstrates that no enemy, whether human or spiritual, can overcome His protective hand.

New Testament Affirmations In the New Testament, Jesus' ministry vividly illustrates divine protection. He healed the sick, calmed storms, and raised the dead, showing that His power over nature and evil is unmatched. Jesus reassured His disciples with the promise that, as they trust in Him, they will find refuge even amid trials. The early church, too, experienced God's protection through miraculous deliverances, as seen in Acts with Peter's escape from prison, reinforcing that God's guardianship is both personal and active.

43.3 Theological Reflections on Divine Protection

Protection Amidst Suffering While believers do face trials and even persecution, God's protection guarantees that no ultimate harm can befall them. As Paul reminds us in Romans 8:31—"If God is for us, who can be against us?"—the protective care of God turns even the harshest challenges into opportunities for growth and spiritual refinement. His protection is not a promise of a trouble-free life, but an assurance that every trial serves a greater redemptive purpose.

Balancing Free Will and Divine Guardianship Some ask why, if God is our Protector, suffering still exists. The answer lies in the balance between divine protection and human free will. God permits human choices and the consequences of a fallen world, yet His sovereign care ensures that these actions never thwart His ultimate plan. His protective presence weaves even our pain into a larger tapestry of redemption.

43.4 Common Misconceptions

"God as a Cosmic Bodyguard" A common misunderstanding is to view God as a mere "bodyguard" who prevents all harm. This perspective can lead to a prosperity-gospel mentality, where faith is measured by the absence of suffering. However, Scripture shows that while God protects us, He also allows challenges that refine our faith and character. His protection is not a guarantee of an effortless life but a promise of ultimate security and eternal deliverance.

Limited to Physical Protection Another error is to reduce God's protection solely to physical safety. Yet the Bible speaks of God shielding our minds, hearts, and spirits from despair, shame, and moral decay. His care extends to the emotional and spiritual realms, providing inner peace and guiding believers toward righteousness.

Negating Personal Responsibility Some mistakenly believe that if God protects us, we need not act prudently. However, biblical teaching encourages vigilance and wisdom alongside reliance on God. Believers are called to "be wise as serpents and innocent as doves" (Matthew 10:16), which means partnering with God's protective work by making thoughtful, ethical decisions.

43.5 Pastoral and Practical Implications

Comfort in Trials The promise of God's protection offers profound comfort during life's storms. When faced with illness, loss, or injustice, believers can draw strength from the assurance that God's unfailing care will see them through. Pastoral counseling often emphasizes that, though hardships are real, they are temporary and ultimately part of a divine plan that transforms suffering into hope.

Motivating Obedience and Moral Living Understanding that God is our Protector instills a sense of responsibility and ethical clarity. When we recognize that our security rests in His unchangeable nature, we are motivated to live righteously—making choices that honor His guidance and reflect His character.

Building Strong Communities Churches that embrace God's protective nature cultivate environments of mutual care and accountability. When members trust in a God who is a steadfast shield, they are more willing to support one another through prayer, counseling, and practical help. This communal reliance strengthens bonds and creates a unified witness to the world.

Empowering Global Mission and Social Justice The conviction that God protects the vulnerable drives believers to advocate for justice and peace. Global humanitarian efforts, social justice movements, and interfaith collaborations often draw on the assurance of divine protection to challenge oppression and support those in need. By mirroring God's protective love, Christians become instruments of hope in a fractured world.

43.6 Global and Cultural Reflections

Universal Relevance God's protective care transcends cultural, national, and religious boundaries. From war-torn regions to impoverished communities, the promise that "God is our refuge and strength" (Psalm 46:1) offers a universal message of hope. This truth unites believers worldwide and serves as a foundation for international peace and humanitarian initiatives.

Cultural Expressions of Protection Different cultures have their own traditions of seeking protection and refuge. When Christians share the biblical vision of God as Protector, it resonates across these diverse contexts, providing common ground for interfaith dialogue and mutual support. Testimonies of miraculous deliverance and personal rescue serve as powerful evangelistic tools, highlighting the tangible reality of God's care.

43.7 Personal Transformation Through Divine Protection

Overcoming Fear and Insecurity Embracing God as our Protector transforms personal fear into confidence. Believers who internalize the truth that no threat—whether physical, emotional, or spiritual—can overcome God's ultimate care develop resilience and courage. This secure foundation helps shift the focus from self-reliance to trust in the Almighty.

Empowering a Life of Purpose and Service Recognizing God's protective hand inspires believers to engage actively in their communities and the world. When we know that we are shielded by a loving God, we are emboldened to take righteous risks, stand up against injustice, and serve the marginalized. Our actions become an extension of divine protection, transforming personal struggles into opportunities for ministry and outreach.

Cultivating Gratitude and Worship Every instance of deliverance—big or small—reinforces the reality of God's protection, fostering a spirit of gratitude. Personal and corporate worship that acknowledges God's safeguarding presence nurtures a deep, abiding trust and motivates us to share that assurance with others. As we recount stories of rescue and renewal, our collective testimony becomes a beacon of hope and unity.

In conclusion, the biblical portrayal of God as our Protector offers profound assurance and hope amid life's uncertainties. From the steadfast metaphors of Psalm 18 and Proverbs 18 to the narrative of deliverance throughout Scripture, we learn that God's care extends over every realm of our existence—physical, spiritual, emotional, and relational. His protective presence is not a guarantee of a trouble-free life, but a promise that no threat can ultimately derail His redemptive plan.

Understanding God as Protector transforms how we face adversity, motivating us to live with courage, ethical integrity, and a deep sense of community. This truth provides personal comfort in times of distress, inspires proactive ministry and social justice, and unites believers across cultures and nations under a common banner of divine care.

As we embrace this protective reality, our lives become a testament to a God who is not distant but intimately involved in every struggle and joy. We are empowered to face challenges with unwavering confidence, knowing that our future is secure in His mighty hands. In every prayer, every act of service, and every moment of vulnerability, we can rest in the promise that the Almighty is our steadfast shield—a refuge in which we find strength, healing, and hope.

Chapter 44: Unstoppable (Irresistible in Will)

God's will is utterly unstoppable—no force, whether human, spiritual, or cosmic, can thwart His divine purpose. Rooted in Scriptures like Job 42:2 ("I know that you can do all things, and that no purpose of yours can be thwarted") and Isaiah 46:10 ("My counsel shall stand, and I will accomplish all my purpose"), this doctrine assures us that God's plans are unfailing and His authority supreme. Unlike human efforts, which often stumble under limitations, God's will proceeds with perfect wisdom, infinite resources, and absolute moral integrity, shaping history and individual lives for ultimate redemption.

44.1 Understanding Divine Unstoppability

Defining Unstoppable Will To say that God is "unstoppable" means that every purpose He initiates will inevitably come to pass. This isn't about blind force but a reflection of His infinite wisdom, justice, and love. His will brings about the ultimate good for creation and the glory of His name. Even in the midst of human failure and opposition, God's decree remains unwavering and thoroughly righteous.

The Scope of Divine Sovereignty God's unstoppable will is an outworking of His complete sovereignty. He governs the entire cosmos with authority that transcends all earthly powers. His control isn't exercised by brute force but through a masterful orchestration of events and relationships that fulfill His redemptive plan. No matter the scale of opposition—be it demonic rebellion, human sin, or natural disaster—His purposes persist, weaving even the darkest events into a grand tapestry of redemption.

44.2 Biblical Foundations of Divine Victory

Victory in 1 Corinthians 15:54–57 Paul proclaims in 1 Corinthians 15:54–57 that "when the perishable has been clothed with the imperishable... death has been swallowed up in victory." This passage encapsulates the Christian hope: through Christ's resurrection, death—the ultimate enemy—is defeated. Paul presents this victory as both a future promise and a present reality, empowering believers to live with boldness, knowing that God's redemptive plan is active in our midst.

The Apocalyptic Vision in Revelation 19:11–16 Revelation 19:11–16 offers a dramatic image of Christ as the conquering King, riding a white horse with eyes like blazing fire and a sword from His mouth. This vivid portrayal confirms that every force of evil will ultimately be subdued under His righteous rule. It serves both as a comfort to believers and a sober warning to those who oppose God's will.

Victory Through the Incarnation and Resurrection The life, death, and resurrection of Jesus Christ stand as the definitive demonstration of divine victory. In becoming human, Jesus confronted sin and death head-on. His sacrificial death paid the penalty for sin, and His resurrection conquered death. This redemptive act guarantees that no setback or sorrow can thwart God's transformative power, ensuring that His purposes are achieved both in history and in the lives of believers today.

44.3 Theological Reflections

Integrating Sovereignty, Omnipotence, and Love Divine victory reflects the harmonious interplay of God's sovereignty, omnipotence, and love. His power is perfect and eternal, ensuring that every act of creation and redemption is flawless. Yet, this power is never exercised without love—His victorious will is aimed at restoring and redeeming creation, not oppressing it. Christ's humble yet triumphant journey on the cross exemplifies this balance: divine power meets sacrificial love, conquering sin through mercy.

Human Agency and Divine Will While God's will is unstoppable, humans still exercise genuine moral responsibility. The unstoppable nature of divine purpose sets the grand narrative of redemption, but individual choices matter within that framework. This tension invites believers to align their lives with God's plan without undermining their freedom. Our decisions contribute to the unfolding story of salvation, even as God's ultimate purposes remain unalterable.

Eschatological Fulfillment The promise of divine victory culminates in the eschatological vision where every enemy is vanquished and God's kingdom is fully realized (see Revelation 19:11–16). This future hope reassures believers that, despite present challenges, God's triumph is assured. It calls us to live righteously, persevere through trials, and work for justice and peace, knowing that our efforts are part of an eternal, unstoppable plan.

44.4 Addressing Common Misconceptions

Victory as a One-Time Event vs. Ongoing Reality Some mistakenly view Christ's resurrection as a singular historical event, but divine victory is continuous. It empowers us daily to overcome struggles, knowing that the triumph of God is an ever-present force sustaining our lives.

Not Merely Political or National Divine victory transcends political or national boundaries. It is not about one nation's triumph but the complete overcoming of sin, evil, and death for all who believe. This universal scope of victory unites believers across cultures and underscores the global relevance of the gospel.

Avoiding Complacency Assuming that God's victory negates the need for personal effort is another error. While divine victory assures us of the final outcome, it challenges us to actively resist sin and pursue holiness. The promise of victory fuels our perseverance, inspiring us to engage in both personal and communal transformation.

44.5 Pastoral and Practical Implications

Finding Hope in Adversity Believers gain immense comfort knowing that God's victorious plan is unassailable. In times of personal crisis or societal turmoil, the assurance that "death has been swallowed up in victory" transforms despair into hope. Pastoral care often emphasizes that no challenge, however daunting, can derail the redemptive work of Christ.

Empowering Ethical Living Understanding God's unstoppable will compels us to live ethically. When we know that our actions are part of an unbreakable divine plan, we are motivated to pursue integrity, compassion, and justice. Our lives become a testimony to the transformative power of divine victory, influencing our personal choices and public engagements.

Building Unity Within the Church Church communities that embrace divine victory experience a deep sense of unity. Sharing in the assurance that God's ultimate plan cannot be thwarted dissolves internal divisions and inspires collaborative mission. United in purpose, believers support one another and collectively work toward a just and redeemed world.

Global Engagement and Social Transformation On a global scale, the message of divine victory challenges prevailing narratives of despair. It encourages international efforts in humanitarian aid, peace-building, and social justice, as believers trust that no oppression or injustice can withstand the power of God's redemptive plan. This conviction fuels movements for systemic change, underscoring that every act of service aligns with an eternal, victorious purpose.

44.6 Personal Transformation and the Call to Victory

Overcoming Personal Limitations Embracing divine victory inspires us to overcome our own limitations. Knowing that the same power that raised Christ is at work within us, we are encouraged to step beyond fear and failure. This internal transformation leads to greater resilience, deeper faith, and a more purposeful pursuit of holiness.

Living as Ambassadors of Victory Believers are called to reflect the victorious nature of God in their daily lives. This means standing firm against injustice, advocating for truth, and demonstrating love in the face of adversity. As ambassadors of Christ's victory, our lives serve as a powerful witness to a world in need of redemption.

Cultivating an Eternal Perspective Understanding that God's victorious plan transcends present struggles encourages us to adopt an eternal perspective. Life's setbacks become temporary hurdles in a grand narrative leading to eternal restoration. This eternal hope empowers us to live with courage and to pursue lasting change, both personally and communally.

In conclusion, the doctrine of divine victory proclaims that God's will is irresistible and His redemptive plan is unfailing. From Paul's triumphant declaration in 1 Corinthians 15 to the apocalyptic vision in Revelation 19, Scripture assures us that no force—human, spiritual, or cosmic—can thwart God's purposes. This truth transforms our lives by infusing us with hope, resilience, and a commitment to ethical living.

Understanding that God is victorious reassures us that every trial, every setback, is part of a grand, unchangeable design. It motivates us to act boldly in our personal lives, to build communities rooted in unity and justice, and to engage globally in the pursuit of peace and transformation.

As ambassadors of Christ's victory, we are invited to live in unwavering confidence, knowing that our struggles are temporary and that the ultimate end of all things is secured in God's eternal plan. May our lives reflect the unstoppable, redemptive power of a God who conquers sin, death, and every force of evil, and may we continually draw strength from the assurance that, indeed, His victory is everlasting.

Chapter 45: Supreme Authority

God's supreme authority is a central tenet of Christian theology. It proclaims that God is the ultimate power over every realm—spiritual and material—and that His sovereign rule is both personal and purposeful. This authority is not distant or arbitrary; rather, it is exercised in perfect justice, love, and wisdom, guiding history and individual lives toward redemption. Scriptures like Psalm 47:2 ("For the LORD, the Most High, is to be feared, a great king over all the earth") and Matthew 28:18 ("All authority in heaven and on earth has been given to me") affirm that no part of creation lies outside God's governance.

45.1 Understanding Supreme Authority

Defining Supreme Authority

To say that God possesses supreme authority means that His power and governance are unmatched by any human or spiritual force. This authority implies not just raw power but the legitimate right to rule, grounded in divine holiness, justice, and love. God's authority underpins every aspect of existence—from the laws of nature to the moral order—because He is the Creator who spoke the universe into being and continues to sustain it.

Power, Right, and Love Intertwined

God's authority is exercised with a balance of power, moral rightness, and compassion. Unlike human rulers, who may falter or become corrupt, God's rule is characterized by perfect justice and benevolence. His authority is not coercive but redemptive; He governs not to subjugate but to nurture, restore, and transform His creation. This divine leadership invites relationship, urging humanity to live in alignment with His righteous and loving will.

45.2 Biblical Foundations

Old Testament: God as King of All

The Old Testament frequently depicts God as the supreme King. Psalm 47:2 declares that "the LORD, the Most High, is to be feared, a great king over all the earth," highlighting His universal dominion. From the creation narrative in Genesis to the deliverance of Israel from Egypt and the giving of the Law at Sinai, God's sovereign interventions show that His word governs nature and history. Even when earthly powers challenge Him—like Pharaoh's resistance or rebellious kings—God's authority ultimately prevails, demonstrating that no human institution can rival His eternal reign.

New Testament: The Authority of Christ

The New Testament amplifies the concept of divine authority through Jesus Christ. In Matthew 28:18, the resurrected Christ asserts that "all authority in heaven and on earth has been given to me," indicating that He shares fully in the divine sovereignty. Jesus' miracles, teachings, and acts of healing consistently reveal a power that commands nature, delivers from demonic forces, and forgives sins. His commission to make disciples of all nations is founded on this authority, affirming that the church's mission is an extension of God's unstoppable governance. Paul's letters further affirm that every knee will bow to Christ (Philippians 2:9–11), reinforcing that His rule is universal and unchallenged.

Eschatological Fulfillment

The final victory of God's authority is vividly portrayed in the Book of Revelation. In Revelation 19:11–16, Christ is depicted as a conquering King, whose authority is recognized by all creation at the final judgment. This apocalyptic vision assures believers that, although earthly powers may rise and fall, the ultimate resolution of history is secured by the unassailable rule of God.

45.3 Theological Reflections

Sovereignty, Freedom, and Love

Divine authority encompasses both the irresistible power of God and His benevolent, just nature. Although some argue that absolute power negates human free will, many theologians maintain that God's sovereign plan incorporates genuine human responsibility. Our choices have real moral weight, yet they are ultimately woven into God's redemptive narrative. His authority, exercised through love, invites us into partnership rather than mere subjugation.

The Infallibility of Divine Will

God's supreme authority is inseparable from the infallibility of His will. His decisions and plans are executed without error because they flow from an infinitely wise and morally perfect nature. Even when we face chaos or injustice, we can trust that God's unerring plan will prevail—a truth powerfully demonstrated in the resurrection of Christ, which transformed apparent defeat into triumphant victory.

45.4 Addressing Misconceptions

Authority Versus Love

Some mistakenly believe that authority implies domination, while love implies gentleness, viewing these as contradictory. However, biblical revelation shows that God's authority is always exercised in love. His rulership is characterized by justice, mercy, and the desire to restore rather than oppress. Christ's leadership, for example, is marked by humility and self-sacrifice, which redefines authority as a force for service and redemption.

Human Autonomy and Divine Control

Another concern is that God's supreme authority undermines human freedom. Yet Scripture teaches that while God's overarching plan is unchangeable, human beings still possess genuine agency and moral responsibility. Our choices contribute to the unfolding of God's redemptive history, and our free will is integrated into His sovereign design without compromising His ultimate control.

Coercion Versus Persuasion

Critics sometimes equate divine authority with coercion, suggesting that an all-powerful God would force obedience. In reality, God's authority is persuasive rather than manipulative. He invites, warns, and calls His people to repentance, respecting the dignity of human freedom while ensuring that His final judgment aligns with His righteous, unyielding plan.

45.5 Pastoral and Practical Implications

Reassurance in Adversity

Understanding that God's authority is supreme provides immense comfort in times of crisis—whether during personal hardship, societal conflict, or global turmoil. When we face challenges, we can rest in the assurance that our lives are under the care of a sovereign God who orchestrates every detail for ultimate good. This trust transforms suffering into a stage for divine intervention, encouraging perseverance and hope.

Motivating Obedience and Ethical Living

Acknowledging God's supreme authority motivates believers to live with integrity and moral clarity. When we recognize that the commands of Scripture come from the ultimate King, obedience becomes an act of heartfelt devotion rather than mere rule-following. This commitment to righteousness influences our personal decisions, business practices, and public engagements, ensuring that our lives reflect the unchangeable standard of divine justice and love.

Fostering Unity in the Church

Church communities that embrace divine sovereignty experience profound unity. Knowing that all members are under the same ultimate authority dissolves divisions based on ego or social status. Such a community, united in its mission, can more effectively address internal conflicts and engage in collective mission work. This shared confidence in God's authority strengthens the church's witness to the world and fosters an environment of mutual support and cooperation.

Engaging Culture with Confidence

When believers engage with broader culture, the recognition of God's supreme authority provides a solid foundation for addressing moral and ethical issues. It encourages Christians to speak truth to power and advocate for justice and peace without resorting to hostility. By representing a standard that is higher than any earthly system, we can influence public discourse and promote policies that reflect eternal values.

45.6 Global and Cultural Dimensions

Universal Scope of Divine Authority

God's authority is universal, extending over all cultures, nations, and peoples. Scriptures affirm that no part of creation is outside His dominion. This universal reign calls believers to engage globally with a message that transcends national and cultural boundaries. Christian missions and global humanitarian efforts are rooted in the conviction that divine authority provides a foundation for justice and peace across all human societies.

Inspiring Intercultural Dialogue and Reform

The doctrine of divine supremacy challenges prevailing narratives of power and corruption. It inspires movements for social reform, peace-building, and human rights, encouraging global cooperation to address injustice. Recognizing that true authority is rooted in divine, unchanging truth motivates believers to promote ethical standards that honor human dignity and foster unity among diverse communities.

45.7 Personal Transformation and the Call to Victory

Overcoming Fear and Anxiety

On a personal level, understanding that God's authority is supreme diminishes fear and anxiety. When we know that every event—whether a personal setback or a global crisis—is part of God's unerring plan, we find peace and courage to face adversity. Daily prayer and reflection on God's sovereignty can reshape our outlook, enabling us to navigate challenges with confidence and resilience.

Living with Purpose and Resilience

Believers are encouraged to see their lives as integral parts of God's grand narrative. This understanding imparts purpose to our daily actions, transforming even setbacks into opportunities for growth. Trusting in divine sovereignty inspires bold, ethical living, motivating us to work for justice and peace, and to serve others as part of God's redemptive mission.

45.8 Embracing an Eternal Perspective

Eschatological Fulfillment

The promise of God's supreme authority reaches its climax in the eschatological vision of a restored creation, where every knee bows and every tongue confesses that Christ is Lord (Philippians 2:10–11). This ultimate fulfillment reassures believers that despite present struggles, the final outcome is secure under the divine reign. It transforms our present trials into steps toward an eternal, unshakable kingdom.

Living with Eternal Confidence

Embracing divine supremacy equips us to face life's uncertainties with eternal assurance. While political powers and cultural trends may shift, our faith rests on the unchangeable will of God. This eternal perspective reorients our priorities, inspiring us to invest our time, talents, and resources in endeavors that reflect a higher, lasting truth. It gives us the resilience to endure and the hope to act boldly, knowing that our efforts are part of an everlasting plan.

In conclusion, the doctrine of God's supreme authority is foundational to Christian faith, affirming that no force can thwart His redemptive plan. From the Old Testament's declarations to the New Testament's portrayal of Christ's authority and the eschatological promises of Revelation, Scripture presents a God whose rule is absolute, righteous, and infused with love. This truth offers profound comfort amid life's challenges, motivates ethical and purposeful living, and unites the church in a common mission.

By understanding that every facet of our existence is under the governance of a sovereign and loving Creator, believers can face adversity with confidence and work for a world that reflects divine justice and mercy. This doctrine not only shapes our personal lives but also inspires global efforts for peace and reform, reminding us that true authority is eternal and transformative.

As we journey through life, may we continually affirm that God's supreme authority is our rock, our guide, and our ultimate hope—a reality that calls us to live with unwavering faith, steadfast integrity, and a passion for justice that echoes the eternal reign of our righteous King.

Chapter 46: Absolute

God's attribute of being "Absolute" declares that He is entirely self-sufficient, independent, and unerring in His word and will. Unlike created beings who depend on external factors and are prone to error, God's nature is the ultimate standard of truth, power, and goodness. His declarations are final and unchallengeable, as seen in Scriptures such as Isaiah 46:10—"My counsel shall stand, and I will accomplish all my purpose"—and Psalm 135:6—"Whatever the LORD pleases, he does, in heaven and on earth, in the seas and all deeps." In this chapter, we explore the nature, biblical foundations, theological significance, common misconceptions, and practical implications of divine absoluteness.

46.1 Understanding Divine Absoluteness

Defining "Absolute"

To call God "Absolute" is to affirm that He is the ultimate foundation of all reality, independent and self-derived. God's being is not contingent on anything external; His existence, wisdom, and will come from Himself alone. This renders His authority, judgments, and promises unassailable. Unlike human decisions, which are subject to error and change, every word and deed of God is flawless and permanent.

Self-Sufficiency and Sovereignty

God's self-sufficiency means that He requires nothing to sustain His power or guide His actions. As the Creator and Sustainer, He exercises supreme authority over every aspect of existence—from the laws of nature to the moral order governing human life. His rule is exercised with moral perfection, ensuring that His decrees always align with justice, love, and righteousness.

Authority with Love

Divine absoluteness is not harsh or arbitrary; it is expressed through benevolence and redemptive love. God's power is wielded not to oppress but to protect, nurture, and redeem. His authoritative commands are the basis for our moral order, yet they invite us into a loving relationship rather than a mere exercise of force.

46.2 Biblical Foundations

Old Testament Witness

The Old Testament frequently highlights God's unchallengeable rule. In Psalm 47:2, we read that "the LORD, the Most High, is to be feared, a great king over all the earth." From creation in Genesis—where God speaks the universe into order—to Israel's deliverance from Egypt and the giving of the Law at Sinai, Scripture affirms that God's word governs all of history. Even when human rulers defy Him, God's sovereign plan ultimately prevails, proving that no earthly power can rival His.

New Testament Affirmation

The New Testament intensifies this message in the person of Jesus Christ. In Matthew 28:18, the resurrected Jesus declares, "All authority in heaven and on earth has been given to me." His miracles, teachings, and sacrificial death underscore that divine authority extends to every corner of creation. Paul's letters reinforce that Christ is supreme (Colossians 1:16–20) and that every knee shall bow (Philippians 2:9–11), assuring believers that His rule is absolute and eternal.

Eschatological Fulfillment

The ultimate expression of divine authority appears in the Book of Revelation, where Christ is depicted as the victorious King who defeats all opposition. This final vision confirms that God's unyielding plan will culminate in a restored creation—a future where every power and rebellion is subdued under His eternal reign.

46.3 Theological Reflections

Integrating Sovereignty, Freedom, and Love

God's absolute authority intertwines with His sovereignty, omnipotence, and love. While His power is limitless, it is exercised with perfect justice and compassion. Though human beings have genuine freedom, our choices are ultimately woven into God's redemptive narrative. His absolute will provides the framework within which human agency operates meaningfully, ensuring that even our failures contribute to a greater, unchangeable plan.

Infallibility of Divine Will

Because God is absolute, His will is infallible. His declarations, promises, and actions are free from error and doubt. Even in the presence of evil and suffering, God's perfect plan moves steadily toward its redemptive end. The resurrection of Christ is the decisive demonstration that no force—however dark—can thwart God's ultimate purpose.

46.4 Addressing Common Misconceptions

Authority Versus Love

A common error is to see authority as synonymous with domination. However, God's absolute authority is exercised in love. His reign is marked by justice and mercy; He calls us to follow Him not through coercion but through an invitation to relationship. Christ's ministry exemplifies this balance—He heals, forgives, and redeems, showing that divine authority is both commanding and compassionate.

Human Autonomy and Divine Control

Some fear that God's absolute rule negates human freedom. Yet, Scripture clearly teaches that while God's ultimate plan is unchangeable, humans still make meaningful choices with real moral consequences. This balance affirms that our free will operates within the secure framework of God's sovereign design.

Coercion vs. Persuasion

Another misconception is that absolute authority equates to coercion. God's rule does not force obedience; instead, He persuades and invites. His commands are given out of love and a desire for our ultimate good, allowing us the freedom to choose while ensuring that His redemptive purposes prevail.

46.5 Pastoral and Practical Implications

Reassurance in Trials

Believers find comfort in knowing that no matter the adversity—illness, financial hardship, or relational strife—God's supreme authority remains unshaken. This truth transforms our suffering into a context for divine intervention, assuring us that every trial is under the watchful eye of a loving, sovereign God.

Motivation for Obedience and Ethical Living

Recognizing God's ultimate authority instills a deep sense of moral responsibility. When we understand that God's commands are unerring, our obedience becomes an act of love and trust rather than mere duty. This conviction inspires ethical living, compelling us to pursue justice, integrity, and compassion in all areas of life.

Building Unity in the Church

Churches that embrace divine authority experience profound unity. Knowing that every member answers to the same ultimate King dissolves divisions and fosters mutual submission and collaboration. This unified community becomes a powerful witness to the world, showcasing a collective commitment to God's unassailable, redemptive plan.

Engaging Culture with Confidence

In public life, the recognition of God's supreme authority empowers believers to engage with society confidently. Rather than being swayed by transient cultural trends, Christians can advocate for justice, peace, and ethical governance, assured that their efforts align with a higher, eternal standard.

46.6 Global and Cultural Dimensions

Universal Scope of Authority

God's absolute authority extends over every culture, nation, and aspect of creation. This universality challenges human leaders and institutions, affirming that no earthly power can rival the sovereign rule of the Creator. Christian missions and global humanitarian efforts are inspired by this truth, as believers seek to reflect divine justice and mercy worldwide.

Influencing Global Movements

The message of divine supremacy galvanizes movements for peace, social justice, and reconciliation. By upholding the belief that all of history is guided by an unchangeable divine purpose, Christians can confront corruption and oppression with hope and determination, knowing that every act of resistance is part of a larger, unstoppable plan.

46.7 Personal Transformation and the Call to Victory

Overcoming Fear and Anxiety

On a personal level, the assurance of God's absolute authority diminishes fear and anxiety. Recognizing that every event unfolds according to God's perfect plan brings peace and resilience, enabling believers to navigate life's uncertainties with unwavering confidence.

Living with Purpose and Resilience

Understanding that our lives are woven into God's grand narrative transforms our outlook. Every challenge becomes an opportunity to serve and glorify the Creator, fostering resilience and a sense of purpose that propels us to act for justice and compassion.

46.8 Embracing the Eternal Perspective

Eschatological Fulfillment

The ultimate manifestation of God's supreme authority is seen in the eschatological vision where every knee bows and every tongue confesses (Philippians 2:10–11). This future promise assures believers that, despite present hardships, God's final victory over sin and death is guaranteed, offering hope that transcends all temporal challenges.

Living with Eternal Confidence

Embracing divine supremacy shifts our focus from the transient to the eternal. Our decisions, relationships, and efforts gain lasting significance as we trust in a God whose authority is absolute and whose plan is unchangeable. This eternal perspective equips us to live boldly and ethically, knowing that our lives are part of an everlasting, redemptive story.

In conclusion, the doctrine of God's supreme authority affirms that no power—human, spiritual, or cosmic—can thwart His unerring, redemptive plan. From the Old Testament's declaration of God as the great King over all the earth to the New Testament's revelation of Christ's all-encompassing power, Scripture portrays a God whose authority is absolute, righteous, and expressed through love.

This truth provides profound comfort and hope amid personal and global crises, motivates ethical and purposeful living, and unifies the church in a shared mission. By recognizing that every aspect of our existence is governed by a sovereign, loving Creator, we are empowered to face life's challenges with confidence and resilience. Our faith is anchored in the certainty that no adversity can derail God's plan and that every effort aligned with His will carries eternal significance.

Ultimately, embracing divine supremacy calls us to live as ambassadors of a righteous King—engaging culture with humility, standing firm in our convictions, and working tirelessly for justice and peace. In doing so, we not only reflect God's unchangeable authority but also participate in His everlasting purpose, secure in the promise that His redemptive reign will prevail forever.

Chapter 47: Creative

God's creative nature is at the very heart of Christian belief. From the opening verse of Genesis—"In the beginning, God created the heavens and the earth"—to the worshipful declaration in Revelation, Scripture reveals a God whose creativity is both foundational and ongoing. This attribute is not merely about the initial act of creation but also about the continual sustenance and renewal of all that exists. Understanding God as the ultimate Creator helps us appreciate His purpose, order, and the inherent beauty in the world around us, while also inspiring us to use our own creative gifts in ways that honor Him.

47.1 The Scope of Divine Creativity

Creator of All

The Bible begins by asserting that God is the originator of everything: the cosmos, nature, and life itself. His creative act is not a one-time event but a dynamic process that sustains the universe every moment. The phrase "heavens and the earth" encompasses every visible and invisible aspect of existence—from the vast galaxies to the intricate workings of microscopic life. This expansive vision underscores that God's creative power is limitless and intentional.

Beyond Material Creation

Divine creativity extends beyond the physical realm. It includes the establishment of natural laws, the intricate design of ecosystems, and the orchestration of the cosmos in perfect harmony. Moreover, it manifests in the redemptive transformation of human lives. When God brings forth new life—both physically and spiritually—it is an act of renewal that mirrors the original creative impulse. This dual aspect shows that God's creativity is both the origin of the universe and the ongoing force of transformation in our lives.

47.2 Biblical Foundations of Divine Creativity

Genesis: The Inauguration of Creation

The opening chapters of Genesis set the stage for understanding God's creative power. "In the beginning, God created..." is not just a statement of origin but a declaration that everything comes from a purposeful, intelligent, and loving Creator. Each day of creation reveals an ordered progression—from light, sky, and land to living creatures and humanity—highlighting both the beauty and the intentionality behind every aspect of the universe.

Revelation: Worship in the Heavens

In Revelation 4:11, the heavenly host proclaims, "Worthy are you, our Lord and God, to receive glory and honor and power, for you created all things, and by your will they existed and were created." This vision confirms that God's creative work is the basis of His worthiness to be worshiped. It ties divine creativity directly to His sovereign authority and eternal nature, reminding believers that creation itself testifies to His glory.

Redemptive Creativity in Christ

The New Testament brings the concept of divine creativity into sharper focus through the incarnation. In Jesus Christ, God's creative power takes on a new dimension as He enters human history, transforms lives, and establishes a new creation through His death and resurrection. As Paul writes in 2 Corinthians 5:17, those in Christ are "a new creation." This redemptive creativity underscores that God's power to create is not limited to the past—it continues to bring forth renewal and hope in every individual.

47.3 Theological Significance

The Divine Artist

God is portrayed as the ultimate Artist—an infinitely imaginative Creator who brings forth beauty and order from chaos. Unlike human artists who work with pre-existing materials, God creates ex nihilo (out of nothing). His work reflects His character: it is original, purposeful, and imbued with moral and aesthetic perfection. Every element of nature, from the delicate bloom of a flower to the majesty of the stars, is a canvas on which God's artistry is displayed.

Creativity and the Trinity

The doctrine of the Trinity deepens our understanding of divine creativity. The Father initiates creation, the Son—the Word—brings it into being, and the Holy Spirit sustains and renews it. This relational creativity reveals a God who works in unity and communal love, inviting believers to participate in His creative mission. In this view, human creativity is a reflection of the divine image (imago Dei), a spark of the infinite that enables us to innovate, imagine, and contribute to the world's beauty.

Redemption and New Creation

God's creative work is not static but redemptive. The transformation of the world through Christ's life, death, and resurrection is the pinnacle of divine creativity. It demonstrates that even in the midst of brokenness, God can bring forth renewal and restoration. This redemptive creativity calls believers to hope and to actively participate in God's ongoing work of reconciliation and transformation.

47.4 Addressing Common Misconceptions

Creation as a Past Event

Some mistakenly view creation as a one-time historical event. However, the concept of *creatio continua* teaches that God is continuously at work sustaining and renewing His creation. The natural order—its cycles and rhythms—reflects an ongoing creative process that underpins life itself.

A Mechanical or Distant Creator

The Bible rejects the deistic notion of a Creator who sets the universe in motion and then withdraws. Instead, Scripture portrays God as intimately involved with His creation. From His sustaining power in nature to the incarnate presence in Jesus, God remains personally active and relational, caring for every detail of our lives.

Human Creativity Equals Divine Creativity

While humans are made in God's image and share in a spark of divine creativity, our creative abilities are limited and fallible. Divine creativity is perfect and purposeful, transcending human innovation. This distinction reminds us to use our creativity responsibly—to honor God's design and contribute to His redemptive work rather than merely pursuing personal acclaim.

47.5 Pastoral and Practical Implications

Inspiration for Worship and Art

Understanding God as the ultimate Creator enriches our worship. When we contemplate the vast beauty of creation—from the grandeur of the cosmos to the delicate intricacies of nature—we are moved to praise and adoration. This perspective inspires artistic expression and innovation, as individuals and communities seek to reflect the divine creativity in music, visual arts, literature, and architecture.

Stewardship and Environmental Responsibility

Recognizing that the world is God's masterpiece carries a profound stewardship mandate. Believers are called to protect and care for creation, ensuring that our actions honor the Creator's design. This involves sustainable practices, conservation efforts, and a commitment to addressing environmental challenges as part of our responsibility to safeguard God's handiwork.

Encouraging Human Creativity for Kingdom Purposes

Embracing the divine creative impulse encourages believers to develop and use their talents in ways that serve the kingdom of God. Whether through innovative technology, community projects, or artistic endeavors, our creative efforts can be acts of worship when they aim to glorify God and promote the well-being of others. This participatory aspect of creation invites us to collaborate in the ongoing work of renewal and transformation.

47.6 Global and Cultural Reflections

Uniting Diverse Cultures Through Creative Expression

God's creative nature is a universal language that transcends cultural and linguistic barriers. Artistic expressions—whether music, art, or literature—offer a way to communicate the beauty and wonder of the Creator. Such expressions foster interfaith dialogue and cultural exchange, inviting people of all backgrounds to appreciate the shared human experience of encountering divine beauty.

Catalyzing Social Innovation

The biblical vision of a creatively sustained world inspires initiatives that address societal challenges. From innovative solutions in healthcare and education to community-driven efforts to combat poverty and injustice, the principle of divine creativity encourages believers to approach problems with fresh perspectives and bold ideas that reflect God's inventive spirit.

47.7 Personal Transformation and Community Impact

Fostering Personal Growth

Recognizing God's creative power can transform our inner lives. When we understand that our existence is the result of a divine, purposeful act, we are empowered to develop our unique talents and pursue our calling with confidence. This realization nurtures a sense of purpose, encouraging personal growth, resilience, and an enduring hope in God's redemptive work.

Building a Vibrant, Creative Community

Churches and faith communities that embrace the concept of divine creativity tend to be dynamic, innovative, and inclusive. They cultivate environments where every member is encouraged to use their gifts in service to others. Such communities prioritize collaboration, celebrate diverse talents, and engage in creative ministry that not only worships God but also transforms society.

In conclusion, the doctrine of divine creativity reveals a God who is not only the originator of all things but who continually sustains, renews, and transforms creation. From the majestic declarations of Genesis to the redemptive power of Christ and the ongoing work of the Holy Spirit, God's creative nature is the wellspring of beauty, order, and hope.

This understanding enriches our worship, informs our stewardship of the earth, and inspires us to use our own creative gifts for kingdom purposes. It challenges us to view our lives as part of a grand, ongoing masterpiece—one in which we are both recipients of divine grace and active co-creators with God.

Embracing God as the ultimate Creator invites us to live with awe, to pursue innovation in service of His purposes, and to engage the world with a spirit of collaborative transformation. As we marvel at the intricacy of nature and the splendor of human creativity, we are reminded that every good and perfect gift comes from the Creator who continues to shape a world that reflects His glory.

In a world that often values the superficial and the temporary, the truth of God's creative nature offers a lasting foundation for hope and purpose—a foundation upon which we can build lives of beauty, justice, and love that honor our magnificent Creator.

Chapter 48: Comforter

God as Comforter is a central biblical theme that reveals a Creator who actively meets us in our pain, bringing solace, healing, and strength in every season of life. Far from being a distant ruler, God is deeply involved in our daily struggles. His comforting presence reassures us that no tear, fear, or heartache goes unnoticed. Scriptures such as Isaiah 51:12 ("I, I am he who comforts you") and John 14:16 (Jesus promises to send the Helper, the Holy Spirit) testify to a God who not only rules with power and wisdom but also stoops to embrace our brokenness with tender care.

48.1 Understanding Divine Comfort

What It Means to Be a Comforter: To call God our Comforter is to affirm that He actively shares in our burdens and brings transformative relief. Divine comfort is more than kind words or temporary relief—it is an unchanging, life-giving presence that meets us at our point of deepest need. God's care is holistic, addressing our physical, emotional, spiritual, and relational needs. As a loving Father, He listens intently, understands our innermost pain, and offers guidance and renewal through His redemptive power.

Active Versus Passive Comfort: God's comfort does not promise the complete removal of suffering. Instead, it empowers us to endure hardship, grow in resilience, and ultimately find hope. Rather than an escape from reality, divine comfort reorients us—transforming sorrow into strength and despair into a catalyst for spiritual renewal.

48.2 Biblical Foundations

Old Testament Testimonies: The Old Testament abounds with images of God's intimate care. In Isaiah 51:12, God declares, "I, I am he who comforts you," assuring His people in times of exile and distress. Similarly, Psalm 34:17 proclaims that "when the righteous cry for help, the LORD hears and delivers them out of all their troubles." From His guidance of Moses in the wilderness—providing manna, water, and direction—to His steadfast covenant with Israel despite their repeated rebellion, God's comfort is woven throughout His dealings with His people.

New Testament Revelations: In the New Testament, divine comfort reaches its fullest expression in Jesus Christ. Jesus' ministry—healing the sick, feeding the hungry, and forgiving sins—demonstrates a heart moved by compassion. In John 14:16, He promises the arrival of the Holy Spirit, who will continue His work of comforting and guiding believers. The Spirit indwells every follower, offering daily reassurance and strength. The parable of the prodigal son (Luke 15) illustrates a father's patient, enduring love—a picture of God's long-suffering comfort that welcomes us back regardless of our past.

48.3 Theological Reflections

Comfort as an Expression of Divine Love: God's comfort is a direct outflow of His nature as a loving and merciful Father. Unlike human sympathy, which can be limited and conditional, divine comfort is rooted in an infinite reservoir of love and wisdom. Because God is all-knowing and ever-present, He meets our needs with precision and care. His comfort is not a passive bystander but an active, restorative force that reclaims brokenness and nurtures growth.

Redemptive Dimension: Divine comfort is also redemptive. It prepares our hearts for transformation and renewal, leading us from despair to hope. The Holy Spirit's work in comforting believers encourages forgiveness and reconciliation—enabling us to extend the same grace to others. In this way, God's comfort builds not only personal healing but also stronger, more compassionate communities.

Interplay with Justice and Discipline: True divine comfort does not ignore sin or injustice; rather, it goes hand in hand with God's righteous discipline. Just as a loving parent corrects a child for their own good, God's comfort often comes with gentle correction that steers us back to a path of truth and holiness. This balanced approach—comfort paired with moral guidance—ensures that we grow not in complacency but in maturity and accountability.

48.4 Addressing Common Misconceptions

Comfort as a Means of Escape: Some mistakenly believe that calling God our Comforter encourages passivity or escapism. In reality, divine comfort empowers us to face our challenges head-on. It provides the strength to endure hardship while inspiring proactive steps toward healing and restoration.

Emotional Balm or Comprehensive Renewal: While God's comfort certainly soothes our emotions, it also transforms our minds and spirits. It reorients our perspective, enabling us to see beyond immediate pain to a future filled with hope. This holistic comfort—integrating emotional, intellectual, and spiritual renewal—prepares us for genuine transformation rather than mere temporary relief.

Intimacy Without Intrusion: Critics sometimes worry that if God is so intimately involved in our lives, He might overstep our personal boundaries. However, divine comfort respects our autonomy. God's approach is inviting and compassionate, never coercive. He offers solace and guidance without violating our dignity, allowing us to willingly embrace His care.

48.5 Pastoral and Practical Implications

Personal Transformation: Understanding God as our Comforter transforms our inner lives. It fills us with hope, reduces anxiety, and fosters resilience. In prayer and meditation, we experience a deep, personal connection that reassures us in our darkest moments. This transformative comfort encourages us to let go of guilt and despair, replacing them with gratitude and renewed purpose.

Modeling Compassionate Relationships: The reality of divine comfort inspires us to extend that same care to others. Whether in families, friendships, or community interactions, when we reflect God's compassionate presence, we build stronger bonds. Practical acts—such as listening, offering support, and forgiving—mirror the comfort we receive from God, transforming relationships and nurturing a culture of empathy and mutual care.

Church Community and Beyond: Churches that embody the principle of divine comfort become sanctuaries of hope and healing. Through support groups, counseling services, and communal worship, these communities provide practical care for those in distress. Such environments not only support individuals but also serve as powerful testimonies to a world in need of genuine compassion. When a community gathers to pray, share, and care, it reflects the intimate, transformative comfort of God.

Global and Cultural Impact: On a broader scale, the message that God is our Comforter transcends cultural and national boundaries. In regions affected by war, poverty, or natural disasters, the promise of divine comfort offers hope and resilience. This universal need for solace can unite people across differences, fostering interfaith dialogue and collaborative humanitarian efforts that echo the compassionate heart of God.

48.6 Living Out Divine Comfort

Integrating Comfort in Daily Life: Living in the assurance of God's comfort means incorporating practices that nurture a continuous, personal connection with Him. Regular prayer, reflective meditation, and engagement in supportive community activities allow us to experience His presence daily. In moments of joy or sorrow, turning to God's comforting word becomes a source of strength and renewal.

Becoming Agents of Comfort: As we receive God's comfort, we are called to share it with others. This can manifest in simple acts of kindness, pastoral care, or organized community support. By becoming conduits of divine comfort, we help create a ripple effect of healing and compassion that reaches beyond our immediate circles and into the wider world.

Encouraging Resilience and Hope: In times of crisis, the reassurance that God is always listening and caring provides an anchor of hope. Whether facing personal trials or communal challenges, this eternal promise empowers us to persevere. Our faith in a Comforter who is ever-present transforms our approach to adversity, enabling us to live with resilience, courage, and unwavering trust.

In conclusion, the doctrine of God as Comforter reveals a deeply personal and transformative aspect of His nature. From the tender assurances of Isaiah 51:12 to the promise of the Holy

Spirit in John 14:16, Scripture paints a picture of a God who actively shares in our sorrows and rejoices in our joys. Divine comfort is not a fleeting sentiment but a profound, enduring presence that redefines our relationship with suffering, hope, and redemption.

Understanding that God is our Comforter invites us to trust Him more fully, to engage in honest, heartfelt prayer, and to cultivate communities that mirror His compassionate care. It challenges us to extend that same comfort to a hurting world—transforming our personal lives and our cultural landscapes through acts of kindness, empathy, and resilience.

Ultimately, embracing God as Comforter empowers us to face life's challenges with a spirit of hope and unwavering faith. As we experience His comforting presence, we are transformed from the inside out, becoming beacons of His love and agents of healing in our communities and beyond. May we continually draw near to the God who listens, cares, and redeems, and may our lives reflect the enduring, redemptive solace of our Comforter.

Chapter 49: Fatherly

In Scripture, God is portrayed not as an impersonal force but as a loving Father who nurtures, protects, and guides His children. Passages like Matthew 6:9 ("Our Father in heaven") and 1 John 3:1 ("See what kind of love the Father has given to us, that we should be called children of God") reveal that God's fatherly care is at the heart of the Christian faith. This chapter explores the biblical, theological, and practical dimensions of divine fatherhood, and how this understanding reshapes our identity, relationships, and community.

49.1 Understanding Divine Fatherhood

Defining Divine Fatherhood To say God is Fatherly means we view Him as the ultimate model of paternal care—one who embodies perfect love, guidance, and protection. Unlike human fathers, whose love can be imperfect, God's fatherhood is marked by flawless compassion and justice. He cares for our emotional, spiritual, and physical needs with both discipline and tenderness. Though expressed using human imagery, "Father" highlights a relationship of intimacy and belonging, not limited by gender but pointing to the nurturing, protective, and authoritative aspects of God's nature.

Fatherhood Versus Distant Authority Unlike impersonal or authoritarian rulers, God's fatherly nature is characterized by closeness and relational involvement. He is not a remote monarch issuing decrees from afar but a caring Parent who walks with His children through every joy and trial. This personal relationship redefines authority: God leads by example, balancing discipline with grace, and inviting us into a secure, transformative bond.

49.2 Biblical Foundations

"Our Father in Heaven" (Matthew 6:9) Jesus' teaching in the Lord's Prayer reorients our approach to the divine. By calling God "Father," Jesus invites believers to see Him as a personal, accessible guide rather than a distant deity. The term "Abba," used by Jesus, conveys deep intimacy and trust, encouraging us to approach God with childlike openness. This communal address—"Our Father"—also unites the church as one family under His care.

Children of God (1 John 3:1) The apostle John marvels at the love of God that allows us to be called His children. This profound privilege transforms our identity: we are not merely creations but cherished members of God's family. This relationship brings security and a call to reflect divine holiness and love in our lives.

Covenantal Encounters in the Old Testament From the calling of Abraham, where God established a personal covenant with promises and guidance, to the intimate encounters of Moses at Sinai and the personal revelations in the Psalms (e.g., Psalm 139), the Old Testament consistently portrays God as actively involved in human history. These narratives emphasize that God's care is not abstract but is demonstrated in direct, relational interaction.

The Incarnation in the New Testament The fullest revelation of divine fatherhood is seen in the Incarnation of Jesus Christ. In becoming human, God entered into the deepest parts of our experience—sharing in our joys, sorrows, and struggles. Jesus' ministry of healing, teaching, and forgiving reveals a God who is not aloof but is personally engaged with His people. Through His actions, He provides a model of love and compassion that defines true fatherhood.

The Indwelling of the Holy Spirit After Jesus' ascension, the promise of the Holy Spirit ensures that God's intimate care continues. The Spirit dwells in believers, guiding and comforting them, and deepening the personal relationship between God and His children. This ongoing presence is a constant reminder that God remains near, attentive, and active in our lives.

49.3 Theological Implications

Love, Authority, and Discipline God's fatherly nature intertwines love with rightful authority. His discipline, as seen in passages like Hebrews 12, is not punitive but designed to guide and refine His children. This balance ensures that while God corrects, He does so with compassion—motivating growth rather than inducing fear.

Adoption and Identity The concept of adoption in Scripture (Romans 8:15–17) underscores that believers are not born into a family by chance but are graciously adopted into God's household. This redefines our identity, offering us both security and responsibility. As children of God, we are invited to reflect His character in our lives, thus extending the legacy of divine love and holiness.

Relational Transformation Understanding God as Father reshapes our relationships. It calls us to emulate His care by being patient, compassionate, and forgiving. The intimate bond we share with God should inspire us to build genuine, supportive relationships that mirror the unity and love of the divine family.

49.4 Addressing Common Misconceptions

Avoiding Negative Projections of Earthly Fatherhood Some may struggle to accept the concept of God as Father due to experiences with flawed human fatherhood. However, divine fatherhood in Scripture transcends human shortcomings. God's care is perfect, unconditional, and restorative, offering a model that heals our wounds and redefines our understanding of love.

Not Limited to a Male Perspective While "Father" is a masculine term, it is used metaphorically to communicate care, protection, and authority. God's fatherly nature encompasses qualities of both nurturing and discipline, and is not confined to human gender norms. Complementary maternal imagery in Scripture further enriches our understanding of God's relational care.

Encouraging Maturity, Not Immaturity The fatherly model does not foster dependency or spiritual immaturity. Instead, it calls believers toward growth and accountability. Just as a loving parent guides a child toward independence while providing support, God's fatherhood encourages us to mature in our faith, embracing responsibility and ethical living.

49.5 Pastoral and Practical Implications

Emotional Healing and Security Recognizing God as a loving Father provides profound comfort to those burdened by fear, shame, or loneliness. Pastoral counseling often focuses on helping individuals understand that their worth and identity are secure in God's familial love—a love that heals and restores, regardless of past wounds or present challenges.

Family Life and Parenting For Christian families, God's fatherly example sets a high standard for parenting. Parents are encouraged to emulate divine attributes—combining authority with warmth, discipline with unconditional love—to foster households where children grow in faith and character. Such an environment not only nurtures the child's spiritual well-being but also builds a legacy of care and respect that extends to the broader community.

Fostering Community and Unity Church communities grounded in the reality of God's fatherly care naturally exhibit strong bonds of fellowship and accountability. When believers see themselves as part of a spiritual family, they are more likely to support one another, resolve conflicts with grace, and work together for the common good. This shared identity as children of God breaks down barriers of division and fosters an inclusive, compassionate community.

Empowering Mission and Social Justice The message of divine fatherhood compels believers to extend care beyond themselves. Mission and social justice efforts are fueled by the conviction that every person is a beloved child of God. This perspective inspires initiatives that address poverty, injustice, and marginalization, reflecting a commitment to uphold the dignity and well-being of all individuals.

49.6 Global and Cultural Reflections

Cross-Cultural Resonance of Divine Fatherhood The concept of a caring, protective Father resonates across cultures, offering a common ground for interfaith dialogue. While human experiences of fatherhood vary widely, the biblical portrayal of God as Father challenges flawed models by offering a vision of perfect, restorative love. This universal appeal fosters connections among diverse peoples, encouraging mutual respect and collective efforts for peace and justice.

Addressing Fatherlessness In societies where dysfunctional human fatherhood is prevalent, the biblical message of God's perfect fatherhood provides hope and a model for transformation. Ministries that focus on mentoring, foster care, and community support demonstrate how divine principles can reshape social structures and heal the wounds of absent or harmful paternal figures.

Overcoming Insecurity and Fear Embracing God's fatherly care helps individuals overcome deep-seated fears and insecurities. Knowing that we are cherished and guided by a loving Father transforms our self-image and replaces anxiety with a secure sense of belonging. This transformation is often experienced through prayer, reflection on Scripture (such as 1 John 3:1), and supportive relationships that echo God's nurturing presence.

Fostering Authentic Relationships Understanding God as our Father encourages us to build authentic relationships grounded in trust and mutual care. As we experience His unconditional love, we are inspired to extend that same love to others—cultivating friendships, marriages, and community bonds that reflect divine values. This authenticity breaks down barriers and builds a culture of empathy and respect.

Pursuing Spiritual Maturity The fatherly model calls believers not only to receive care but also to grow in independence and moral responsibility. As we mature in our relationship with God, we learn to balance reliance on divine guidance with personal initiative, thereby becoming more resilient, wise, and compassionate. This process of sanctification is central to the Christian journey and empowers us to serve others more effectively.

In conclusion, the biblical portrayal of God as Fatherly reveals a loving, compassionate, and authoritative presence that is intimately involved in every aspect of our lives. From the personal intimacy expressed in Psalm 139 and John 10 to the communal identity of being "children of God," Scripture presents a Father whose love transforms, heals, and unites. This divine fatherhood redefines our understanding of authority—not as oppressive control, but as nurturing guidance that fosters growth, discipline, and redemption.

For individuals, the assurance of God's fatherly care brings deep healing, security, and a renewed sense of identity. It invites us to approach God with the confidence of a beloved child and to extend that same grace in our relationships. For the community, this understanding creates bonds of unity and compassion, inspiring collective efforts to address social injustices and support one another in the journey of faith.

Globally, the message of divine fatherhood transcends cultural and social divides, offering hope and a universal standard of care that challenges the shortcomings of human models. As believers, embracing God's fatherly nature calls us to live with humility, accountability, and a passion for justice—reflecting the redemptive love of our Heavenly Father in every sphere of life.

Ultimately, to know God as Father is to experience a transformative relationship that redefines our purpose and destiny. It is an invitation to a life marked by intimate communion, ethical living, and the confident assurance that we are cherished by a God whose love is perfect and everlasting. May our lives continually mirror the grace and compassion of our divine Father, as we nurture relationships, build communities, and work toward a world that reflects His holy, redemptive love.

Chapter 50: Healer

God as Healer is one of the most transformative and comforting images in Scripture. He heals not only the body but also the heart, mind, and spirit, restoring us from all forms of brokenness. From Psalm 147:3—"He heals the brokenhearted and binds up their wounds"—to Isaiah 53:5, which proclaims, "by his wounds we are healed," the Bible reveals a God whose healing power reaches into every dimension of life. This chapter explores the biblical foundations, theological significance, common misconceptions, and practical outworkings of God's healing nature.

50.1 Understanding Divine Healing

The Nature of Divine Healing Divine healing is a holistic restoration that goes beyond physical recovery. It is the process by which God mends emotional scars, heals spiritual wounds, and reconciles broken relationships. His healing is rooted in love and compassion, reflecting His desire to restore creation to its original wholeness. This process addresses the root causes of pain, transforming suffering into opportunities for growth and renewal.

Healing as Restoration Healing in Scripture means becoming whole again—body, mind, and spirit are renewed. God's intervention reorders our lives, turning despair into hope, and chaos into order. His restorative work assures us that no wound is too deep to mend, and every sorrow is given purpose in His redemptive plan.

50.2 Biblical Foundations of Divine Healing

Healing in the Psalms The Psalms vividly portray God as the healer. Psalm 147:3 encapsulates this truth: He "heals the brokenhearted and binds up their wounds." Here, the focus is not only on physical repair but also on the deep emotional and spiritual care God provides. The language of the Psalms invites believers to trust in God's constant presence in times of distress.

The Ministry of Jesus Jesus' earthly ministry is the ultimate demonstration of divine healing. He healed the sick, restored sight to the blind, and even raised the dead—acts that revealed His compassion and authority over sin and death. Beyond physical miracles, Jesus healed spiritual brokenness by forgiving sins and offering hope to the downtrodden. His encounters— with the woman caught in adultery or the Samaritan woman at the well—show that true healing transforms lives, restoring relationships and dignity. The cross, too, is a profound symbol of healing: through His suffering and resurrection, Christ conquered sin, offering a path to eternal restoration.

Healing Through the Holy Spirit After Jesus' ascension, the Holy Spirit continued His healing work. The early church witnessed numerous miracles that affirmed God's power to heal both body and soul (Acts 3:6–8). Today, the indwelling Spirit renews minds and transforms hearts, providing believers with ongoing comfort and strength. This continual presence ensures that divine healing is not confined to past events but is a living, everyday reality.

50.3 Theological Reflections on Divine Healing

Healing as an Expression of Divine Compassion At its core, divine healing reflects the compassionate nature of God. His willingness to bind up our wounds is an expression of unconditional love and mercy. This healing is deeply intertwined with redemption, as seen in Christ's atoning sacrifice, which offers forgiveness and restoration for all humanity. The cross is not only a symbol of judgment but also a beacon of hope where brokenness meets transformative love.

Healing and Redemption Together Divine healing and redemption are inseparable. While healing restores the body and spirit, redemption reconciles us to God. Many who experience physical healing also report spiritual renewal—an inner transformation that reorients their lives toward God's purposes. This dual process shows that God's ultimate aim is holistic restoration, bringing every aspect of our being into alignment with His perfect design.

The Transformative Impact of Healing God's healing power transforms individuals from the inside out. It shifts our focus from our limitations to the possibilities of new life in Christ. Those who experience His healing often find a renewed sense of purpose, deeper gratitude, and a stronger commitment to live out their faith. This transformation is not merely personal but ripples outward, equipping believers to minister healing and hope to others.

50.4 Common Misconceptions and Clarifications

Healing as a Magic Formula One common misconception is that divine healing is a formula for instant, effortless recovery. While God can perform miraculous healings, His healing process is often gradual and transformative. It involves faith, repentance, and the deep work of inner renewal. Sometimes the healing journey is slow, requiring believers to grow in trust and endurance.

Healing Only in the Physical Sense Another error is to confine healing solely to physical ailments. Although many biblical accounts detail physical miracles, divine healing encompasses emotional, mental, and spiritual restoration. True healing mends relationships, alleviates despair, and renews the mind and spirit, reflecting God's comprehensive care.

Healing as a Guarantee Against Suffering Some believe that if God is the Healer, believers should be free from suffering. However, while God's healing brings ultimate restoration, it does not necessarily eliminate all trials in this life. Instead, His healing provides the strength to endure suffering, transforming pain into a pathway for spiritual growth and deeper reliance on His grace.

50.5 Pastoral and Practical Implications

Comfort in Times of Loss For those experiencing grief or personal crisis, the promise of divine healing offers profound comfort. Pastoral care often centers on the assurance that God is near to the brokenhearted, providing a steady hope that transcends immediate pain. This understanding helps individuals reframe their struggles within the larger narrative of God's redemptive work.

Fostering a Community of Healing Church communities that embrace God as Healer create supportive environments where members share their burdens and find encouragement. Through support groups, counseling, and prayer partnerships, the healing work of God is experienced collectively. Such communities not only offer emotional relief but also build resilience and deepen faith through shared testimonies of restoration.

Promoting Holistic Wellness Understanding God as the ultimate Healer encourages believers to pursue holistic wellness—caring for body, mind, and spirit. Practical programs like health workshops, spiritual retreats, and mental health counseling complement divine healing by equipping communities to live out a balanced, restored life. This integrated approach ensures that all facets of well-being are nurtured.

Empowering Mission and Outreach Experiencing divine healing transforms believers into effective ministers of hope. Personal testimonies of healing can become powerful tools for evangelism and social justice. When the church extends care through humanitarian initiatives—such as crisis intervention, support for the marginalized, or global missions—it echoes the redemptive message of healing that restores dignity and builds lasting hope.

50.6 Global and Cultural Dimensions

Healing Across Cultures The promise of divine healing transcends cultural boundaries. In various societies, the desire for restoration and wholeness is universal. The biblical vision of God as Healer offers a common ground for interfaith dialogue and global humanitarian efforts, inspiring communities worldwide to work together for the well-being of all.

Integrating Faith and Science in Healing Modern advancements in medicine and psychology complement the biblical narrative of healing. Many Christians view scientific progress as a means through which God's healing power is manifested, while ultimately affirming that true restoration comes from His redemptive work. This integration encourages a holistic approach that values both empirical knowledge and spiritual transformation.

Addressing Global Crises with Hope In regions ravaged by conflict, natural disasters, or systemic injustice, the assurance of God's healing provides long-term hope. Global initiatives that combine relief efforts with spiritual care demonstrate that divine healing extends beyond immediate physical needs, offering a vision of restoration that encompasses communities and nations.

From Brokenness to Wholeness On a personal level, encountering God as Healer brings profound transformation. Many testify that divine healing has redefined their lives—turning deep wounds into testimonies of grace. This healing process involves confronting past traumas, embracing forgiveness, and experiencing a renewed sense of purpose that aligns with God's redemptive plan.

Cultivating Resilience and Joy Trust in God's healing fosters a resilience that enables believers to endure life's challenges with hope. Even amid pain, the assurance of divine restoration empowers individuals to view suffering as temporary, fostering a deep-seated joy that coexists with hardship. This resilient faith transforms despair into opportunities for growth and renewal.

Living Out a Legacy of Healing As individuals experience healing, they are compelled to share that gift with others. This legacy of compassion becomes a dynamic cycle where those healed become agents of healing in their communities. Whether through mentorship, counseling, or simple acts of kindness, living out divine healing creates ripple effects that strengthen both personal and communal bonds.

In conclusion, the biblical portrayal of God as Healer is a powerful testament to His boundless compassion and redemptive power. Scripture reveals a God who not only mends physical ailments but also heals emotional scars, restores spiritual integrity, and reconciles broken relationships. This holistic healing—epitomized in passages like Psalm 147:3 and Isaiah 53:5, and fully manifested in the life, death, and resurrection of Jesus Christ—offers believers deep hope and a transformative pathway from pain to wholeness.

Understanding God as the ultimate Healer reshapes our approach to suffering and brokenness. It reassures us that no wound is too deep for His touch and that every trial can become an opportunity for divine restoration. For individuals, this promise provides comfort, resilience, and a renewed sense of purpose. For communities, it fosters environments of mutual care and collective healing, strengthening the church's witness to a world in need of hope. Globally, the message of divine healing transcends cultural boundaries, inviting a holistic dialogue that bridges faith and science and encourages sustainable initiatives for recovery and justice.

Ultimately, embracing the healing work of God means entering a relationship where our deepest hurts are met with His loving, redemptive grace. As we journey through life, may we always trust in the One who heals all our wounds, transforms our sorrows into joy, and restores every broken piece of our existence—so that we may, in turn, become instruments of His healing love in the world.

Chapter 51: Gentle and Lowly

One of the most endearing portraits of Christ is His self-description as "gentle and lowly in heart" (Matthew 11:29). Rather than an aloof or harsh ruler, Jesus reveals Himself as a compassionate Savior who offers rest, forgiveness, and renewal to all who are weary. This depiction is echoed throughout the Gospels and in apostolic teachings like Philippians 2:5–7, where Christ's self-emptying humility serves as a model for believers. In this chapter, we explore the biblical foundations, theological insights, and practical implications of Christ's gentle and lowly nature, and how His example transforms personal faith and community life.

51.1 Understanding "Gentle and Lowly"

Defining the Terms

To describe Christ as "gentle and lowly" means that He embodies a spirit of kindness, humility, and approachability.

- **Gentleness** implies a disposition free of harshness, characterized by empathy and a readiness to forgive.

- **Lowliness** denotes a self-lowering humility, where Christ does not cling to divine privilege but engages with humanity as a servant.

These qualities demonstrate that divine power does not rely on force or intimidation but is expressed through compassionate service. Christ's leadership is marked not by coercion but by a willingness to heal broken hearts and restore those in need.

An Invitation to Rest

Jesus invites the weary to find rest in Him (Matthew 11:28–30). His yoke is "easy," and His burden is "light"—not because life is without challenges, but because His presence transforms hardship into a journey of hope and renewal. His gentle approach contrasts sharply with the oppressive legalism of His day, offering instead a relational path where disciples learn from a Master who is both patient and supportive.

51.2 Biblical Foundations

Old Testament Insights

The Old Testament lays the groundwork for understanding divine intimacy.

- **God's Personal Engagement:** Throughout narratives—from the calling of Abraham to Moses at Sinai—God reveals His desire for a close relationship with His people. The psalmist in Psalm 139 marvels at God's intimate knowledge of every thought and action.

- **Covenantal Relationship:** God's interactions with Israel demonstrate a commitment to nurture, guide, and restore His people, even amid their failures.

New Testament Revelation

The New Testament brings Christ's intimate nature to its fullest expression.

- **Jesus' Self-Description:** In Matthew 11:29, Jesus declares, "I am gentle and lowly in heart," revealing that His humility is central to His identity. This sets Him apart from the religious elites, offering an alternative that comforts and uplifts.

- **Kenosis in Philippians 2:5–7:** Paul highlights Christ's self-emptying—His choice to take on human form and live as a servant. This humility did not diminish His divine authority; instead, it enabled Him to reach out with compassion to the marginalized and suffering.

- **The Holy Spirit's Role:** After Jesus' ascension, the Holy Spirit continues His work, indwelling believers and guiding them with gentle wisdom, ensuring that divine intimacy remains a daily experience.

51.3 Theological Reflections

Gentleness as Strength

Christ's gentleness is not weakness but a refined strength. His power is exercised with calm authority that heals and restores rather than dominates by force. This gentle strength—exemplified in His healing miracles, His rebukes of hypocrisy, and His calm in the face of adversity—embodies the truth of "the meek shall inherit the earth" (Matthew 5:5). True power, then, is not measured by loudness or aggression, but by the ability to transform lives through compassion.

The Mystery of the Incarnation

The humility of Christ, as seen in His humble birth, His life among ordinary people, and His sacrificial death, reveals that divine greatness is not incompatible with lowliness. By taking on human flesh, Jesus demonstrated that no aspect of human experience is too insignificant for divine attention. His willingness to serve—symbolized by His washing of the disciples' feet (John 13)—challenges conventional ideas of leadership, replacing dominance with servant-heartedness.

The Transformative Role of Divine Intimacy

Divine intimacy is designed to bring about transformation. It invites believers to enter into a relationship where vulnerability is met with unconditional love, leading to personal healing and growth. This intimate encounter with Christ reshapes hearts, turning pain into opportunities for forgiveness, renewal, and a deeper commitment to live out God's values.

51.4 Addressing Common Misconceptions

Gentleness Does Not Mean Permissiveness

Some mistakenly equate gentleness with leniency toward sin. However, while Jesus is compassionate and forgiving, He also confronts sin and calls for repentance. His gentle approach in guiding sinners toward transformation demonstrates that true gentleness upholds moral truth without harshness.

Lowliness Is Not Weakness

Christ's lowliness is sometimes misunderstood as a sign of frailty. In reality, His humility coexists with divine authority. Jesus remained resolute and courageous in the face of injustice (e.g., His encounter with Pilate in John 18:36) and in His commitment to righteousness. His lowly demeanor is a deliberate choice that opens the door to genuine relationship without compromising strength.

Emotional Authenticity Over Stoicism

To be gentle and lowly does not mean suppressing emotions. Jesus' own expressions of compassion, grief, and even righteous anger illustrate that true intimacy includes genuine emotional engagement. His approach invites us to experience a balanced, authentic range of emotions that ultimately draws us closer to the divine.

51.5 Pastoral and Practical Implications

Personal Rest and Healing

Jesus' invitation—"Come to me, all who labor and are heavy laden" (Matthew 11:28)—offers a profound promise of rest. Believers experiencing guilt, stress, or grief find solace in knowing that a compassionate Savior walks with them. This rest is not passive; it is the refreshing of a soul burdened by life's challenges, leading to inner healing and renewed strength.

Discipleship and Community Growth

Christ's gentle and lowly approach sets the tone for discipleship. Leaders who embody these qualities nurture an environment of trust and support, where individuals feel safe to share their struggles and grow in faith. Such communities—whether through small groups, mentoring, or collective worship—become living expressions of Christ's relational love, fostering unity and resilience.

Serving the Marginalized

Ministries that prioritize gentleness are especially effective in reaching out to the marginalized—prisoners, refugees, victims of abuse, and the homeless. By reflecting Christ's tender care, believers open pathways to healing and restoration. Acts of service, from providing shelter to offering a listening ear, manifest the transformative power of a Savior who meets people where they are.

Global and Cultural Engagement

Across cultures, the model of a gentle and lowly Savior challenges aggressive power structures and promotes peace, justice, and reconciliation. Christian organizations that adopt this approach find common ground with diverse communities, fostering interfaith dialogue and collaborative solutions to global challenges. In this way, the gentle heart of Christ becomes a beacon of hope in a fragmented world.

51.6 Personal Transformation and Community Impact

Overcoming Pride and Embracing Vulnerability

Cultivating Christ's gentle, lowly disposition helps individuals overcome pride and defensiveness. Embracing vulnerability enables believers to admit weaknesses, seek help, and grow in spiritual maturity. This transformation deepens relationships and fosters an environment where grace flows freely.

Enhancing Prayer and Worship

An intimate understanding of Christ's nature transforms prayer from a mere ritual into a heartfelt conversation. Personal and communal worship that reflects His gentle care leads to a deeper, more authentic relationship with God. This, in turn, nurtures a culture of empathy and sincere devotion within the church.

Living as Agents of Comfort

Believers who internalize the gentle and lowly heart of Christ become effective comforters in their communities. Their approach to conflict resolution, counseling, and daily interactions reflects a commitment to healing and reconciliation. This ministry of consolation extends beyond formal settings, influencing workplaces, families, and neighborhoods.

In conclusion, the biblical portrait of Christ as "gentle and lowly in heart" presents a Savior who embodies both divine strength and compassionate humility. Far from being an aloof ruler, Jesus' self-description invites us into a relationship marked by empathy, forgiveness, and authentic care. His example redefines true authority—not by dominance, but by service; not by coercion, but by gentle persuasion.

For the individual, this intimate relationship with Christ offers profound rest, healing, and transformation. It encourages us to shed pride, embrace vulnerability, and seek growth through honest, heartfelt prayer. For the community, the model of gentle, lowly leadership fosters unity, resilience, and a spirit of mutual care that stands as a testament to the redemptive power of the Gospel.

Globally, the compassionate, accessible nature of Christ's fatherly love challenges cultural norms and inspires initiatives for peace and justice. It provides a bridge in interfaith dialogue and offers a counter-narrative to systems of power that value aggression over empathy.

Ultimately, the call to embrace the gentle and lowly heart of Christ is an invitation to live a life transformed by divine grace. It is a call to be agents of comfort and healing in a hurting world, to embody a faith that uplifts the broken, and to reflect the profound, redemptive love of our Savior. May we, in our daily lives, strive to mirror this extraordinary disposition, drawing others into the warm, restorative embrace of a God who is as gentle as He is mighty.

Chapter 52: Purposeful

Scripture portrays God as acting with deliberate intention and foresight, ensuring that nothing is left to chance. His purposeful nature assures believers that every event, from creation to redemption, fits into an unchanging, redemptive plan. Passages like Isaiah 46:9–10 ("I am God... My counsel shall stand, and I will accomplish all my purpose") and Ephesians 1:11 ("[God] works all things according to the counsel of his will") affirm that nothing in the cosmos is random or wasted. This chapter explores the dimensions of divine purposefulness, its biblical foundations, theological implications, common misconceptions, and its practical impact on personal lives, church communities, and the world at large.

52.1 Understanding Divine Purposefulness

What It Means to Be Purposeful

To say that God is purposeful is to affirm that His actions are not haphazard but flow from an overarching, coherent design. Unlike human plans—subject to error, limited knowledge, and resource constraints—God's plan is founded on perfect wisdom and love. His purposeful work is evident in the orderly progression of creation, the unfolding of salvation history, and the consistent moral order throughout time. Nothing is random; every event, whether triumphant or tragic, is woven into the divine tapestry.

Consistency and Unity

Divine purposefulness implies that God's actions always align with His character. Whether through creation, discipline, or redemption, His deeds consistently reflect His nature—holy, just, and loving. This ensures that every moment of history and every personal journey fits seamlessly into His unassailable plan, uniting all things toward a final consummation in Christ.

52.2 Biblical Foundations

Isaiah 46:9–10 – "My Counsel Shall Stand"

Isaiah 46:9–10 powerfully declares God's absolute control: "I am God, and there is none like me... My counsel shall stand, and I will accomplish all my purpose." Set against Israel's context of captivity and the rise of empires, this passage assures believers that, despite human frailty and shifting political powers, God's plan remains secure and unthwarted. His counsel, more than mere foreknowledge, actively orchestrates history toward redemption.

Ephesians 1:11 – "Works All Things According to the Counsel of His Will"

Paul's message in Ephesians 1:11 reinforces that every blessing in Christ—from redemption and adoption to the sealing of the Holy Spirit—flows from God's deliberate intent. This verse emphasizes that nothing in our lives is coincidental; every aspect of our existence is part of a larger, divinely ordained narrative that culminates in Christ's redemptive work.

Purpose in Creation and Redemption

The biblical narrative consistently shows that from creation to the final restoration, God's actions are methodical and intentional. Genesis reveals a cosmos brought into order by divine command, while the redemptive arc—from Abraham's covenant through the prophets to the incarnation, crucifixion, and resurrection of Christ—demonstrates that even what seems like the darkest moment (Calvary) is central to God's plan of salvation.

52.3 Theological Reflections

Integrating Sovereignty, Omniscience, and Goodness

God's purposefulness arises from His sovereignty (absolute authority), omniscience (complete knowledge), and goodness (moral perfection). These attributes ensure that His plan is both inevitable and inherently good. Divine purposefulness is not mere determinism; it accounts for the complexities of free will and sin, yet guarantees that every action contributes to a redemptive outcome. Even acts of rebellion or human injustice are ultimately integrated into God's grand design.

Human Agency Within the Divine Plan

While God's plan is unstoppable, Scripture affirms that human choices have genuine consequences. Our moral decisions shape our lives and contribute to the unfolding of the divine narrative, though they cannot override God's ultimate purpose. This dynamic encourages humility and responsibility, reminding us that we are both participants in and subjects to a larger, unchanging divine plan.

Mystery and Paradox

The tension between divine purpose and human experience introduces mystery. Believers may struggle to understand suffering or injustice, yet the Bible teaches that God incorporates even these complexities into His redemptive work. The story of Job, for example, illustrates how adversity can lead to spiritual growth and revelation. While we may not grasp every detail, we trust that God's overarching plan is wise and purposeful.

52.4 Addressing Common Misconceptions

Misinterpreting Purpose as Fatalism

Some equate divine purposefulness with fatalism, suggesting that all events are predestined and human effort is irrelevant. However, Scripture shows that while God's plan is assured, it works in tandem with human response. Prayer, repentance, and moral effort are vital parts of our relationship with God—they are the means by which we participate in His plan, not obstacles to it.

Minimizing Present Suffering

Another error is to assume that if God has a purpose, current suffering must be insignificant. Yet, divine purposefulness does not trivialize pain; it recontextualizes it. God's plan often includes periods of hardship that refine character and produce ultimate good. Recognizing that nothing is wasted under God's counsel invites us to trust that our struggles are temporary and serve a higher, redemptive aim.

Viewing God as a Remote Architect

Finally, some mistakenly see God's purposefulness as a detached, mechanical orchestration that ignores human experience. In reality, God's plan is relational; He cares deeply about each person's journey. His purposeful actions are not distant decrees but intimate interventions aimed at restoring and renewing His creation.

52.5 Pastoral and Practical Implications

Comfort and Assurance in Trials

Believers find profound comfort knowing that nothing in their lives is random. Even when facing personal or collective crises—illness, loss, injustice—the assurance that God is orchestrating every detail provides hope and resilience. Pastoral counseling often emphasizes that even the most painful experiences are woven into a larger tapestry of divine redemption.

Motivation for Perseverance and Moral Living

Understanding God's purposeful plan inspires perseverance. Believers are encouraged to continue acts of kindness, prayer, and justice, trusting that every effort contributes to the unfolding of God's redemptive story. This perspective fosters ethical living, as individuals align their choices with a higher, unchanging standard.

Shaping Leadership and Community Vision

Church leaders can harness the concept of divine purpose to unify and inspire their communities. By "discerning God's will," congregations can set aside personal agendas to work toward common, Spirit-led goals. Such unity enhances both local outreach and global missions, reinforcing the truth that every endeavor aligned with God's plan carries eternal significance.

Encouraging a Missional Outlook

The conviction that God's plan is purposeful empowers missions and evangelism. Believers are driven to share the gospel with confidence, knowing that every soul has a part in God's grand narrative. Local and global mission efforts are thus seen as integral components of the unstoppable movement toward ultimate redemption.

52.6 Global and Cultural Dimensions

Affirming Universal Values

God's purposeful nature challenges cultural relativism by affirming that every event has meaning within His redemptive design. This truth undergirds universal values such as justice, human dignity, and the pursuit of peace. When societies base laws and ethics on a transcendent standard, they reflect the enduring order of God's purpose.

Inspiring Social Justice and Transformation

The assurance that nothing is wasted under God's plan motivates believers to address systemic injustices. By viewing their efforts in education, healthcare, and social reform as part of a divine narrative, Christians are emboldened to work for lasting change. This global perspective fosters unity and resilience, as communities collaborate to transform even the most entrenched issues through the lens of divine purpose.

52.7 Personal Transformation Through Divine Purpose

Reframing Personal Struggles

For individuals, recognizing that God's purpose governs every aspect of life can reframe personal suffering and setbacks as opportunities for growth. Like the stories of Joseph or Paul, personal tragedies can lead to transformative ends when seen as part of God's larger, redemptive plan. This perspective transforms despair into hope and encourages ongoing spiritual development.

Integrating Daily Life with Divine Vision

Believers are invited to see every aspect of life—work, relationships, leisure—as part of God's purposeful design. Engaging in spiritual disciplines such as prayer, meditation on Scripture, and communal worship helps align personal choices with divine will, fostering a sense of partnership in the Creator's grand narrative. This integrated outlook imbues everyday actions with lasting significance and joy.

Leaving a Legacy of Faith and Hope

A life lived in alignment with God's purpose not only transforms the individual but also leaves a legacy for future generations. When believers model resilience, ethical integrity, and compassionate service, they inspire others to pursue a similar path. This legacy of faith and hope contributes to a culture that values purpose over chance and meaning over randomness.

In conclusion, the doctrine of divine purposefulness reassures believers that nothing in the universe is random or wasted. From the creation narratives in Genesis to the redemptive work of Christ and the promise of eternal restoration, Scripture consistently affirms that God's actions flow from a deliberate, unchanging plan. This assurance transforms our understanding of life's challenges, infusing us with hope, moral clarity, and a renewed commitment to align our actions with His eternal design.

Understanding that every joy, every trial, and every tear is part of God's purposeful tapestry provides comfort amid adversity and motivates us to persevere in faith. It shapes our ethical decisions, informs our leadership, and unites communities in a shared mission for justice and renewal. Globally, the belief that nothing is wasted under God's plan challenges cultural relativism and inspires social transformation through the universal values of dignity and righteousness.

Ultimately, living in light of divine purpose empowers us to see our lives as integral threads in a grand, redemptive narrative—a narrative where every detail matters and every effort contributes to the unfolding of God's unassailable, loving plan. As we navigate life's uncertainties, may we trust that our Creator's purpose is perfect and unchanging, and may we joyfully participate in His eternal, purposeful work.

Conclusion

Throughout this book, we have journeyed through a rich tapestry of divine attributes that reveal the multifaceted nature of God. Each chapter has offered a glimpse into His character—from His unfathomable wisdom and redemptive love to His steadfast provision, protective care, and healing grace. Together, these themes form a holistic portrait of a God who is both transcendent and intimately involved in our lives.

We began by exploring the mystery of God's incomprehensibility, a truth that reminds us our finite minds can only ever grasp a portion of His infinite nature. Yet, even in our limitations, God chooses to reveal Himself through creation, Scripture, and the ultimate revelation in Jesus Christ. This partial unveiling invites us into a humble relationship, marked by continual wonder and trust.

The book then illuminated God's role as Provider—a benevolent Creator who meets every need with wisdom and abundance. From the promise of Jehovah Jireh to the practical outworking of divine provision in our daily lives, we learned that nothing is wasted in God's economy. His provision extends beyond material blessings to include emotional, spiritual, and relational sustenance, offering hope even in the darkest times.

Next, we delved into God's protective nature, which assures us that no threat—whether physical, spiritual, or emotional—lies beyond His watchful care. The imagery of God as a rock, fortress, and strong tower echoes throughout Scripture, providing a secure refuge amid life's storms. His protection encourages us to face adversity with confidence and to embrace our responsibilities with resilience and determination.

We also examined the intimate nature of God, particularly as revealed in the person of Jesus. His gentle and lowly heart, exemplified in His teachings, miracles, and sacrificial love, redefines divine leadership. Jesus' invitation to "come to me" transforms our understanding of discipleship, replacing harsh judgment with compassionate care and fostering an environment where true relationship and healing can flourish.

Moreover, we reflected on God's supreme authority, which undergirds His other attributes. His unassailable power, perfect wisdom, and unconditional love converge to form an authority that governs all of creation. This assurance of divine sovereignty dispels fear and doubt, guiding our ethical decisions and empowering our collective mission.

Finally, the healing work of God encapsulates His transformative power. Whether through physical miracles, emotional restoration, or spiritual renewal, His healing brings wholeness to our broken lives. It is not merely a temporary relief but a dynamic, redemptive process that calls us to grow in faith, hope, and compassion.

In summary, this book has revealed a God who is absolute in His character and purpose, inviting us into a profound relationship with Him. His attributes are not isolated traits; they interweave to form a comprehensive narrative of redemption—a story in which every moment, every trial, and every triumph is part of a grand, purposeful design. As we embrace these truths, we are encouraged to reflect His nature in our own lives, becoming beacons of hope, agents of transformation, and ambassadors of divine love. May we continue to trust in, worship, and emulate the One who is truly beyond measure, guiding us toward eternal fulfillment and unity in His everlasting kingdom.

www.ingramcontent.com/pod-product-compliance
Lightning Source LLC
LaVergne TN
LVHW061257060426
835508LV00015B/1398